Social Movements

Social Movements

SUZANNE STAGGENBORG

New York   Oxford

OXFORD UNIVERSITY PRESS

2011

Oxford University Press, Inc., publishes works that further Oxford University's
objective of excellence in research, scholarship, and education.

Oxford   New York
Auckland   Cape Town   Dar es Salaam   Hong Kong   Karachi
Kuala Lumpur   Madrid   Melbourne   Mexico City   Nairobi
New Delhi   Shanghai   Taipei   Toronto

With offices in
Argentina   Austria   Brazil   Chile   Czech Republic   France   Greece
Guatemala   Hungary   Italy   Japan   Poland   Portugal   Singapore
South Korea   Switzerland   Thailand   Turkey   Ukraine   Vietnam

Copyright © 2011 by Oxford University Press, Inc.

Published by Oxford University Press, Inc.
198 Madison Avenue, New York, New York 10016
http://www.oup.com

Oxford is a registered trademark of Oxford University Press

Library of Congress Cataloging-in-Publication Data

ISBN 978-0-19-537508-4

Printed in the United States of America
on acid-free paper

CONTENTS

PREFACE

Social movements are important means of bringing about political and cultural changes through collective action. The study of social movements helps us to understand how movements can achieve change, and how they are limited in doing so, by examining political and cultural opportunities and obstacles, organizational dynamics, resources, collective action frames, and strategies and tactics. The field of social movements is an exciting one, and scholars continue to produce new studies of a wide array of social movements in many different countries, while activists also regularly provide accounts of their experiences in social movements. Relevant to both activists and social scientists, the area is one that students find important and interesting.

Given the proliferation of social movement scholarship in recent decades, it is a daunting task to attempt to capture the field in a short book. Thus, my goal is simply to introduce students and other readers to some interesting history, ideas, and questions about social movements. No single researcher can be an expert on all of the many social movements that might be covered in such a book, and I have limited myself to some of the movements that I have followed for many years in teaching and researching in the area. Because an earlier edition of this book, published by Oxford University Press Canada, was part of a series on themes in Canadian sociology, it contained more Canadian content. In this American edition of the book, I have added a chapter on right-wing movements, which are particularly important in the United States. I also considered adding a chapter on the civil rights movement, which is obviously very important as well to the United States, but I decided instead to expand somewhat the material on the civil rights movement in my chapter on the protest cycle of the 1960s. My rationale for doing this instead of including a whole chapter on the civil rights movement is that there is so much excellent scholarship available on the movement, which instructors can easily use to supplement my brief treatment. Hopefully, students will find this selection of contemporary protest movements interesting and will learn enough about theoretical ideas and approaches to movements to be able to apply this knowledge to other movements of interest.

ACKNOWLEDGMENTS

I would like to thank Sherith Pankratz, my editor at Oxford University Press in New York, for inviting me to do an American edition of the book. She completely surprised me by getting no fewer than eight scholars in the area to provide detailed comments on the Canadian version of the book and advice on a possible American edition. When I received these extremely constructive and encouraging reviews along with the invitation to do an American edition, it was difficult for me to turn down the opportunity to make general improvements to the book as well as to revise it for an American audience. I am grateful to the following reviewers, as well as one anonymous reviewer, for their many helpful comments:

> Benigno E. Aguirre, University of Delaware
> Andrew W. Martin, Ohio State University
> Holly McCammon, Vanderbilt University
> David S. Meyer, University of California, Irvine
> Ziad Munson, Lehigh University
> Benita Roth, Binghamton University
> David Walls, Sonoma State University

Although I could not follow all of their advice, I did take quite a bit of it into account in revising the book, and I think it is greatly improved as a result. I also thank Sherith Pankratz for her useful suggestions as I decided how to reshape the book and for her patience in waiting for me to finish it.

The invitation to do an American edition of the book also coincided with my own move back to the United States after 15 years in Canada. This increased my interest in addressing American students, though I remain very interested in social movements in my adopted country of Canada as well as in the United States. As readers will see, I have not eliminated all of the Canadian content from the book, as I think much of this material, as well as material on movements in other countries, should be of interest to American as well as to Canadian students. Because the two countries are similar in many ways, comparisons between the United States and Canada are often very useful. But I have also added more American examples in all of the chapters as well as in the new chapter on the New American Right.

Finally, I am greatly indebted to my family for their help and support. My husband, Rod Nelson, read and commented on several chapters and dug up helpful material for me, both in the library and online. My daughter Laura also read and commented on some of the chapters, telling me where I was unclear and where I needed examples. My son Charlie spent hours typing and fixing the references for me and catching a number of mistakes. The book is dedicated, with love, to all three of them.

CHAPTER 1

Introduction

Social movements around the world have used a wide variety of protest tactics to bring about enormous social changes, influencing cultural arrangements, public opinion, and government policies. Consider the following examples:

- At the beginning of the twentieth century, British "suffragettes," impatient with the failure of their government to give women the vote, protested in Parliament, marched in the streets, chained themselves to the railings outside the prime minister's residence, and went on hunger strikes. Numerous suffragettes were jailed and force-fed, and many were beaten by police when they participated in demonstrations. The militancy and bravery of the suffragettes inspired movement activists around the world. By the 1920s, suffrage movements had won the vote for women in many different countries, but struggles for a full range of women's rights continued. Today, the women's movement continues to combat problems such as violence against women and to fight for access to education, employment, and citizenship rights for women around the world.
- In the southern United States, civil rights activists in the 1950s and 1960s used boycotts, sit-ins, mass demonstrations, "freedom rides" on public transportation, and voter registration drives to secure basic rights for blacks. Activists were jailed, beaten, and murdered as they combated a society in which African Americans were denied service in many public establishments, forced to sit in the back of buses and give up their seats to whites, and disenfranchised by threats of violence when they attempted to vote. After the civil rights movement won battles over desegregation of public facilities and voting rights, blacks became a political force in the South and African Americans served as mayors of cities that once denied them basic rights, such as Atlanta, Georgia, and Jackson, Mississippi. In 2009, Barack Obama took office as the first African-American President of the United States.
- In Canada, a group calling itself the Association for Social Knowledge formed in Vancouver in 1964 to begin the long process of creating a positive gay identity at a time when gays and lesbians were denied basic rights such as employment and were often arrested simply for socializing

1

together in bars and other public places. By 1971, the low-key approach of the early activists gave way to a gay liberation movement that marched on Parliament Hill to demand the "freedom to love." Since the 1970s, gay and lesbian rights groups have lobbied for inclusion in human rights codes, filed lawsuits to secure legal protections, and staged numerous "gay pride" parades and demonstrations. In 2005, after many years of equality-seeking work by the lesbian and gay rights movement, same-sex marriage became legal throughout Canada.

- In 1999, a seemingly new movement for global justice burst on the scene with large demonstrations against the World Trade Organization meetings in Seattle, which virtually closed down the WTO conference. In Quebec City in 2001, activists stormed the fence that had been erected to keep protestors from disrupting meetings to establish a Free Trade Area of the Americas (FTAA). These and other demonstrations around the world helped to raise public consciousness about the impacts of the trade and monetary policies of global institutions. The global justice movement works to unite local and international activists and organizations from a variety of different social movements and attempts to influence international labor, environmental, and human rights standards.

In all of these examples, individuals banded together in collective efforts to create social change by presenting demands for justice and pressuring authorities to respond. Movements have organized to protect the environment, oppose wars, and advocate for the rights of more and more groups, including workers, women, gay men and lesbians, students, children, disabled people, senior citizens, and many racial and ethnic groups. Social movements are important vehicles for social and political change, yet it is not always apparent how it is possible to bring together a variety of groups and individuals with varying interests and ideologies to form a cohesive movement capable of effecting real changes. Thus, social movement theorists attempt to answer a variety of questions about the growth and impact of movements, which are relevant to activists and policymakers as well as to social scientists. Key questions include why movements originate when they do, how they attract and maintain support, how they present issues and formulate strategies and tactics, how they structure organizations, why they generate opposition and sometimes decline, and how and why they succeed or fail in achieving cultural and political changes.

This book introduces students and other readers to the study of social movements by looking at some influential theories in the field, the issues they raise, and how they help to explain the mobilization and outcomes of social movements. I review major theories of social movements and collective action and identify important theoretical issues that we will explore in connection with a selection of substantive movements. I also discuss the cluster of protest movements that arose in many countries in the 1960s, creating strategies and changes that continue to influence collective action in the twenty-first century. Chapters on women's, gay and lesbian, environmental, right-wing, and global justice movements analyze general issues in the study of social movements as they apply to each movement, including how these social movements originate, mobilize participants, and bring about social change. In this introductory chapter, we consider the concept of social movements and related ideas, and place the study of contemporary movements in historical context.

THE ORIGINS OF THE SOCIAL MOVEMENT

The social movement, as we know it today, is a relatively recent means of organizing for social change. Charles Tilly, who did extensive historical research on the origins of the social movement in the Western world, quotes from an account of a "movement" in 1682 in Narbonne, France, to make this point:

> [T]here was a little movement in Narbonne on the occasion of the collection of the *cosse* tax, which had been ordered by an act of the royal council. Many women gathered with the common people, and threw stones at the tax collectors, but the Consuls and the leading citizens hurried over and put a stop to the disorder. (Tilly 1984: 297)

Although this seventeenth-century incident is referred to as a "little movement," it bears scant resemblance to what we think of today as a "social movement." The term *petit mouvement* was part of the vocabulary of the time, used to refer to "a localized collective action by ordinary people which the authorities considered necessary and proper to end by force" (Tilly 1984: 298). Tilly points out that today we would not consider this type of action a **social movement** unless it were more enduring, part of a series of collective actions rather than one incident, and enacted by participants with common interests and a distinct identity, who had broader goals than stopping a particular tax. He uses the concept of a **repertoire of collective action** to get at the idea that limited forms of protest are familiar during a given time. Using the repertoire of tactics available to them, activists engage in what Tilly calls **claim-making performances** in interaction with targets. Repertoires and performances evolve over time "through incremental transformation in use" (Tilly 2008: 13). When we compare long periods of history, we can see major changes in repertoires; our contemporary protest repertoire has changed dramatically since the women of Narbonne stoned their tax collectors.

Collective action in Western countries such as France and England (Tilly 1986, 1995, 2004a, 2008) was once localized and defensive. People got together within their communities to defend local interests, using protest forms drawn from local culture and typically directed at particular individuals. For example, the **charivari** was a traditional form of collective action directed towards individuals who had transgressed community norms, such as a married man who got a single woman pregnant. The guilty party would be subject to a noisy demonstration designed to humiliate him or her before the community. As historian Edward

Shorter (1975: 219) describes, there were many variations of the charivari, based on local tradition:

> Sometimes the demonstration would consist of masked individuals circling somebody's house at night, screaming, beating on pans, and blowing cow horns (which the local butchers rented out). On other occasions the offender would be seized and marched through the streets, seated perhaps backwards on a donkey or forced to wear a placard describing his sins. Sometimes the youth would administer the charivari; on other occasions villagers of all ages and sexes would mix together.

Despite such variations, the charivari shared characteristics in common with other forms of protest in the traditional repertoire, which also included food riots, grain seizures, and land revolts (Tarrow 1998: 32–36). All of these traditional forms of action were short in duration and local in scope; even when a national issue such as taxation was involved, the targets of the protest were local authorities and the actions were particular to the local community (Tilly 1995: 45). In contrast to this traditional repertoire, a new repertoire of collective action, consisting of tactics such as large-scale demonstrations, strikes, and boycotts, began to develop in Europe and North America in the late eighteenth century and became firmly established in the nineteenth century. The new repertoire was cosmopolitan rather than parochial, with protests often targeted at national rather than local authorities. The tactics of the new repertoire were "modular" (Tarrow 1998) in that they could easily be transported to many locales and situations, rather than being tied to local communities and rituals. For example, the boycott and the mass petition were tactics that could be aimed at any target with regard to any type of grievance. The nineteenth-century abolition movement was one of the first social movements to use these tactics, organizing a boycott of sugar grown with slave labor and sending petitions signed by large numbers of supporters to the British Parliament (Tarrow 1998: 38–39).

The story of how this shift in repertoires came about is a complicated one (Tarrow 1998; Tilly 1995, 2004a, 2004b, 2008), but it involved the expansion of nation-states and the spread of capitalism. With the development of national electoral politics, special-purpose associations formed to represent the interests of various groups, including dissident aristocrats and bourgeois activists who sometimes formed alliances with dissatisfied workers. These coalitions adopted new means of making claims, such as mass petitions and disciplined marches, to replace the often violent direct actions, such as food riots and grain seizures, that had been central to the older repertoire and were more likely to be repressed by authorities. With the spread of wage labor, workers gained independence from particular landlords and masters, and were freer to engage in political activities (Tilly 2004b: 27). The repertoire of collective action gradually changed, and the social movement became part of the new repertoire.

Thus, the social movement emerged in a particular historical period as a result of large-scale social changes and political conditions that made it possible.

Although there have been some innovations in protest forms, social movements still select tactics from essentially the same repertoire of contention that became established in the nineteenth century. Tilly notes, however, that the social movement and its repertoire are products of historical circumstances and could change as political conditions change. For example, insofar as centralized nation-states are replaced with transnational bodies, the national social movement may become a less effective form of political organization (Tilly 2004b: 14). Indeed, transnational movements and organizations are already significant, and new forms of action, such as Internet-based protests, have developed with new technologies and processes of globalization.

DEFINING SOCIAL MOVEMENTS

Research by Charles Tilly and others on the origins of the social movement has been influential in promoting a political view of social movements (McAdam et al. 2001). In this view, social movements are one form of **contentious politics**:

> contentious in the sense that social movements involve collective making of claims that, if realized, would conflict with someone else's interests, political in the sense that governments of one sort or another figure somehow in the claim making, whether as claimants, objects of claims, allies of the objects, or monitors of the contention. (Tilly 2004b: 3)

According to Tilly, social movements as they developed in the West after 1750 came to consist of sustained **campaigns** that made collective claims aimed at authorities. They typically created special-purpose associations or coalitions and engaged in tactics such as demonstrations, petition drives, public statements, and meetings—various *contentious performances* drawing on the modern *social movement repertoire* (Tilly 2008). Movement actors attempt to represent themselves publicly as worthy, unified, numerous, and committed (Tilly 2004b: 3–4).

Based on this contentious politics approach, Sidney Tarrow (1998: 4) provides a succinct definition of social movements as "*collective challenges, based on common purposes and social solidarities, in sustained interaction with elites, opponents, and authorities.*" Social movements are *sustained* in that they consist of multiple campaigns or at least multiple episodes of collective action within a single campaign. Movement campaigns consist of *interactions* among movement actors, their targets, the public, and other relevant actors. The targets of movement claims are often government authorities, but they may also be other types of authorities, such as business owners or religious leaders (Tilly 2004b: 4). Certainly, not all social movements target the state.

Nor are social movements the only form of contentious politics. McAdam et al. (2001) include in their definition of contentious politics various public and collective political struggles, such as revolutions, nationalism, and strike waves, as well as social movements. They also consider actions by established political actors within institutions as contentious politics, provided the action is episodic and departs from the everyday, noncollective action that goes on within institutions. For example, the activities of the National Commission on Terrorist Attacks Upon the United States (also known as the 9/11 Commission), backed by collective action on the part of family members of victims of the September 11, 2001, terrorist attacks, might be considered a form of contentious politics, though perfectly legal and using an established political forum. McAdam et al. (2001: 7–8) distinguish between *contained contention* by established political actors and *transgressive contention*, which involves at least some "newly self-identified political actors" and/or "innovative collective action" by at least some parties.

Although the distinction between social movements and other phenomena such as *political parties* and *interest groups* is not always sharp, movement scholars have generally regarded movements as *challengers* that are, at least in part, *outsiders* with regard to the established power structure (Gamson 1990 [1975]; Tilly 1978). Political parties and interest groups, in contrast, are *insiders* with at least some degree of access to government authorities and other elites. However, political insiders may engage in (usually) contained contention, and movements may become **professionalized** in the sense that they include fairly stable organizations, often headed by paid leaders, and may have memberships consisting largely of financial contributors, or "paper members," rather than activists (McCarthy and Zald 1973). It may be difficult to distinguish between a professional movement organization and an established interest group.

Some social movement theorists have distinguished between social movements and the organized entities that typically populate movements. John McCarthy and Mayer Zald (1977: 1217–1218) define a social movement as "a set of opinions and beliefs in a population which represents preferences for changing some elements of the social structure and/or reward distribution of a society" and a **countermovement** as "a set of opinions and beliefs in a population opposed to a social movement." In this view social movements are "preference structures" or sets of opinions, beliefs, and goals, which may or may not be turned into collective action, depending on preexisting organization and on opportunities and costs for expressing preferences. Movements supported by populations that are internally organized through communities or associations are most likely to generate organized structures (McCarthy and Zald 1977; Oberschall 1973). A **social movement organization (SMO)** is defined as "a complex, or formal, organization which identifies its goals with the preferences of a social movement or a countermovement and attempts to implement those goals" (McCarthy and Zald 1977: 1218). Movements differ from one another in the extent to which they are organized by formal organizations and in the extent to which they trigger organized opposition or countermovements. McCarthy and Zald refer to the collection of organizations within a movement as a **social movement industry** and to all of these "industries" in a society as the **social movement sector**.

McCarthy and Zald's definition of the social movement as a preference structure differs from most other definitions, including the contentious politics view of movements as collective challenges, in that McCarthy and Zald separate preferences for change from organized collective action. They argue that this approach has the advantage of recognizing that movements are "never fully mobilized" and that the size or intensity of preferences may not predict the rise and fall of the organized movement (McCarthy and Zald 1977: 1219). Collective action may depend less on the grievances of unorganized groups than on social movement leaders who act as "entrepreneurs" in mobilizing—and perhaps even creating—preferences (McCarthy and Zald 1973). Moreover, McCarthy and Zald's approach leads us to focus on social movement organizations and the interactions of these organizations within the context of a particular social movement. Organizations have different structures, which affect their strategies and longevity, and they may cooperate or compete with one another. In some instances, organizational interests may interfere with the attainment of movement goals or preferences.

The distinction between a social movement and a social movement organization is important because major social movements typically include multiple organizations, and internal organizational dynamics and interorganizational alliances are critical to movement strategies and outcomes. For example, the environmental movement in North America includes organizations such as Greenpeace, the Sierra Club, the Nature Conservancy, the World Wildlife Fund, and Earth First!, to name only a few of the many active organizations. These organizations have different ideologies and strategic approaches and may compete with one another for members and funding, despite their common commitment to environmental protection. Coalitions of movement organizations are often difficult to form and maintain, particularly among those with different structures and strategic preferences. However, many movements face organized countermovements, which increase the urgency of coalition work (Staggenborg 1986). Movement-countermovement interactions, as well as interactions with the state, are an important topic for social movement research and often involve organizational dynamics (Meyer and Staggenborg 1996; Zald and Useem 1987).

At the same time that analyses of social movement organizations are critical to social movement theory, scholars have recognized that movements consist of more than politically motivated organizations with an explicit mandate to seek change in public policy. The notion of a **social movement community** captures the idea that movements consist of networks of individuals, cultural groups, alternative institutions, and institutional supporters as well as political movement organizations (Buechler 1990; Staggenborg 1998). Moreover, movements also consist of more than the public protest events emphasized by the contentious politics approach. Although the contentious politics approach recognizes that movements can target authorities other than the state, critics charge that movements such as religious and self-help movements tend to be neglected along with less visible forms of collective action, such as efforts to change institutions and create new forms of culture. Consequently, a number of theorists have called for broadening our conception of social movements.

Mayer Zald (2000) suggests that we should view "ideologically structured action" as movement activity. He argues that movement-related activity occurs within such organizations as political parties, government agencies, and religious institutions, and that families and schools are important in socializing movement supporters. In short, action shaped by movement ideology can be found in a variety of institutions and structures of everyday life. David Snow (2004) argues that movements can be conceived as "collective challenges to systems or structures of authority," including various types of organizations and institutions and also sets of cultural beliefs and understandings. These theorists and others argue that movement activity occurs in a wide range of venues, through a variety of forms of collective action. Movements consist of informal networks as well as formal organizations, and they produce culture and collective identity as well as political campaigns (cf. Armstrong 2002; Diani 1992; Melucci 1989, 1996; Polletta and Jasper 2001; Rupp and Taylor 1999).

The danger, as Tilly (2004b: 10) points out, is that "one may see social movements everywhere." He argues that it is better to stick to a definition of movements as consisting of sustained campaigns directed at authorities, which use the social movement repertoire of tactics and create public displays of worthiness, unity, numbers, and commitment. Then, movements can be compared to other forms of contentious politics such as conflict over policy within institutions. This approach has the merit of keeping the definition of social movements tied to the historical origins of the social movement that Tilly has so carefully documented. Nevertheless, studies of contemporary social movements such as the women's movement show that we cannot completely understand the maintenance and outcomes of important social movements without looking broadly at their cultural, institutional, and political manifestations (Staggenborg and Taylor 2005).

The above discussion might suggest that social movement analysts disagree about the very definition of social movements. The field is certainly a lively one in which new perspectives and ideas compete with existing approaches. However, the different conceptions of social movements do share some common ground. As Richard Flacks (2005: 5) argues, "I think there is agreement in the field on the following definition of social movements: they are collective efforts, of some duration and organization, using noninstitutionalized methods to bring about social change." (Of course, movements also use institutionalized methods, but most would agree that they need to employ at least some noninstitutionalized methods to qualify as social movements.) Beyond this general understanding, varying definitions of social movements lead to different emphases in the study of particular movements. The contentious politics definition of the social movement—as a sustained challenge to elites or other opponents by shifting coalitions of collective actors through a series of public campaigns—points to the political nature of social movements and their role in putting issues on the public agenda and changing public policies. McCarthy and Zald's view of social movements as preference structures leads us to focus on how preferences get transformed into organized movements through the enterprise of leaders and the creation of different types of movement organizations. Conceptualizations of social movements as including ideologically structured action, social movement communities, and challenges to different types of institutional authorities all point to the multiple arenas in which movements operate. These different emphases are not necessarily incompatible, and their usefulness depends in part on the nature of the movement being studied.

OUTLINE OF THE BOOK

The field of social movements is an exciting one that contains a healthy mix of interesting theoretical ideas and empirical studies of real social movements. The best way to introduce the field is to look at some important movements, using the tools of social movement theory. The book highlights a few contemporary movements, including the women's movement, the gay and lesbian rights movement, the environmental movement, the New American Right, and the global justice movement. Because right-wing or conservative movements have been particularly influential in the United States, I have added a chapter on the New American Right to this American edition of the book. My selection of the other movements is based on my own expertise and interest, and I make no claim of providing a comprehensive survey of social movements. However, the book does attempt to equip readers with an understanding of the theoretical questions and issues involved in studying social movements, which can be applied to a wide variety of movements. The substantive chapters in this book provide examples of how several important movements have been analyzed by social movement theorists. Although the book focuses on movements in the United States, it also draws on some studies from other Western countries, with some attention to global developments. It should be noted, too, that although there is a growing body of literature on movements outside the West (Oliver et al. 2003), this book is limited largely to studies from North America and Western Europe, which still dominate the field.

Before delving into the specifics of particular movements, I discuss the theoretical approaches, and issues stemming from those perspectives, that guide social movement theorists. Chapter 2 provides a review of several major theoretical traditions in North America and Western Europe: collective behavior theory; resource mobilization and political process perspectives; and new social movement theory. I note various attempts to synthesize ideas from these approaches, as well as efforts to go beyond them. My goal is to familiarize readers with the ideas in these perspectives and to highlight the contributions as well as limitations of each. Theories about social movements are important because they direct researchers to different types of questions regarding movements. Chapter 3 elaborates on the general types of issues studied by social movement theorists, which come out of the theoretical perspectives and guide studies of substantive movements. Because of the importance of the mass media to the movements described in the book, a section of the chapter is devoted to the role the media play in modern social movements.

In Chapter 4, before examining selected movements in detail in subsequent chapters, I discuss the historical importance of the cycle of protest of the 1960s for contemporary social movements. I describe the American civil rights movement, which had a worldwide impact on strategies of protest and political consciousness, and the New Left student and antiwar movements of the 1960s in North America and Western Europe. This discussion is important to subsequent chapters because the movements to be discussed were part of this cycle of contention or were strongly influenced by the 1960s protest cycle. Right-wing movements also have roots in the 1960s, and reaction to the leftist movements of the sixties was an important impetus for mobilization of the New American Right.

In Chapter 5, I focus on the key question of what has happened to the contemporary women's movement since the 1960s. I examine the origins of the contemporary movement, the range of feminist activities, and how the women's movement has survived and changed over time, including its development within institutions, other social movements, and cultural venues. I also look at the role of antifeminist countermovements in challenging feminist goals and channelling movement activism. The chapter demonstrates and explains the continuity and growth of feminism, as evidenced by recent developments such as third-wave feminism and expansion of the global women's movement.

Chapter 6 discusses the origins and strategies of the contemporary gay and lesbian movement and the role played by factors such as political opportunity, state repression, and countermovement campaigns. The chapter examines a variety of different movement approaches, including liberationist, equal rights, and queer politics, and the outcomes that have been achieved in the United States and other countries.

Chapter 7 takes up the problem of maintaining a movement that can deal with serious and ongoing environmental problems over many years. The chapter examines problems of winning and maintaining public interest and individual participation, combating countermovements, and creating effective organizations and strategies. After discussing recent debates on movement strategy, the chapter looks at the mass media–focused efforts of Greenpeace, green lobbies and consumer boycotts, and grassroots direct-action campaigns.

Chapter 8 examines the emergence and development of the New American Right in the United States. I have placed this chapter after the chapters on three progressive movements that were part of the cycle of protest of the 1960s because the issues raised by those movements were strongly implicated in the rise of the New American Right. The chapter expands on discussions of countermovement activity in earlier chapters, showing how antifeminist, antigay, and antienvironmental campaigns were important to right-wing mobilization.

In Chapter 9, I focus on the recent movement for global justice that came to public attention with the demonstrations against the WTO meetings in Seattle in 1999. After examining the origins of this new global movement, I discuss the strategic and organizational challenges facing the movement as it brings together local and international activists and organizations from a variety of different social movements and attempts to influence international labor, environmental, and human rights standards.

My conclusion, Chapter 10, ties together themes from the previous chapters and lays out important challenges for social movements. It stresses the importance of social movements in bringing about social and political changes.

DISCUSSION QUESTIONS

1. Which definition of social movements is most useful for understanding contemporary movements such as the environmental movement?
2. How do different definitions of social movements focus our attention on different aspects of movements?
3. What are the major tactics within the contemporary repertoire of collective action? What explains the use of these tactics in our society? How are these tactics changing with new communications technologies?

SUGGESTED READINGS

McCarthy, John D., and Mayer N. Zald. 1977. "Resource Mobilization and Social Movements: A Partial Theory." *American Journal of Sociology* 82(6):1212–1241. This is one of the seminal statements on resource mobilization theory.

Tarrow, Sidney. 1998. *Power in Movement: Social Movements and Contentious Politics*, 2nd ed. Cambridge: Cambridge University Press. This book provides an important synthesis of theoretical and substantive themes in the field.

Tilly, Charles. 2004. *Social Movements, 1768–2004*. Boulder, CO: Paradigm Publishers. This book is a very good summary of Tilly's extensive historical work on social movements.

CHAPTER 2

Theories of Social Movements
and Collective Action

Several major theoretical approaches have influenced the thinking of social movement scholars in Europe and North America. These theoretical approaches are important as perspectives that guide students of social movements to focus on particular issues, questions, and methods of inquiry. Often, researchers borrow from different theoretical approaches in carrying out their studies, and in recent years theorists have attempted to synthesize the major approaches. In the study of social movements, few scholars have aimed to build universal theories that attempt to make general statements about movements across time and place. Rather, researchers have generally recognized the importance of historical context and cultural differences, at the same time building a body of ideas about how movements operate within particular circumstances. Before the 1980s, European and North American scholars developed analytical approaches, for the most part independently of one another, with "new social movement theory" originating in Europe and "collective behavior" and "resource mobilization" theories coming mostly from the United States. Many cross-national collaborations and influences between Europeans and North Americans have since resulted in extensions and integrations of these theories.

This chapter begins with overviews of collective behavior theory, resource mobilization and political process theories, and new social movement theory, showing how each of these approaches raises different types of questions and points to different ways of describing and analyzing social movements. After summarizing these major theoretical approaches, I look at efforts to fill gaps in these theories, integrate approaches, and create new ones. In Chapter 3, I discuss further some of the important issues raised by the theories outlined below.

COLLECTIVE BEHAVIOR THEORY

A number of different perspectives are included in the category of **collective behavior theory**, which is often referred to as the classical model of social movements. Collective behavior theories have also been labeled *strain* or *breakdown theories* because they typically posit that collective behavior comes about during a period of social disruption, when grievances are deeply felt, rather than being a standard part of the political process (Jenkins 1981; Marx and Wood 1975; McAdam 1999 [1982]; Morris and Herring 1987). Collective behavior theorists have studied a wide variety of phenomena, including crowds, panics, mobs, riots, crazes, fads, religious cults and revivals, social movements, and revolutions. The study of "crowds" dates back to the late nineteenth century when European theorists such as Gustave Le Bon (1895) tried to explain crowd behavior by analyzing the psychology of the collective or large gathering. Le Bon emphasized the irrationality and abnormality of crowds, and his work has often been invoked by scholars trying to disavow the supposed tendency of collective behavior theory to treat social movement participants as irrational and pathological. In fact, most collective behavior theorists reject the view that collective behavior is irrational, although many are concerned with the psychological states of participants and the spontaneous dynamics of collective actions outside established structures.

In general, collective behavior theories share several assumptions (Morris and Herring 1987: 145). First, they see collective behavior as existing outside of institutionalized structures, though some theorists note the linkages between institutional and noninstitutional actions. Various forms of collective behavior are connected insofar as they are all unstructured situations unbound by established norms. Second, collective behavior theorists argue that social movements and other forms of collective behavior arise as a result of some type of structural or cultural "breakdown" or "strain" such as a natural disaster, rapid social change, or dramatic event. Third, collective behavior theorists assign an important role to the shared beliefs of participants in analyzing the emergence of social movements and other forms of collective behavior. Although preexisting organization and strategy are typically mentioned by collective behavior theorists, they are not a major focus, whereas the psychological states of participants and emergent ideologies and forms of organization receive much attention. Beyond these similarities, there are major differences among collective behavior approaches.

The Chicago School Approach to Collective Behavior
The Chicago School approach to collective behavior was initiated in the 1920s by Robert Park and Ernest Burgess (1921) and was developed by a number of other sociologists associated with the symbolic interactionist approach at the University of Chicago, including Herbert Blumer (1951), Ralph Turner and Lewis Killian (1957, 1972, 1987), and Kurt and Gladys Lang (1961). **Symbolic interactionism** is a social psychological theory that focuses on how actors construct meanings through social interaction. According to the Chicago School perspective, collective behavior develops in situations where established systems of meaning and sources of information have broken down, forcing participants to construct new meanings to guide their behavior (Morris and Herring 1987: 147). Collective behavior theorists are concerned with how participants in social movements manage to act collectively, creating goals, new organizational structures, and new culture.

Turner and Killian emphasize the role of the "emergent norm" as a shared view of reality that justifies and coordinates collective behavior. In the case of social movements, which are complex and sustained forms of collective behavior, emergent norms may become "highly elaborated ideologies such as the environmentalist's view of the consequences of ecological imbalance and the Marxist's view of class struggle" (Turner and Killian 1987: 8).

Thus, Chicago School collective behavior theorists focus on the emergence of social movements and the creation of new forms of activity and organization. Collective behavior is a means of bringing about social change, and emergent forms of social order develop through the interactions of individuals in social movements. Ideology plays an important role in highlighting injustices and guiding collective behavior, but the beliefs that govern this behavior are not fixed; systems of belief emerge and develop as social movement actors interact with one another, the public, opponents, and authorities. Emergent norms may develop in response to a precipitating event or some type of extraordinary condition as individuals within preexisting or new groups interact with one another and try out forms of action, revising their ideas and actions in response to changing events and opportunities (Turner and Killian 1987: 10).

Smelser's Theory of Collective Behavior

In his influential book *Theory of Collective Behavior* (1962), Neil Smelser presents a model consisting of six determinants. The model is "value added" in that each determinant or social condition adds value to the explanation; the conditions operate within the context of one another and together explain collective behavior. First, conditions of *structural conduciveness* permit or encourage certain types of collective behavior. For example, panics occur in money markets, rather than in financial systems where property is tied to kinship and cannot be easily transferred (Smelser 1962: 15). Second, conditions of *structural strain* create real or anticipated deprivation; this strain, such as the threat of economic deprivation, combines with the condition of conduciveness. Third, the *growth and spread of a generalized belief* makes the situation meaningful to potential participants in collective behavior; the generalized belief identifies the source and nature of the strain and suggests possible responses. Fourth, *precipitating factors*, such as a dramatic event, give the generalized beliefs a concrete target for collective action. For example, an incident of police brutality might provoke a race riot when it occurs in the context of conduciveness, strain, and a generalized belief (Smelser 1962: 17). Fifth, *mobilization for action* must occur, and Smelser notes that leadership is particularly important in mobilizing participants. Sixth, *social control* may act to prevent the collective behavior, perhaps by minimizing strains, or to limit the scope of the collective behavior. The potential or actual episode of collective behavior will be affected by the actions of police, the courts, the press, community leaders, and other agents of social control.

Theorists have found the idea of a value-added model useful, and a number of studies have shown the factors identified by Smelser to be important in predicting collective action. However, scholars have also raised a number of criticisms. Smelser's theory, along with other breakdown theories, has been criticized for relying too heavily on structural strains to explain social movements. Critics have argued that no clear criteria exist for identifying "strain" in a society; once a social movement or other form of collective behavior occurs, it is always possible to find some type of strain, making the argument tautological (Useem 1975: 9; Wilson 1973: 35). Moreover, the theory seems to assume that societies are normally stable and that strains, and the social movements that accompany them, are unusual. In fact, strains may be a fairly constant feature of societies, and the rise of movements may be better explained by factors such as political opportunities, resources, and organization. Critics have also objected to Smelser's characterization of generalized beliefs as "short-circuited" in the sense of bypassing normal routines and controls and "akin to magical beliefs" insofar as expectations of the consequences of collective action may be unrealistic (Smelser 1962: 8). Smelser and other collective behavior theorists have often been lumped with Le Bon and accused of treating participants in collective behavior as "irrational." However, collective behavior theorists have vehemently denied this charge, arguing that their approaches do not assume irrationality on the part of movement participants (Killian 1994; Smelser 1970; Turner 1981).

Mass Society Theory

One version of collective behavior theory, **mass society theory**, does view collective behavior as an extreme response to social isolation. Mass society theory takes off from the Durkheimian notion that social stability is maintained by the existence of common values that are transmitted and sustained through various social institutions. A "mass society" is one in which there are few secondary or intermediate groups, such as religious groups or community organizations, to bind people together and keep them attached to the mainstream society. In *The Politics of Mass Society*, William Kornhauser (1959) argued that social changes, such as rapid industrialization and urbanization or economic depressions, uproot people from their normal associations, as in the case of new immigrants to cities or unemployed workers. Consequently, individuals become isolated from social and political institutions. This creates social "atomization" and feelings of "alienation and anxiety" that make people susceptible to recruitment by social movements such as the German Nazi movement. In a popular version of mass society theory, Eric Hoffer (1951) argued in *The True Believer* that alienated, fanatical, and irrational individuals participate in social movements as a means of finding an identity and sense of belonging in a rapidly changing society.

A large body of empirical research has challenged mass society theory, showing that the theory is essentially wrong (Jenkins 1981: 92–93). In fact, it is not isolated individuals who are most likely to be drawn into social movements, but just the opposite. Research shows that individuals who are tied into social networks, and who participate in organizations, are most likely to be recruited into social movements. Whereas mass society theorists viewed organizations as playing a conservative role in keeping individuals from participating in collective action, they failed to appreciate the role of preexisting organizations in mobilizing participants for social movements (Morris and Herring 1987: 155). For example, black churches provided a preexisting organizational base through which the civil rights movement mobilized local African-American communities, refocusing the cultural content of the churches on movement messages (Morris 1984: 96–97).

Relative Deprivation Theory

Relative deprivation theory is based on the observation, made by Alexis de Tocqueville and others, that people often rebel when things are improving; it is not the most deprived groups that engage in collective action, but those who seem to be improving their positions or who are among the best off within an aggrieved group. When conditions start to improve, expectations rise, but when the rate of improvement does not match expectations, people feel deprived. For example, Freeman (1975) argues that support for the women's movement increased as women gained access to education but did not achieve commensurate access to high-paying occupations. Deprivation is *relative* because people feel dissatisfied with their situations relative to what they think they deserve, and they assess what they deserve by comparing their progress to that of other groups. Thus, college-educated women might compare themselves to men of the same educational levels in assessing their occupational satisfaction. Social changes such as large-scale economic shifts generate feelings of relative deprivation in that people's expectations rise, they experience change, and then they are frustrated by the gap between their expectations and their actual situations. When people become angry and frustrated, according to relative deprivation theory, they rebel.

Relative deprivation theories were popular in the 1960s and 1970s (e.g., Davies 1962, 1971; Gurr 1970), but they have since been strongly criticized on a number of grounds (Gurney and Tierney 1982; Jenkins 1981). One difficulty is that relative deprivation studies typically infer psychological states of relative deprivation from objective indicators such as unemployment rates. Studies designed to test the theory have found little evidence that such objective measures of relative deprivation are good predictors of various types of rebellions; instead, factors such as organizational capacities and governmental sanctions are better predictors of collective action (Jenkins 1981: 100–101). Although feelings of relative deprivation may be present, they are not likely to generate collective action in the absence of other factors such as resources and organization. Moreover, feelings of relative deprivation may be generated through participation in a movement rather than being a precondition for the movement (Jenkins 1981: 103). For example, women who worked in the New Left began to feel deprived relative to their male comrades, who occupied the most important roles in the movement and ignored women's complaints (Freeman 1975: 57–62).

RESOURCE MOBILIZATION AND POLITICAL PROCESS THEORIES

In the 1970s, the focus of North American social movement research began to shift away from the concerns of collective behavior theory to those raised by newly emerging **resource mobilization** and **political process** approaches (Gamson 1990 [1975]; McAdam 1999; McCarthy and Zald 1973, 1977; Oberschall 1973; Tilly 1978). These new models of social movements and collective action resulted in part from the experiences of social movement theorists with movements of the 1960s and their criticisms of classical collective behavior theories for inadequacies in explaining the new wave of protest. Although the criticisms did not apply equally to all versions of collective behavior theory, they helped to shape the new perspectives, which departed from past theories in important ways (Jenkins 1983). First, collective behavior theory explanations for the rise of social movements and collective action were considered wrong or inadequate. Mass society theory, as we have seen, was not supported by empirical studies, and resource mobilization theorists argued that socially connected people, rather than social isolates, are most likely to be mobilized for collective action. Strain theories also failed to explain the rise of social movements insofar as neither large-scale strains in social systems nor individual discontents lead directly to collective action. The extent of movement mobilization and participation in a population cannot be predicted by the amount of frustration or suffering experienced by people. Second, resource mobilization and political process theorists rejected what they perceived as a sharp disjuncture in collective behavior theory between "normal" or routine actions and collective action. The newer perspectives emphasized the continuities between collective actions and institutionalized actions, as social movements were seen as a continuation of the political process, albeit by disorderly means (Gamson 1990: 139). Whereas collective behavior theories, by emphasizing the motivations of individuals, focused on social movements as psychological phenomena, the newer perspectives treated social movements as political phenomena (McAdam 1999: 11–19). Individual participants were seen as rational actors pursuing their interests and it was argued that movements arise out of preexisting organization, engaging in both institutionalized and noninstitutionalized forms of action.

Resource Mobilization Theory

Early resource mobilization theorists argued that strains or grievances can nearly always be found; the mobilization of social movements requires resources, organization, and opportunities for collective action. As the label "resource mobilization" suggests, **resources** are seen as central to successful collective action in this approach, and a wide variety of studies demonstrate linkages between resource availability and collective action (Edwards and McCarthy 2004). Resources include both *tangible* assets, such as funding, and *intangible* assets, such as the commitment of participants (Freeman 1979). Edwards and McCarthy (2004: 125–128) identify various types of resources used and created by social movements: *moral resources*, such as legitimacy; *cultural resources*, including tactical repertoires and strategic know-how; *social-organizational resources*, including movement infrastructures, networks, and organizational structures; *human resources*, such as the labor and experience of activists; and *material resources*, such as money and office space.

In their seminal articles advancing an entrepreneurial-organizational version of the theory, McCarthy and Zald (1973, 1977) argue that **movement entrepreneurs** play an important role in defining movement issues by drawing on public sentiments and increasing public demand for change. While stressing the importance of resources such as skills, money, and time for movement mobilization, they note that resources do not necessarily come from aggrieved groups (the *beneficiaries* of a movement), but may come from **conscience constituents**, who contribute to movements but do not personally benefit from their achievements (McCarthy and Zald 1977: 1221–1222). In some instances, the ability to mobilize conscience constituents determines movement effectiveness. For example, Jenkins and Perrow (1977) compared a successful attempt to organize American farm workers in the 1960s and early 1970s with an earlier failed attempt, arguing that outside support from a coalition of liberal organizations was essential to the successful challenge. Other researchers, however, emphasize the importance of internal resources for oppressed groups. In the case of the American civil rights movement, Aldon Morris (1984) found that black churches and other community institutions provided indigenous resources that were critical to movement success.

Social movement organizations and their leaders are typically important in mobilizing resources for movements, whether from **beneficiary constituents** or conscience constituents. Resource mobilization theorists have called attention to the varying structures of social movement organizations, which influence their longevity and strategic choices. Studies have suggested that organizations with more formalized or bureaucratic structures are better able to sustain a movement over time, whereas informal organizations are better at innovating tactics and taking quick action in response to events (Gamson 1990; Staggenborg 1988, 1989). For example, in the environmental movement, loosely structured groups such as Earth First! have organized blockades to prevent logging and have engaged in other acts of civil disobedience to protect the environment, whereas bureaucratic organizations such as the Sierra Club are more involved in lobbying governments and are better able to raise funds to maintain a large organization with paid staff. In addition to political movement organizations, theorists have identified various other types of **mobilizing structures**, including formal and informal networks, groups, and organizational vehicles, which movements use to recruit participants and organize action campaigns (McAdam et al. 1996: 3). Morris (1984) shows the importance in the American civil rights movement of a type of mobilizing structure that he terms a "movement halfway house." For example, the Highlander Folk School was founded in the 1930s as a place where oppressed people could participate in educational programs that would draw on their own experiences and allow them to devise strategies of social change, and in the 1940s and 1950s many civil rights movement leaders attended the school and participated in developing a successful mass education program for the movement (Morris 1984: 141–149).

Political Process Theory

The political process approach emphasizes the interactions of social movement actors with the state and the role of political opportunities in the mobilization and outcomes of social movements. Political process theorists argue that social movements are most likely to emerge when potential collective actors perceive that conditions are favorable. The concept of **political opportunity** refers generally to features of the political environment that influence movement emergence and success, but specific definitions of political opportunity differ considerably (Meyer 2004). Sidney Tarrow's (1998: 77–80) elaboration of the elements of political opportunity is perhaps the most widely employed schema. He conceives of political opportunity as including the extent of openness in the polity, shifts in political alignments, divisions among elites, the availability of influential allies, and repression or facilitation by the state. When opportunities expand generally, a variety of movements may mobilize, resulting in a **cycle of contention**, which is "a phase of heightened conflict across the social system" (Tarrow 1998: 142). For example, during the 1960s a large number of protest movements mobilized in Europe and North America, including the civil rights movement, women's movement, gay rights movement, environmental movement, and antiwar movement. Moreover, movements are not only influenced by political opportunities; they can also create opportunities for themselves and other movements. Tarrow suggests that movements that are "early risers" in a protest cycle may open up opportunities for later movements by demonstrating that targets are vulnerable to collective action.

In addition to affecting the emergence of social movements, political opportunities may alter the strategies and outcomes of protest. However, opportunities for mobilization and opportunities to effect change are sometimes different (Meyer 2004: 136–137). Social movement theorists have recognized that *threats* are as likely as opportunities to mobilize activists by creating feelings of outrage and urgency. It may be more difficult to mobilize participants when authorities or other elites are sympathetic to movement goals because supporters may feel that there is no need for collective action. When threats arise or negative outcomes occur, there may be little opportunity for effecting change but great opportunity for mobilization as movement supporters become alarmed by unfavorable changes. When a countermovement mobilizes to oppose movement goals, movement supporters are likely to respond with heightened activity. For example, the rise of a strong antiabortion movement in the United States helped to keep abortion rights activists mobilized, even after they had won legalization of abortion through the 1973 Supreme Court ruling in *Roe v. Wade* (Staggenborg 1991).

A Synthetic Approach

By the 1980s and 1990s, resource mobilization and political process approaches dominated North American social movement theory. The two approaches were sometimes treated as distinct models (McAdam 1999) and sometimes as two variants of resource mobilization theory, with a political process version of resource mobilization theory associated with theorists such as William Gamson, Anthony Oberschall, and Charles Tilly and an entrepreneurial-organizational version of resource mobilization theory formulated by John McCarthy and Mayer Zald (McCarthy and Zald 2002; Perrow 1979). Increasingly, however, resource mobilization and political process approaches could be seen as part of one evolving perspective, with many of the same theorists contributing to each and attempting to synthesize the model (McAdam et al. 1988, 1996). Key elements of the synthetic approach became so essential to social movement studies that McAdam et al. (2001) went so far as to refer to the synthesis as the "classical social movement agenda."

The synthetic resource mobilization/political process model views social movements as political entities aiming to create social change. Scholars have analyzed various features of the movement environment and of movement organizations and strategies that influence the mobilization and outcomes of collective action. The approach initially downplayed grievances and ideology, as these were thought to be overemphasized by collective behavior theorists, who focused on individual discontent as the driving force behind collective action. As the newer approach developed, however, this lacuna began to be addressed. In particular, theorists sympathetic to resource mobilization/political process theory developed the concept of **collective action frames** as a way of capturing the importance of meanings and ideas in stimulating protest (Benford and Snow 2000). Collective action frames are interpretations of issues and events that inspire and legitimate collective action and *framing* is an important activity of movement leaders and organizations. The **framing perspective** emphasizes the role of movements in constructing cultural meanings, as movement leaders and organizations frame issues in particular ways to identify injustices, attribute blame, propose solutions, and motivate collective action.

In what is now a large literature on collective action frames, movement theorists have analyzed the role of framing in a variety of movement processes. Snow and Benford (1992) distinguish between **master frames**, which are generic types of frames available for use by a number of different social movements, and movement-specific collective action frames, which can be derived from master frames. They argue that the availability of an innovative master frame helps to explain the emergence of a protest cycle consisting of a number of different social movements. For example, they suggest that the "rights frame" was a master frame used by the civil rights movement and adapted by a number of other movements such as the women's movement and the gay rights movement in the protest cycle of the 1960s. In addition to their role in the growth of a protest cycle, master frames can be used to bring different movements together in coalitions. Gerhards and Rucht (1992) analyze the ways in which organizers of multimovement **campaigns** extended master frames dealing with peace and globalization to address the concerns of a variety of different movement activists such as feminists, environmentalists, and union members. In a study of cross-movement activism in Vancouver, Carroll and Ratner (1996) find that the use of a master frame stressing the "political-economy of injustice" brought together activists from the labor, peace, and feminist movements.

Analysts of collective action framing have also looked at the *frame disputes* that often take place in social movements (Benford 1993). Disputes over frames are common because social movements are not unified actors, but typically consist of many different types of groups and individuals with varying ideological and strategic perspectives. Framing disputes may occur either within or between movement organizations, and their consequences may include the decline of some types of movement organizations, the depletion of resources that could have been used to accomplish goals, factionalism, and lack of cohesiveness in a movement (Benford 1993: 694–697). Although the impacts of frames are often difficult to assess, movements that succeed in creating persuasive and coherent frames appear better able to attract movement participants, form coalitions, win public approval and media attention, and influence authorities. Moreover, effective frames may help movements to overcome a lack of political opportunities (Polletta and Ho 2006).

The concepts of *political opportunities, mobilizing structures,* and *cultural framing* became the core elements of North American social movement theory in the 1990s (McAdam et al. 1996). Attention to political opportunities reflected the state-centered approach of political process theory, and conceptions of mobilizing structures drew on the entrepreneurial-organizational version of resource mobilization theory. The concept of framing provided a means for resource mobilization theorists to bring ideas and cultural elements into social movement theory, but the strategic approach to framing did not satisfy critics who argued for a broader approach to culture and ideology. Consequently, there was a "cultural turn" in social movement theory as scholars began to examine a variety of cultural processes. **Discourse analysis** became important as theorists looked at questions such as how actors construct frames and discursive strategies using the genres available in the contexts where framing occurs (Steinberg 1998: 856). Expanding on the concept of political opportunities, Ferree et al. (2002) use the concept of a **discursive opportunity structure** to examine the factors, such as cultural context and mass media norms, that shape movement discourse in different countries. More broadly, a number of movement theorists have proposed notions of a **cultural opportunity structure** or "cultural opportunities" to refer to elements of cultural environments, such as ideologies, that facilitate and constrain collective action along with political opportunities (McAdam 1994; Noonan 1995). This cultural turn in North American social movement theory has been influenced by European new social movement theories, which emphasize symbolic activities in cultural spheres as well as instrumental actions directed at the state (Buechler 1995: 442).

NEW SOCIAL MOVEMENT THEORY

In Europe, the approach known as **new social movement theory** developed independently of North American theories, emphasizing the new types of social movements that have emerged in "postindustrial" or "advanced capitalist" society, including the peace, environmental, gay and lesbian, student, and women's movements. New social movement theorists have argued that these movements differ in structure, type of constituents, and ideology from the "old" movements of industrial society, notably the labor movement. As is the case with collective behavior and resource mobilization perspectives, however, a number of different views fall under the category of new social movement theory (Buechler 1995; Pichardo 1997). Some theorists have been concerned with how large-scale socioeconomic trends are related to the emergence of new social movements, while others have focused on changes in the sites of conflict and nature of civil society in an "information society."

Scholars concerned with the effects of modernization have argued that new movements mobilized because there are new grievances in a postindustrial society, resulting in new values, new forms of action, and new constituencies (Klandermans 1986: 21). For example, German theorist Jürgen Habermas (1984, 1987) draws attention to the new goals and demands associated with movements in postindustrial societies. He argues that new social movements are concerned with defense of the "lifeworld," the sphere of life not governed by instrumental, economic concerns but where real debate and communication create normative consensus. Because political and economic institutions are interfering in this realm, new movements have arisen to defend against bureaucratic and economic intrusions and to raise issues related to quality of life, democratic participation, and identity. Although economic concerns remain important in new social movement theory, the nature of the economic concerns has changed and new concerns have been added. For example, new international movements have emerged in an era of global capitalism with new kinds of concerns such as the effects of world trade and environmental degradation. "Postmaterialist" values, focusing on quality-of-life issues, are central to new social movements (Inglehart 1990).

Scholars who focus on the new sites of conflict that accompany large-scale transformations have stressed the various processes involved in the creation and ongoing construction of social movements. One important process emphasized by new social movement theorists is the creation of **collective identity**, which refers to the sense of shared experiences and values that connects individuals to movements and gives participants a sense of "collective agency" or feeling that they can effect change through collective action (Snow 2001). Alberto Melucci (1989, 1996) focuses on how collective identities are continually constructed by small groups in the "submerged networks" of everyday life. He sees social movements not as collections of relatively stable movement organizations or as unified actors, but as fluid networks that can erupt into collective action from time to time. To understand how social movements are constructed, we need to look at the formation and maintenance of the cognitive frameworks and social relationships that form the basis of collective action (Melucci 1988: 331). Before a movement becomes visible, there is a period of "latency" when a new collective identity is emerging. For example, American women began to develop a feminist identity within civil rights and New Left student and peace movement networks (Mueller 1994). Once a movement is under way, the "collective" is continually constructed, and failure to maintain solidarity may lead to tensions in the movement and a decline in collective action (Melucci 1988: 333). In the case of the women's movement, different organizations and networks formed around different formulations of movement identity (Mueller 1994: 247–248). As relationships are formed within the submerged networks of new social movements and new collective identities are constructed, activists produce new cultural models and symbolic challenges. For new social movement theorists, these cultural innovations are a key contribution of social movements to social change.

New social movement theory's focus on culture and collective identity has been influential in redirecting North American movement theory. A number of scholars attempting to fill in gaps in resource mobilization and political process approaches have adopted Melucci's (1988: 343) view of collective identity as a process that involves the formulation of cognitive frameworks, the activation of relationships among actors, and the investment of emotions. Recent studies have focused on collective identity to explain how interests get defined and movements emerge; how people are motivated to participate in collective action; how strategic choices are made; and what cultural impacts movements have (Polletta and Jasper 2001: 284). Moreover, theorists interested in culture and collective identity also began to emphasize the role of emotions in protest, which helps to explain such problems as why individuals participate, how collective identity is created, and why movements continue or decline (Goodwin et al. 2001; Jasper 1998). For example, Nepstad and Smith (2001) show how moral outrage was generated among members of the American religious community as credible information about U.S. activities in Central America spread through church networks, motivating many individuals to join the peace movement.

Along with these influences, however, new social movement theory generated much debate among movement theorists. In particular, scholars questioned how "new" the movements in postindustrial societies really are with regard to the forms of collective action employed, organizational structures created, and issues addressed. Charles Tilly (1988) argues that, from a historical perspective, recent social movements such as the environmental movement and the women's movement basically employ the same repertoire of actions as nineteenth-century movements, including forming associations, demonstrating, and petitioning. In response to the claim of new social movement theorists that new social movements are loosely structured, Dieter Rucht (1988) shows that in fact movements such as the environmental movement contain a mix of different organizational forms, including both bureaucratic organizations and grassroots collectives. And, disputing the idea that concerns with identity are new, Craig Calhoun (1993) shows that nineteenth-century social movements such as the labor movement were also concerned with issues of identity as, for example, they mobilized workers with different ethnic and regional backgrounds. Carroll and Ratner (1995) note both the historical importance of collective identity to labor movements and the need for contemporary unions to alter bureaucratic forms of organization and reconstruct collective identities in order to survive large-scale economic globalization and to attract workers such as women and visible minorities. In their research on labor organizations in Vancouver, they find that labor activists were involved in cross-movement coalitions, open to "cultural politics" such as feminist music and gay pride events, and sensitive to the concerns of a variety of different groups.

Thus, the distinction between "old" and "new" social movements may be difficult to defend on the grounds of collective identity and organizational preferences. Nevertheless, new social movement theory has been valuable in directing attention to some central theoretical issues such as the connection between large-scale features of society and social movements and the importance of culture, identity, and everyday life in the mobilization and outcomes of social movements.

NEW DIRECTIONS IN SOCIAL MOVEMENT THEORY

Recent challenges to social movement theory come from different directions, yet voice surprisingly similar concerns. Some critics of the political process approach have argued that the theory is overly structural, focusing on the relatively stable "political opportunity structure" that influences movement mobilization and outcomes (Goodwin and Jasper 1999). According to these critics, the structural focus neglects the agency of movement activists, who respond to opportunities and in some cases create them, as well as cultural elements of movements and their environments. Social networks, for example, are treated as structures that mobilize participants, but the ideas and emotions transmitted through networks are often overlooked. Culture is subsumed under framing activities, while a broader understanding of how culture constrains and facilitates collective action is underdeveloped.

McAdam et al. (2001) argue that the political process model, which they helped to develop, is too static, failing to capture the dynamic interactions of contentious politics. They argue for a new approach that will uncover the underlying mechanisms and processes of change. While political process theory works best in analyzing relatively unified movements in democratic polities, their dynamic contentious politics approach is developed by comparing different types of contentious politics—movements, revolutions, strike waves, nationalism, and so forth—in a wide range of settings. To create a more dynamic model of contentious politics, McAdam et al. argue that opportunities and threats should not be treated as objective structures but as "subject to attribution," recognizing that the perceptions of activists are important. Mobilizing structures should not be treated simply as preexisting organizational sites, but as structures that are actively appropriated by collective actors. Framing, similarly, is not just a strategic tool, but involves "the interactive construction of disputes among challengers, their opponents, elements of the state, third parties, and the media." Collective action involves interaction, and mobilization "occurs throughout an episode of contention" (McAdam et al. 2001: 43–45). McAdam et al. aim to understand how collective actors attribute threats and opportunities, appropriate mobilizing structures, construct frames and meanings, and innovate collective action tactics.

In short, several of the major developers of political process theory agree with their critics that a more social constructionist approach to social movements and collective action is needed to focus on the perceptions and strategies of activists (Kurzman 2004). Or, as Oliver et al. (2003) note, "there is a growing appreciation for the need to integrate structural political theories of movements with constructivist theories rooted in social psychology and cultural sociology." Klandermans (1997) discusses the interaction of structural factors, such as social networks, with social psychological factors, such as cognitive information processing, in the process of recruitment to social movements. Buechler (2000, 2002) proposes a "structural approach to social movements" that recognizes the interrelationships of large-scale patterns and human agency. Polletta (1997, 2004) argues that social movement theorists have erred in treating "culture" and "structure" as distinct entities, tending to equate culture with agency and structure with politics. In reality, culture, defined as "the symbolic dimensions of all structures, institutions, and practices" (Polletta 2004: 100), constrains as well as enables collective action, and political opportunities have cultural dimensions.

CONCLUSION

Theorists of social movements and collective action continue to grapple with how best to integrate culture and politics, emotions and interests, macro-level changes and micro-level interactions. Ultimately, theories are important insofar as they help us to understand the rise, development, and decline of social movements and to investigate key issues in the study of collective action. Despite efforts at synthesis, different theories focus on different aspects of social movements and lead to different research questions. Table 2.1 outlines the differing views on origins, focuses, and outcomes of the major theoretical approaches to understanding social movements. Collective behavior theories are important in pointing to the grievances and breakdowns in routine that may result from critical events and social changes and the importance of ideologies in mobilizing activists around these grievances. They tend to see protest as occurring outside the normal political process and as resulting in new forms of organization and new social understandings. Resource mobilization and political process theories

Table 2.1 Major Theories of Social Movements

THEORETICAL PERSPECTIVE	ORIGINS OF MOVEMENTS	IMPORTANT FEATURES AND FOCUSES	KEY OUTCOMES OF MOVEMENTS
Collective Behavior	Social disruptions, strains, grievances; precipitating events	Social psychology of protest; emergent organization and norms; protest outside institutional structures	New meanings and forms of organization
Resource Mobilization and Political Process	Pre-existing organization; resources; political opportunities and threats; master frames	Connections between social movements and political process; mobilizing structures; framing strategies; institutional and non-institutional forms of action	New resources, organizations and frames; cultural and political changes
New Social Movement	Large-scale changes; everyday networks and organizational structures; new types of grievances	Collective identity; submerged networks; new types of structures, constituents and ideologies	New types of values, identities and organizations; cultural innovations

focus much more on the role of preexisting organizational structures, resources, and political opportunities in explaining the origins of movements, and they focus on the mobilizing structures, framing efforts, and opportunities that affect the maintenance and outcomes of movements. In this approach, social movements are an ordinary part of the political process, although they tend to employ disorderly protest strategies rather than the established practices of insiders with routine access to the political system. In the new social movement approach, theorists emphasize both how large-scale changes affect the organization and goals of movements and how movements create new cultural forms and identities and develop ideas and strategies within the structures of contemporary society. Their approach leads to an emphasis on the ongoing creation of movement identities and movement cultures that sustain social movements and allow for periodic protests.

These major theories of social movements all contribute to the formulation of research questions by social movement scholars. In investigating different issues related to theoretical approaches, scholars add to a growing body of knowledge about the mechanisms and processes underlying movement mobilization and outcomes. In the following chapter, I identify some of the important issues that scholars have examined in studying various social movements and elaborate on some of the themes touched upon in describing the major theoretical approaches.

DISCUSSION QUESTIONS

1. How might a theory of social movements influence how a movement is studied and analyzed?
2. What different questions about movements and ways of analyzing them are raised by collective behavior, resource mobilization/political process, and new social movement theories?
3. How are large-scale social changes important to each of the major theories of social movements?

SUGGESTED READINGS

Jenkins, J. Craig. 1981. "Sociopolitical Movements." pp. 81–154 in *Handbook of Political Behavior*, vol. 4, edited by S. L. Long. New York: Plenum Publishers. This is a very good review essay detailing theoretical approaches to social movements.

McAdam, Doug, John D. McCarthy, and Mayer N. Zald, eds. 1996. *Comparative Perspectives on Social Movements*. New York: Cambridge University Press. This important collection of writings highlights the concepts of political opportunity, mobilizing structures, and collective action framing.

Pichardo, Nelson A. 1997. "New Social Movements: A Critical Review." *Annual Review of Sociology* 23:411–430. This is a good review essay dealing with New Social Movement theory.

CHAPTER 3

Issues in the Study of Social
Movements and Collective Action

Theories such as those reviewed in the previous chapter aim to explain the origins, growth and decline, and consequences of social movements and collective action. In this chapter, I identify key issues and elaborate on theoretical ideas about these concerns, drawing on the major theories of collective action. The issues explored by social movement scholars range from macro-level questions about large-scale structural changes to meso-level organizational dynamics and micro-level questions about individual decisions and interactions. Table 3.1 lists the kinds of questions that are asked in each of these three levels of research. One of the challenges for theorists is to connect these levels of analysis in their explanations of social movements and collective action. The various issues to be covered are interrelated, and the following discussion is organized around the central categories of movement emergence, maintenance and decline, and outcomes. Under each of these broad headings, more specific problems are discussed. A separate discussion of social movements and mass media is also included because this topic is particularly relevant to several subsequent chapters dealing with specific movements. Following discussion of these substantive topics, I provide a short discussion of some of the methods used to study issues in social movement research.

MOVEMENT EMERGENCE: MOBILIZATION
AND RECRUITMENT

Movements typically do not emerge suddenly, and new movements are often linked to previous ones. **Mobilization** is the process whereby a group that shares grievances or interests gains collective control over resources (Tilly 1978: 54). The **recruitment** of individuals to movements is part of the broader process of mobilization, involving the commitment of individual resources, such as time, money, and skills, to a cause. Mobilization and recruitment are ongoing processes rather than one-time events, as groups challenging the social and political status quo need

Table 3.1 Key Issues in the Study of Social Movements

Macro (large-scale) level

- how large-scale changes and events alter resources and organizational structures and create grievances that stimulate collective action
- how cultural and political opportunities facilitate the emergence of social movements
- how cycles of contention arise and spread
- how master frames originate and diffuse into a culture
- how changing political, cultural, and economic conditions affect the ongoing strategies and growth, maintenance, and decline of a social movement
- how social movements contribute to large-scale cultural and political changes, which affect subsequent collective action
- how countermovements emerge in response to social movements

Meso (organizational) level

- what resources are available to groups and what organizational structures tie group members together prior to movement emergence
- how leaders use mobilizing structures, master frames, and cultural and material resources to organize movements
- how leaders and movement organizations frame injustices and recognize opportunities for collective action
- how collective identities are developed within structures of everyday life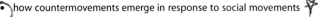
- how the organizational structures of movement organizations affect maintenance and strategies
- how collective campaigns are mobilized and how they affect subsequent movement organization and collective action
- how coalitions are formed and maintained within and across social movements
- the impact of interactions of movement organizations with other organizations such as countermovement groups, established interest groups and institutions, government agencies, and mass media

Micro (individual) level

- how social networks lead individuals to movement organizations
- how individuals come to believe that collective action is necessary and effective
- how outrage and other emotions are generated to motivate participation
- how individuals decide that the benefits of collective action are worth the costs
- how individuals take on collective identities and feel solidarity with a group
- why individuals sustain or terminate their participation in social movements
- how individuals are affected by their participation in social movements

to continually maintain control over resources and keep individuals involved following their initial recruitment. We begin by looking at major factors in the mobilization of a social movement and then turn to the issue of individual recruitment and participation.

Influences on Mobilization

A number of factors are involved in mobilization, including large-scale socio-economic and political changes, opportunities and threats, critical events, pre-existing or emergent organization, leadership, resources, and frames. Collective behavior, political process, and new social movement theorists all have pointed to the importance of large-scale social changes in stimulating social movements. Urbanization, for example, creates social problems such as poor housing conditions that lead to grievances among particular groups. While grievances do not automatically lead to mobilization, large-scale changes can also affect the organization and resources of groups. Leaders can organize participants through preexisting structures as well as new movement organizations, using the cultural and material resources associated with them. In the case of the American civil rights movement, studies point to the importance of socio-economic and political changes for the rise of the movement. The decline of cotton as a cash crop in the United States had a number of important consequences that created favorable conditions for the emergence of a civil rights movement (McAdam 1999: 77), including the migration of many southern blacks to cities, where they were concentrated in black neighborhoods and could support indigenous institutions.

Both the resources controlled by a group and the extent of organization among members of a group or collectivity prior to movement mobilization are important factors. If individuals already share membership in some of the same organizations, they have a preexisting communications network, resources, and leaders that can be mobilized; in some cases, blocs of people may be recruited rapidly through preexisting organizations (Oberschall 1973: 125). Numerous studies find that social networks help to recruit individuals into social movements. Leadership is also important, either in the form of indigenous leaders or movement entrepreneurs who define issues and create movement organizations (McCarthy and Zald 1973, 1977). McCarthy and Zald suggest that entrepreneurs may even be able to mobilize movements in the absence of preexisting grievances. Where grievances are long-standing and preexisting organization exists, this type of entrepreneurial leadership is less likely to matter (Jenkins 1981: 121), but leaders remain important in framing injustices and recognizing opportunities for collective action (Morris and Staggenborg 2004).

Political process theorists suggest that political opportunities or threats lead to the emergence of a social movement. As Sidney Tarrow (1998: 71) argues:

> Contention increases when people gain the external resources to escape their compliance and find opportunities in which to use them. It also increases when they are threatened with costs they cannot bear or which outrage their sense of justice. When institutional access opens, rifts appear within elites, allies become available, and state capacity for repression declines, challengers find opportunities to advance their claims. When combined with high levels of perceived costs for inaction, opportunities produce episodes of contentious politics.

In this view, people are more likely to engage in collective action when they think they have a chance of succeeding. Moreover, social movement activists create opportunities for themselves and others by demonstrating the effectiveness of protest, in some cases spurring a cycle of protest.

Even when political opportunities exist, however, potential collective actors do not always take advantage of them. The framing activities of leaders and organizations are important in diagnosing problems and suggesting collective solutions. Collective action frames translate grievances into broader movement claims, and they help to create the sense of injustice and the emotional energy that make individuals willing to participate in collective action (Tarrow 1998: 111). Frames point to collective solutions and encourage people to adopt a collective identity associated with a movement, which involves a shared sense of being part of a group and a feeling of "collective agency" that invites collective action (Snow 2001: 2213). Movements that frame issues in a way that resonates with the existing culture can sometimes mobilize support even in the absence of political opportunities. In a study of the American suffrage movement, McCammon (2001) examined differences between states where suffrage associations formed and those that lacked suffrage associations. Although some states offered political opportunities, such as a receptive legislature, McCammon found that culturally resonant frames, together with resources, were more important than political opportunities in arousing support for women's suffrage. In particular, suffrage associations were likely to form when activists used frames that emphasized the importance of bringing women's unique perspective to the political arena rather than arguments that emphasized women's rights as citizens.

Such studies suggest that mobilization is a complicated process, involving meso-level collective action framing and micro-level perceptions as well as large-scale opportunities and changes. The case of the gay and lesbian movement discussed in Chapter 6 provides a particularly interesting example of the relationship between large-scale changes and strategic actions; even in the absence of political opportunity, activists used the master "rights" frame to raise the consciousness of constituents and build movement support, allowing the movement to take advantage of subsequent political opportunities.

Individual Recruitment and Participation

If movements need activists to mobilize, what makes individuals willing to commit their time, money, and skills to a social movement? The answer to this question may seem obvious in that participants typically believe in the particular cause and want it to succeed. Yet not all **adherents** to a cause, defined as those who believe in the cause and want to see movement goals achieved, become **constituents**, defined as supporters who contribute resources to a movement (McCarthy and Zald 1977: 1221). Collective behavior theories stress the importance of grievances and individual discontent in generating collective action, but not everyone who is aggrieved, upset, or even outraged about a problem becomes an activist. There are many more adherents of social movements than there are constituents. For example, as we will see in Chapter 7, many people support environmental measures, but few of them contribute to environmental organizations.

One important argument for why this is the case comes from **rational choice theory**, which focuses on the costs and benefits of collective action for individuals. According to this theory, many latent groups have grievances, but few of them mobilize because the costs for the individual typically outweigh the benefits of participation. The problem of getting individuals to participate in social movements or other collective action is known as the **free-rider problem**. In his influential book *The Logic of Collective Action* (1965), the economist Mancur Olson argued that rational individuals will be free riders because the goal of collective action is a **collective good**, such as clean air or water, which the individual will receive regardless of whether or not he or she works to achieve it. Olson argues that members of a latent group, such as women, may have a common interest in obtaining a collective good, such as pay equity, but they do not have a common interest in paying the cost of obtaining the collective good. Because the contribution of any one individual typically makes no difference to the outcome of the collective action, and because the collective good will be received—or not received—regardless of personal participation in efforts to secure it, the rational individual will be a "free rider" and allow others to pay the cost of obtaining the collective good. Olson argues that rational actors will voluntarily participate in collective action only under two conditions: (1) if they are offered **selective incentives**, which are benefits available exclusively to those who participate in collective action, or (2) if they are in a *small group situation*, where an individual might be motivated to pay the entire cost of obtaining the collective good or where his or her contribution might make a significant difference. Otherwise, individuals will be free riders unless forced into participation through coercion.

This logic presented an important challenge to social movement scholars, who responded with various explanations of how the free-rider problem might be overcome. Whereas Olson focused on **material incentives**, other theorists have broadened the notion of selective incentives to include less tangible rewards for participation in collective incentives such as **solidary incentives**, which come from associating with a group, and **purposive incentives**, which come from the sense of satisfaction at having contributed to the attainment of a worthwhile cause (Wilson 1973). McAdam and Friedman (1992) argue that collective identity can act as a selective incentive, as when people participate in movements because they want to share in an identity (e.g., environmentalist) available only to movement activists.

Rather than broadening the definition of selective incentives, other theorists have addressed the free-rider problem by arguing that recruitment is affected not just by individual motivations, but by organizational arrangements and structures such as social networks. McCarthy and Zald (1973, 1977) argue that the free-rider problem may be less salient for modern social movements because many are becoming professionalized. That is, many movements have paid leaders who work full time for movement organizations and they often attract conscience constituents rather than beneficiaries. In the environmental movement, for example, many large organizations have paid staff and members who join by sending in financial contributions rather than by actively participating. When movements rely mainly on paid staff along with financial contributions from "paper members," participation from large masses of people is less critical. Owing to the low-risk commitments required of conscience constituents, many of whom have discretionary income available, the free-rider problem is not particularly important.

However, not all movements involve low-risk activism and many still require participation from sizable numbers of people. Movements such as the civil rights, animal rights, antiabortion, grassroots environmental, and global justice movements have required *high-risk activism* (McAdam 1986). Theorists emphasize the importance of different types of organizational bonds and social ties in recruiting activists to movements. When members of an aggrieved group are tied together by various structural factors that generate group solidarity, individuals are more likely to participate in group actions (Fireman and Gamson 1979). For example, a person who has friends in a group, or who participates in the same social clubs or other organizations with members of a group, is more likely to respond to a call to collective action by the group than someone who lacks such ties. Some individuals, such as visible minorities, may have "no exit" from a group, insofar as they are identified and treated as group members whether they like it or not (Fireman and Gamson 1979: 22). If an individual is closely tied to a group of people engaging in collective action, he or she has a big stake in the group's fate and may find it hard not to participate when everyone else is involved. When collective action is urgent, the person is likely to contribute his or her share even if the impact of that share is not noticeable. Critics of rational choice theory note that decisions about participation in collective action are made not by isolated individuals but by people in group contexts, such as local communities and friendship networks (Klandermans 1997; Marwell and Oliver 1993).

McAdam et al. (1988: 707–709) identify several types of structural factors that increase the likelihood of activism. First, studies suggest that *prior contact with a movement member* makes an individual more likely to become an activist. Often, individuals are asked to come along to a meeting or activity with a friend, and this contact then leads to further involvement. Based on a study of recruitment to religious movements, Snow et al. (1980) argue that social networks are in fact more important than ideological motivations for participation; often, individuals become involved through networks and take on movement beliefs after their initial exposure to a group, through interaction with members. Second, *membership in organizations* makes people more likely to become movement activists insofar as their organizational memberships give them access to information and make them targets of movement recruitment efforts within organizations. Third, a *history of prior activism* increases the likelihood that individuals will participate in subsequent movements. People gain organizing skills that are transferable from one movement to another, and subsequent activism is a way of retaining one's identity as an "activist." Finally, *biographical availability* makes individuals more likely to be recruited to social movements. Individuals who have responsibilities such as young children and demanding jobs are likely to be less available for participation than people with flexible work schedules and fewer domestic responsibilities. Based on case studies of religious movements, Snow et al. (1980) propose a similar concept of *structural availability* to explain the recruitment of some individuals from the streets rather than through social networks. They argue that these individuals were structurally available insofar as they lacked commitments that would prevent their participation. Thus, network ties to activists can draw individuals into movement participation, and a lack of competing ties can also free people to participate.

MOVEMENT MAINTENANCE, GROWTH, AND DECLINE

Social movements, by definition, endure over some length of time, interacting with the broader public, mass media, supporters and opponents, authorities, and other targets. Once initial mobilization occurs, movements have to be maintained, and they may either grow in strength or decline. The commitments of individual participants need to be retained and new supporters must be recruited. As resource mobilization theorists have emphasized, social movement organizations are central to this process. Movement organizations and coalitions of organizations are typically the main organizers of movement campaigns, which are important to the growth of movements and their ability to bring about change. However, movements are not stable and unified entities. They consist of shifting coalitions of actors and, for long-lived movements, there may be periods without a great deal of visible collective action. Movements are maintained not only by formalized organizations but by the more informal networks and cultural groups within social movement communities that keep people with a common collective identity tied together even during times when there is not much movement action going on. Movements can also endure within institutions, other social movements, political parties, and various other venues where ideologically structured action occurs.

The following discussion begins with movement organizations and the characteristics that help them to survive and generate collective action. We then consider collective action strategies and campaigns, and their importance to movement growth and decline. Finally, we examine other types of structures through which movements grow and sustain themselves.

Social Movement Organizations

Social movement organizations (SMOs) play an important role in mobilizing participants for collective action in most modern social movements. One important question is how the structures of these organizations affect their longevity and effectiveness. Scholars have identified some key dimensions on which SMOs vary, including the extent of **bureaucratization** or **formalization** in the organization and the extent of **centralization** (Gamson 1990). Organizations that are more formalized or bureaucratic have established procedures for decision-making, a developed division of labor, explicit criteria for membership, and rules governing subunits such as standing committees or chapters. More informal SMOs have fewer established procedures, rules, and membership requirements and a less-developed division of labor. Decisions in informal organizations are likely to be made on an ad hoc basis and organizational structures are frequently adjusted. Centralized SMOs have "a single centre of power" whereas power is dispersed in decentralized organizations (Gamson 1990: 93). Although formalization and centralization tend to go together, it is possible to have decentralized formal SMOs and centralized informal SMOs.

These differences are important because they affect organizational maintenance, goals, and strategies. Some theorists have argued that formalization leads to a focus on organizational maintenance at the expense of protest, resulting in a decline of insurgency. In their classic study *Poor People's Movements*, Piven and Cloward (1977) look at how movements of relatively disadvantaged people, such as unemployed workers and welfare activists, mobilized in response to opportunities but failed to keep their movements alive. They argue that poor people's movements can succeed only by engaging in disruptive tactics under extraordinary conditions, such as the Great Depression or the turbulence of the 1960s. During such times, poor people, who are ordinarily caught up in the struggle to survive and lacking in resources for collective action, are often compelled to take action. Organizers have often tried to sustain poor people's movements by building large-scale organizations, but Piven and Cloward contend that such efforts are doomed to fail. By focusing on building organizations rather than engaging in mass insurgency that will force elites to make concessions, they argue, leaders will squander the period of opportunity, which is always limited. During the 1960s, for example, urban riots in the United States helped to spawn a relief movement through which more poor people applied for welfare benefits and movement leaders pushed to mobilize the unaided poor, disrupt the system, and end poverty (Piven and Cloward 1977: 275–276). In an attempt to maintain the movement, organizers put their energies into the creation of a National Welfare Rights Organization, but this effort inadvertently hastened the decline of the movement by draining energy away from mass insurgency. Although poor people's movements are inevitably short-lived, Piven and Cloward advocate gaining as much as possible from militancy during extraordinary times rather than building organizations.

Other scholars, writing about other types of groups besides poor people's organizations, point to the benefits of bureaucratization in keeping organizations "combat-ready" and of centralization in preventing internal conflict and factionalism (Gamson 1990; Staggenborg 1988). Rupp and Taylor (1987) document the role of the centralized National Women's Party (NWP) in keeping the American women's movement alive during the "doldrums" between the passage of women's suffrage in 1920 and the "rebirth" of the women's movement in the 1960s. The NWP became a rather exclusive organization of highly committed women with close personal ties who shared the experience of participating in the suffrage movement and maintained a close community. Taylor (1989) shows how such a centralized, "elite-sustained" organizational structure can keep a movement in "abeyance" during a slow period when there is little collective action and it is difficult to recruit new members.

With regard to strategies and tactics, a number of studies suggest that more centralized and formalized structures are associated with the use of institutionalized tactics, such as legislative lobbying, while decentralized and informal structures promote tactical innovation and direct action (Freeman 1975, 1979; Gerlach and Hine 1970; Staggenborg 1988, 1989). In the American civil rights movement, for example, the bureaucratic structure of the NAACP was well suited to legal tactics, but the need to go through proper organizational channels hindered nonviolent direct-action tactics, which often required quick decisions (Morris 1984). Movements such as the women's movement and environmental movement succeed and endure in part because they include a variety of organizational structures with different capacities. In the American environmental movement, for example, a number of national organizations such as the National Wildlife Federation and the Wilderness Society lobby government officials and provide information to the public collected by their professional staffs, while grassroots organizations such as Earth First! engage in direct-action tactics such as blockades of roads and "tree-sits" to prevent logging and create media attention for the movement.

One of the important problems that SMOs face is how to encourage participation while avoiding internal conflict. Leadership is important to this problem insofar as movement leaders play a key role in inspiring commitment, devising strategies, shaping organizational structures, and providing opportunities for activists to participate in decision-making processes. Leaders interact with potential participants and "offer frames, tactics and organizational vehicles that allow participants to construct a collective identity and participate in collective action at various levels" (Morris and Staggenborg 2004: 180). When individuals have an opportunity to contribute meaningfully to organizational decisions about strategies and goals, they tend to develop greater solidarity and commitment to the SMO. Yet, there are often conflicts over who has authority in movement organizations and what structures allow for genuine participation.

Movements such as the civil rights, student, and women's movements have tried to develop forms of "participatory democracy" whereby activists are closely involved in organizational decision making. At its worst, this type of structure can degenerate into what Jo Freeman (1972) describes in her analysis of the "younger branch" of the American women's movement (consisting of radical and socialist-feminist groups) as the "tyranny of structurelessness." Groups that shun "structure," Freeman shows, may nevertheless end up with exclusive informal structures and unaccountable leaders. At its best, however, participatory democracy is a process that helps to build movements by involving participants and developing their political skills, creating solidarity, and encouraging the development of new tactics. In a study of several American movements, including the civil rights movement, the New Left, and the women's movement, Francesca Polletta (2002) found that participatory democracy was beneficial in developing strategy insofar as activists learned to engage in discourse that allowed them to consider different options carefully. Active participation required individuals to take "ownership" of decisions reached collectively.

Research by Polletta and others suggests that successful movement organizations have structures that enable them to develop accountable and diverse leadership and to formulate innovative and effective strategies. In a study of efforts to unionize farm workers in California, Marshall Ganz (2000) shows how the United Farm Workers (UFW) succeeded in the 1960s and 1970s while a better-funded rival union failed. He argues that the UFW was successful because it developed better strategies as a result of access to information and through the ability to generate ideas based on salient information. Ganz finds that several features of organizational structures are important in expanding what he calls "strategic capacity" (Ganz 2000: 1016–1018). First, organizations need to create forums for "regular, open, and authoritative deliberation" among leaders so that they have access to information and the authority to act on decisions. Second, organizations have more flexibility when they draw resources from multiple constituencies rather than from a single source. Third, organizations that hold leaders accountable to their constituents are likely to have politically skilled and knowledgeable leaders. Ganz argues that strategic capacity increases when movement organizations, rather than relying on single leaders, promote interactions among members of a "leadership team" consisting of both "insiders" with links to constituencies and "outsiders" with professional or value commitments. By including leaders with diverse backgrounds and repertoires of collective action, organizations have access to greater knowledge and more ideas about how to mobilize resources and create strategies.

Thus, one of the most important problems for social movements is the creation of organizations that are able to minimize internal conflict and develop effective strategies. SMOs are not the only structures within social movements, but activists often work through movement organizations to direct social movement campaigns. These strategic campaigns are critical not only for achieving movement goals but also for the growth and maintenance of social movements.

Movement Strategies and Campaigns

Social movements are loose and changing coalitions of groups and individuals that interact with opponents, bystanders, and targets through collective action. Movement activists have at their disposal a variety of strategies and tactics within the repertoire familiar at the time. The modern repertoire of collective action includes demonstrations, public meetings, petitions, and press statements, and activists often display "symbols of personal affiliation" and form "specialized associations devoted to pursuit of a cause" (Tilly 2008: 72). Many movements engage in a mix of direct-action tactics, which bypass established avenues of influence, and institutionalized tactics such as lobbying, which use established channels. Activists engage in "contentious performances," which are often part of movement campaigns (Tilly 2008).

Marwell and Oliver (1984: 12) define the **collective campaign** as "an aggregate of collective events or activities that appear to be oriented toward some relatively specific goal or good, and that occur within some proximity in space and time." Social movements typically consist of a series of collective campaigns, which extend beyond single events and are aimed at government officials or other authorities (Tilly 2004b: 4). A campaign at one period of time may alter the conditions for subsequent campaigns by changing political opportunities, creating new networks, and providing models of contentious performances (Tilly 2008). Through strategic campaigns, movement participants engage in dynamic interactions with authorities and third-party opponents and supporters; as these actors respond to movement strategies, movement actors in turn alter their strategies and organizational structures. The women's movement, for example, developed vehicles for new strategies, such as participation in electoral politics, in response to antifeminist countermovements and unreceptive governments (see Chapter 5).

During movement campaigns, various types of interactions affect mobilization, strategies, and outcomes. These include interactions with allies, countermovements and other opponents, and mass media as well as government officials and other authorities. Scholars have conceived of movement organizations as operating within **multi-organizational fields**, which include, in addition to SMOs, a variety of other types of organizations that might either oppose or support the movement (Curtis and Zurcher 1973; Klandermans 1992). Within and across movements, participants may form coalitions and engage in cooperative actions, compete with one another, or come into conflict with one another. Similarly, movements engage in a variety of different types of exchanges with nonmovement adversaries, mediators, and audiences (Rucht 2004). As the frequent targets of protest, government authorities or other elites may facilitate or repress protest campaigns through a variety of means. Movement leaders and organizations adjust their strategies and tactics as they respond to opponents and targets and as they form coalitions or compete with other movement activists and organizations.

The *policing of protest* is a key aspect of state response to movement campaigns. Police handling of protests is more or less repressive or tolerant under different types of governments and in response to different types of collective action, and trends in the policing of protest have important impacts on collective action, in some cases reducing disruption and visibility (della Porta and Fillieule 2004). Studies of policing in Western democracies have traced several trends in the nature of policing, which affect the strategies and outcomes of social movements. During the 1960s, police used an "escalated force" style characterized by "ever-increasing amounts of force to disperse protesters and break up demonstrations" whereas the period from the mid-1970s to the late-1990s was one of "negotiated management" in which police and protesters reached agreements "limiting the scale and scope of demonstrations, but not preventing them from happening" (Gillham and Noakes 2007: 342). After the Seattle demonstrations of 1999, however, policing styles began shifting to a "strategic incapacitation" approach in which police used "a range of tactical innovations aimed at temporarily incapacitating transgressive protesters, including the establishment of extensive no-protest zones, the increased use of less-lethal weapons, the strategic use of arrests, and a reinvigoration of surveillance and infiltration of movement organizations" (Gillham and Noakes 2007: 343). Activists in the global justice movement (see Chapter 9) have made numerous strategic adjustments in response to the policing of large demonstrations at the sites of international meetings.

Movement campaigns may occur in response to **critical events**, and campaigns also generate such events. Critical events focus the attention of movement supporters, members of the public, and authorities on particular issues, creating threats and opportunities that affect movement mobilization and outcomes. There are various types of critical events, including large-scale socioeconomic and political events, natural disasters and epidemics, accidents, policy outcomes, face-to-face encounters between movement actors and authorities or other parties, and strategic initiatives of movements, such as demonstrations (Staggenborg 1993). Some types of critical events are completely outside of movement control, while others are orchestrated by movements. However, even when movements do not control the occurrence of an event, they may be in a position to make use of critical events. Depending on their organizational capacities, movements may be able to plan campaigns that take advantage of unforeseen events. For example, anti–nuclear power activists used the threat and publicity created by the 1979 accident at the nuclear power plant at Three Mile Island near Harrisburg, Pennsylvania, to attract many new supporters to their movement (Walsh 1988). During campaigns, movements may be able to create events, such as dramatic confrontations with police, to call attention to movement issues and spread movement frames.

Movements thrive when participants are engaged in collective campaigns, which allow them to mobilize previously inactive movement supporters and strengthen the commitments of activists to a movement community (Downton and Wehr 1991). As we will see in Chapter 8, campaigns around issues such as the ERA, abortion, and gay rights helped the New Right to mobilize in the 1970s and 1980s. During a campaign, there are more ways for activists to become involved and more opportunities for participants to take leadership roles. Collective identities often undergo expansion during campaigns, incorporating the concerns of new actors, and individuals typically become more identified with the movement as they participate in its campaigns. During the 2000 World March of Women, for example, activists from community organizations and unions in Montreal became active in the women's movement through their participation in the campaign, and many local participants came to identify with global feminism (Staggenborg and Lecomte 2009). Movements that are no longer capable of mobilizing public campaigns, or that find difficulty devising campaigns appropriate for achieving movement goals, are likely to have a hard time maintaining themselves.

McAdam (1983) demonstrates the importance of particular campaigns in the growth of the American civil rights movement. He shows that peaks in movement activity occurred with tactical innovations, which were then countered by opponents, creating the need for new tactics. Bus boycotts sparked movement growth in the 1950s, resulting in some victories but also some effective countertactics that limited continued use of the tactic. Next, the movement experienced dramatic growth with the sit-ins of 1960. After mass arrests helped to diffuse the campaign, movement activity declined until the freedom rides of 1961 revived the movement. When that campaign was neutralized by government action, community-wide protests again revived the movement in southern cities such as Albany, Georgia, and Birmingham and Selma, Alabama. After these campaigns, which resulted in many victories in desegregating public facilities, the movement faltered in devising nonviolent tactics to address more entrenched and systemic problems of economic inequality. The urban riots of 1966–1968 in northern U.S. cities spurred calls for economic reforms, but the civil rights movement found it very difficult to devise campaigns to address issues of race and poverty, leading to a decline in the civil rights movement in the late 1960s.

Other studies also point to the importance of collective campaigns in expanding movements. Lofland (1979) shows how a religious movement achieved "white-hot mobilization" in part by devising campaigns and public events that involved participants and created excitement about the movement. Kleidman (1993) demonstrates how the American peace movement ebbed and flowed in the twentieth century with several major campaigns that created peaks in the movement. Voss and Sherman (2000) show how some labor unions revitalized in recent years through innovative campaigns that encouraged member participation. Often, movements expand during such campaigns through coalition building, as coalitions of organizations within movements and coalitions across movements often are needed to wage extensive campaigns. Particularly when cross-movement coalitions are involved, master frames are critical in providing a common language that can be used to address the concerns of a variety of groups (Carroll and Ratner 1996; Gerhards and Rucht 1992; Van Dyke 2003). In the case of the global justice movement, for example, we will see in Chapter 9 how a master frame focusing on the consequences of neoliberal economic policies helped to unite feminists, environmentalists, labor union members, and other activists.

In some instances, countermovement campaigns generate new movement strategies and new rounds of collective action. Movements and countermovements often respond to one another, and successful action by one side frequently spurs new activity by its opposition. For example, when Canadian abortion-rights activist Henry Morgentaler opened an abortion clinic in Toronto in 1983, anti-abortion activists launched an intensive campaign of daily protests against the clinic, and abortion-rights supporters responded by organizing demonstrations to protect the clinic (Cuneo 1989). When the militant antiabortion group Operation

Rescue mounted major protests of abortion clinics in the United States in the late 1980s and early 1990s (see Chapter 8), the campaign stimulated a great deal of mobilization by abortion-rights groups in response. While countermovements arouse opposition to movement goals, they also help to fuel movement campaigns, as we will see in the cases of the women's movement and the gay and lesbian movement. In federal systems such as the United States and Canada, there are numerous venues in which opposing movements can spar; when one side chooses a particular battleground such as the courts or legislatures, the other side may feel compelled to follow suit (Meyer and Staggenborg 1996, 1998).

Collective action is clearly central to social movements, and movements survive and grow through their ability to generate action campaigns; as collective campaigns ebb, movements contract in size and become less publicly visible. Although no movement can sustain nonstop public campaigns, long-lived movements do not completely disappear between campaigns; they typically remain alive in less visible venues.

Movements within Institutions, Other Social Movements, and Culture

Beyond the visible faces of movements in political organizations and public campaigns, movements survive and grow in numerous other settings, including institutions, other social movements, and cultural groups and activities. A number of studies have examined movements within institutions as forms of **ideologically structured action** that expand movements and secure new advantages. Mary Katzenstein (1998) shows how feminism moved into the U.S. military and Catholic Church in the 1980s and 1990s, as activists established "organizational habitats" or spaces where they could meet and strategize within the institutions. In the case of the Catholic Church, feminist activism took the form of "discursive politics" whereby feminists within the Church raised a broad range of social issues. In the military, activism took the form of "interest group activism" as feminists lobbied Congress and used the courts to secure career advancement for women within the military. Nicole Raeburn (2004) examines lesbian and gay activism within corporations, showing how networks of employee activists influenced their employers to change their policies, winning gay-inclusive benefits from a number of major American corporations. In all of these cases, the movements within institutions were connected to the external movement, both drawing support from the larger movement and contributing to it. As movements gain footholds within institutions, new mobilizing structures are established, which can be used to organize campaigns both inside and outside institutions.

Movements also spread and maintain themselves within other social movements. Activists commonly participate in multiple movements with compatible ideologies, and movements influence one another in various ways. For example, Barbara Epstein (1991) describes how feminists became active in peace and anti–nuclear power movements in the 1970s and 1980s. Meyer and Whittier (1994) look at the "spillover" of feminism into the U.S. peace movement in the 1980s, showing how feminists contributed to the peace movement collective action frames, tactics, and organizational forms along with leaders and activists, while the peace movement helped to maintain and invigorate feminism at a time when there were few visible feminist campaigns. More recently, feminists in North America have become heavily involved in the global justice movement during lulls in feminist campaigns (Rebick 2005: 256).

Cultural activities and the activities of everyday life provide additional venues for the spread of movement ideology and the maintenance of movement networks. In Alberto Melucci's (1989, 1996) view of new social movements, collective identity develops within the structures of everyday life and is transformed from time to time into political action. In her study of the gay rights movement in San Francisco, Elizabeth Armstrong (2002) argues that the movement is sustained by a whole "field" of cultural, political, and commercial organizations. A wide variety of groups such as gay pride parade organizations, gay and lesbian sports teams, gay bars, professional groups, religious groups, and service organizations have helped to create a "gay identity movement." Other researchers have similarly focused on social movement communities, which include cultural groups, alternative institutions, and other groups and events that spread movement ideas and provide spaces for activists to interact (Buechler 1990; Staggenborg 1998, 2001; Taylor and Rupp 1993; Taylor and Whittier 1992).

One of the important issues raised by this conception of social movements is how submerged networks become activated for political campaigns. Depending on the context in which the activities take place and the intentions of participants, cultural activities might either support or detract from political activities. In some cases, cultural strategies are employed to promote political change, and political campaigns reinvigorate cultural rituals. In other instances, culture may be an end in itself. The relationship between cultural and political activities is thus an important topic for social movement research.

MOVEMENT OUTCOMES

Questions about the outcomes or consequences of collective action are the most important of all for social movement researchers; ultimately, we want to know what impact a social movement has on a society. Outcomes are also among the most difficult aspects to evaluate, for several reasons. First, movements produce numerous types of outcomes—intentional and nonintentional, long-term and short-term. Movements affect public policy, political access, culture, institutions, and opportunities for subsequent collective action. They may also provoke countermovements or other forms of opposition that in turn have a variety of impacts. Second, because movements endure for some length of time, they don't produce single outcomes but rather multiple outcomes over time, such as court rulings and legislation. It is important to take into account how the outcomes of one "round" of collective action influence future "rounds" by affecting subsequent resources, tactics, and outcomes (Snyder and Kelly 1979). For example, a positive political outcome at one point, such as the U.S. Supreme Court ruling in *Roe v. Wade* for the abortion rights movement, is not necessarily good for mobilization in the next round as supporters may feel the goals of the movement have already been accomplished. Third, causality is difficult to determine; although social movements no doubt have impacts, other factors, such as large-scale socioeconomic changes, also play a role in many social changes. Certainly, the women's movement helped to open up jobs for women and bring women into the labor force, but so did large-scale changes such as the shift from industrial to service-based economies in many countries. Much of the research on outcomes of social movements looks at political and policy outcomes, which are perhaps the most straightforward changes, whereas fewer studies examine the cultural and institutional effects of social movements, which are harder to assess (Giugni 1998: 373).

To get a handle on the numerous outcomes of social movements, researchers have attempted to specify various types of impacts and to examine how movement strategies and organizational structures influence outcomes. In an influential formulation, Gamson (1990) offered two criteria for evaluating movement success: (1) *acceptance* of a challenging group as a legitimate representative of a constituency, and (2) *new advantages* or success in achieving particular goals, such as passage of legislation. Some theorists have expanded on this formulation by specifying other steps in the political process, such as getting issues on the political agenda, getting new policies implemented, actually having the intended effect, and transforming political structures (Burstein et al. 1995). Others have sought to identify broader cultural outcomes of social movements such as the creation of new pools of activists, new vocabularies and ideas (often disseminated by mass media), new cultural products and practices, and changes in public consciousness (Earl 2004; Gusfield 1981; Mueller 1987; Staggenborg 1995). Gamson (1998) amended his earlier categories to include measures of movement impacts on cultural change through public discourse. Arguing that the mass media are "the most important forum for understanding cultural impact" (Gamson 1998: 59), Gamson suggests that impact in this arena can be measured in terms of (1) *media standing* or acceptance as a legitimate source, resulting in opportunities to provide interpretations that are quoted in the media, and (2) *media discourse* as a reflection of new cultural advantages gained by a movement (see also Ferree et al. 2002).

Looking at movement impacts over time, scholars have examined how different types of cultural, organizational, and political outcomes influence subsequent collective action and outcomes. In a study of the influence of the women's movement on the election of women to public office in the United States, Mueller (1987) finds that the early women's movement did not initially have a direct impact on women's elections through means such as contributions of money and volunteers to campaigns. However, the movement helped to change the "collective consciousness" about the appropriateness of women running for public office as well as the collective identities of politically active women. As a result of the change in their consciousness and identity created by the women's movement, women who previously would have played supportive roles in the campaigns of men decided to run for office themselves. Once elected, feminists helped to bring about changes in policies that benefited women and, as the movement developed, women's movement organizations began supporting feminist candidates more directly. Thus, challenges to existing ideas and cultural practices may be early outcomes of movements that later help to produce more substantive goals (Mueller 1987: 93).

Movement outcomes are influenced by a number of factors both internal and external to movements, including the resources, organizational strength, and strategies of movements and the impacts of political opportunities and ongoing interactions with opponents and elites. In a study of outcomes of the American civil rights movement in the state of Mississippi, Andrews (2004) looked at a range of outcomes in different areas of the state, including electoral participation by blacks, social welfare policies, school desegregation, and election of blacks to public office. He finds that these outcomes are affected by the extent to which the movement has created a lasting infrastructure, by the strategies the local movement employs, and by countermovement mobilization and federal intervention. In places where the movement left behind a "local infrastructure" consisting of networks of grassroots leaders, community centers, and other organizations, as well as a resource base of activists and money, it was able to have a greater impact. The creation of such infrastructures is one of the long-term legacies of a social movement, which affects its ability to respond to opponents and win support from authorities and other elites.

Movements can increase their likelihood of success by taking advantage of opportunities and selecting vulnerable targets of collective action strategies. Opportunities are not only political but also cultural and economic. Moreover, outcomes are influenced not only by movement strategies but also by the strategies of their opponents, including both state and nonstate actors. In a study of animal rights campaigns, Jasper and Poulsen (1993) stress the preexisting vulnerabilities of targets and their strategic responses to movement tactics. A movement campaign that targeted research on cat sexuality at the American Museum of Natural History in New York succeeded in part because the research employed a culturally popular species, cats, for what could be framed as frivolous research, but also because divisions within the museum created "an institutional vulnerability that prevented a united position to protect the research" (1993: 648). In a very different example, which highlights economic opportunities, Luders (2006) examines the vulnerabilities and responses of businesses to civil rights campaigns. He argues that businesses responded to civil rights campaigns based on their assessments of two types of costs: *disruption costs*, which directly result from movement actions (e.g., lost business during demonstrations), and *concession costs*, which are the costs to targets of conceding to movement demands (e.g., lost votes for politicians). When movement campaigns targeted businesses with high disruption costs and low concession costs, they were most likely to succeed.

MOVEMENTS AND MEDIA

The mass media are very important to social movements, yet it is quite difficult for social movements to get their messages across through the mass media because movements are typically less powerful than media organizations in controlling images. Both social movements and media organizations frame issues, but the collective action frames offered by a movement are rarely presented just as the movement would like by mass media. Instead, media organizations have their own interests and routines that influence their coverage and framing of social movements. Movements generally need media coverage more than mass media need to cover movements, creating a "fundamental asymmetry" in the relations of movements with media (Gamson and Wolfsfeld 1993: 116). Often, movement activities are not reported at all, and when they are covered, movement messages are frequently distorted by media frames.

Organizational and resource considerations, and journalistic conventions and values, are among the factors that influence media frames (Gans 1979; Schudson 2003; Sigal 1973; Tuchman 1978). News organizations in Western countries are bureaucracies, located either within public agencies such as the Public Broadcasting Service (PBS) or private profit-making firms, such as the broadcasting networks and cable news channels, and they compete with other news organizations to attract audiences and sell air time, newspapers, and magazines. More material is collected by journalists than can be included in the news, and journalists working within news organizations have to sell their stories to their superiors. In developing stories, journalists work under organizational constraints and conform to occupational norms that do not necessarily work to the advantage of social movements seeking favorable media coverage (Gamson and Wolfsfeld 1993; Kielbowicz and Scherer 1986).

Deadlines and resource considerations are among the organizational constraints that influence news coverage. One important consequence of limited time and resources is the *centralization of news gathering*. Because news agencies cannot afford to have reporters everywhere in the world and must produce news in a timely fashion, they rely on centralized sources, including news bureaus located in central places, such as large cities; agencies, such as the Associated Press, that collect and disseminate news; and news beats in established institutions, such as police headquarters and government legislatures, where reporters routinely are briefed and given press releases. Centralized organizations with accessible spokespersons get the most coverage because they make it easier for reporters to gather information and meet deadlines. Government agencies and officials are by far the most widely used sources, both because they have the resources to continuously provide news to the press and because they are generally seen as credible sources for news stories. The credibility of government officials as news sources does vary historically, however. In the United States, the Vietnam War and the Watergate scandal of the early 1970s both decreased the willingness of journalists to accept presidential statements at face value (Hallin 1989).

The reliance of journalists on official sources creates an obvious problem for social movements in that they are not among the centralized, routine sources used by the media and therefore often do not get covered. In some cases, this results in missed or inaccurate stories by news organizations, which ignore movement frames. In a study of media coverage of the New Left in the United States, for example, Todd Gitlin (1980) notes that Students for a Democratic Society (SDS) existed for five years before the mass media "discovered" the organization in 1965. The group was then portrayed only as an antiwar organization despite the fact that "SDS put itself forward in no uncertain terms as a multi-issue organization which worked in university reform, civil rights, and community organizing, as well as against war and corporate domination of foreign policy" (1980: 34). Movement organizations that are more centralized and professionalized, and that learn how to conform to media norms and provide information or "stories" in a format acceptable to media organizations, are most likely to get coverage. Even for professionalized movement organizations, however, it is difficult to get movement frames represented accurately in the mass media, as journalists and news organizations apply their own frames to events.

Different types of movement organizations have employed different strategies for securing favorable media coverage, with varying degrees of success. In a study of movement organizations in Vancouver, Carroll and Ratner describe the dilemmas associated with the media strategies of different types of organizations. Greenpeace Vancouver put a great deal of effort into planning events that would attract media coverage and bring support to the organization through the free publicity garnered; although the strategy enjoyed some success, it detracted from grassroots organizing and resulted in the use of predictable "media stunts" (Carroll and Ratner 1999: 14). In contrast, a gay and lesbian community service organization used the media less to generate support than to combat homophobia by educating the public; in doing so, the group took a relatively conservative stance that alienated more radical elements in the gay and lesbian community. A third organization devoted to "redistributive justice for the poor" had difficulty in getting across its leftist critique of government policies through the mass media despite use of standard practices such as issuing press releases and making contact with sympathetic reporters (Carroll and Ratner 1999: 24).

Often, movements resort to dramatic tactics that will secure media coverage, but the difficulty is that the standards for coverage may escalate. Gitlin (1980: 182) argues that, as the anti–Vietnam War movement used increasingly flamboyant gestures, there was a rising threshold of rhetoric and violence needed for coverage; whereas "a picket line might have been news in 1965, it took tear gas and bloodied heads to make headlines in 1968." As Gitlin shows in the case of SDS, movement organizations are often ill-prepared for dealing with the media, and media coverage can have extremely negative impacts on movements. Because the mass media have an "event" orientation to deciding what is news (i.e., the "news" is what is happening today), it is difficult for movements to secure coverage of long-term trends and conditions, such as poverty or environmental degradation. They have to stage events, such as an antipoverty march or an Earth Day demonstration, to receive media attention, but even then there is no guarantee of coverage. Because the mass media are always looking for novelty, movements have to continually come up with new tactics to stay in the news, and this may not be helpful for the pursuit of many movement goals. Greenpeace, as Chapter 7 discusses, became adept at using dramatic tactics that attract media coverage, but found itself limited by its media-oriented strategies.

Thus, the issue of how movements can use the mass media effectively is a critical one for social movement studies. One important development is the availability of the Internet as a direct form of mass media for social movements. Movements have always used internal communications such as newsletters to convey their messages, but the Internet provides a quick, low-cost means of reaching a large number of potential supporters and of organizing events through e-mail and Web sites (Ayres 1999; Myers 1994; Schulz 1998). The global justice movement, for example, has made extensive use of the Internet to organize its international campaigns (see Chapter 9). In some instances, collective actions or "e-movements" have been organized strictly on-line with little formal organization (Earl and Schussman 2003; Peckham 1998). The strengths and limitations of this type of organizing, which bypasses the mainstream mass media, are an increasingly important topic for social movement research.

METHODS OF SOCIAL MOVEMENT RESEARCH

The field of social movements has advanced greatly because researchers have conducted extensive empirical research on the key issues discussed above. A wide range of methods are used to study movements, including surveys, interviews, participant observation, content analysis, protest event analysis, and network analysis (Klandermans and Staggenborg 2002). Different methodological approaches allow researchers to examine different causal factors and processes affecting social movements and their outcomes. Although many individual studies employ single methods, some benefit from the use of multiple methods, and most build on other studies using different methods. Each method has its strengths and weaknesses, and social movement theory has been developed through a combination of methods, either within or across studies. The following are a few examples of the key methodological approaches of social movement studies and their payoffs and limitations.

Because social movement researchers are interested in examining collective actions over time, and often want to compare actions across movements or nations, many studies employ *protest event analysis* (Koopmans and Rucht 2002). This method involves the coding of large numbers of protest "events" over time from sources of data such as newspaper accounts or police records. This data, which is often combined with other sources of data, allows researchers to employ statistical techniques to analyze the occurrence and patterns of protest. In one influential study, Kriesi et al. (1995) constructed a data set of protest events coded from major newspapers in France, Germany, the Netherlands, and

Switzerland to explore differences in mobilization patterns across the four Western European countries from 1975 to 1989. Using a political process approach, the researchers were able to examine how the different political contexts of these countries, which they saw as quite similar socially and economically, affected the mobilization of "new social movements." They found, for example, that France is less receptive to new social movements than the other countries owing to the salience of traditional cleavages there, such as social class. Comparing across movements, they found that challengers raising more threatening issues were most likely to be met with repressive actions by authorities in all of the countries. Protest event data allowed the researchers to analyze these and other patterns over time in different political opportunity structures. As Kriesi et al. and other researchers recognize, however, the method is limited insofar as sources such as newspapers provide data on only a limited number and type of protests, and event data does not tell us about many aspects of movements, such as the motivations of participants.

Surveys are another quantitative method commonly used in social movement research. Individual-level surveys are administered to participants or potential participants in social movements about their motivations, attitudes and beliefs, behavior and characteristics, while organizational surveys are given to group spokespersons regarding matters such as organizational structure, strategies and tactics, and policies. Surveys are often conducted at protest events or delivered by phone, mail, or Internet to samples of activists, usually members of movement organizations. Some researchers have employed comparative designs to examine changes in participation or mobilization over time or differences across movements or localities (Klandermans and Smith 2002). For example, Bert Klandermans surveyed participants in the Dutch peace movement at three different points in time, allowing him to "trace changing patterns in who left, who stayed, and who considered leaving" (1994: 175). Surveys such as this help researchers to understand changing individual motivations, using statistical techniques to control for individual characteristics such as gender and social class as well as variables such as social context. However, surveys make it easy for people to provide false information on sensitive matters, and they typically force respondents to select among preset choices without permitting them to explain themselves.

To obtain more detailed accounts from informants, researchers often use *in-depth interviews*. Unlike surveys, which require participants to provide a closed-ended answer using options provided by the researcher or a very short write-in response, in-depth interviews employ open-ended questions that encourage respondents to elaborate on their experiences in their own words. In this type of research, interviewers use a list of questions or topics to guide informants, but they typically add questions to probe answers and encourage elaboration, and they are flexible in allowing the informant to introduce new topics (Blee and Taylor 2002). Often, in-depth interviews are used along with documentary sources to trace the history of movement organizations and campaigns, to understand strategic choices, and to explain movement mobilization and outcomes. For example, Rupp and Taylor (1987) used interviews with surviving members of the National Women's Party, together with archival evidence, to show how the American women's movement survived between 1945 and the early 1960s, when it was widely believed to have died. Taylor (1989) used this data to explain how movements can sustain themselves during periods of "abeyance" when there is little visible movement activity. In-depth interviews help researchers to understand such processes, but the method is limited in a number of ways. Unlike surveys, interviews are usually conducted with relatively small numbers of people and findings typically cannot be generalized to a larger population, although they do help to build movement theories. Moreover, interviews are limited by the ability of informants to provide information about movement dynamics; even when highly motivated to be as honest as possible, interviewees do not always understand all aspects of an organization or movement and they can't always convey in words what they have experienced. For this reason, researchers try to interview people with a range of perspectives (e.g., leaders and rank-and-file members of an organization, volunteers and paid activists), and they also try to use multiple sources of data.

Sometimes it is possible for researchers to observe movement dynamics firsthand by engaging in *participant observation*. This involves participating, to some extent, in a movement or organization, while also observing interactions among participants and between movement activists and their targets. Following periods of observation, participant observers record their observations in detailed field notes, and they both use social movement theory to analyze their observations and use their observations to extend theory (Lichterman 2002). Often, participant observation is done in conjunction with in-depth interviews, with each providing different types of information. For example, Paul Lichterman (1996) studied environmental groups in California using both participant observation and in-depth interviews. While the interviews with participants provided information about how they saw their own activism, participant observation allowed Lichterman to see for himself "how they present themselves in everyday movement settings" (1996: 237) and to develop a theory of different styles of movement participation that he could not have arrived at by interviews alone. At the same time, interviews provide insights into individual motivations and behaviors that cannot necessarily be "seen" by participant observers. Moreover, many topics, such as the history of movement development, cannot be studied through participant observation.

Thus, different methods of social movement research have different strengths and weaknesses, and the use of multiple methods within and across empirical studies has been critical to the development of social movement theory.

CONCLUSION

Movements are faced with numerous obstacles and opportunities as they seek to mobilize and maintain themselves and to have a social and political impact. Large-scale political opportunities and cultural changes, meso-level organization and resources, and micro-level interactions and choices of individuals all affect the emergence, maintenance, and outcomes of social movements. The characteristics of social movement organizations and other mobilizing structures affect the ability of the movement to attract participants and to wage campaigns. Movement campaigns and strategies result in victories and defeats in achieving goals, and they also affect subsequent mobilization. Movements survive through and influence institutions, other social movements, and culture in addition to creating political changes by targeting the state. Social movement scholars study the numerous issues involved in mobilizing effective collective action using a variety of methods, as we will see as we examine substantive movements in the following chapters.

DISCUSSION QUESTIONS

1. How do large-scale changes, organizational structures, and collective action frames influence the mobilization of social movements?
2. Why do individuals sometimes participate in social movements rather than remain "free riders"?
3. What conditions would be necessary for a new movement organization, such as a local environmental group, to get off the ground and engage in collective action? What conditions might lead to failure to mobilize and act?

SUGGESTED READINGS

Gamson, William A. 1990. *The Strategy of Social Protest*, 2nd ed. Belmont, CA: Wadsworth. First published in 1975, this seminal statement of resource mobilization and political process theory remains influential in its approach to studying movement outcomes.

Klandermans, Bert, and Suzanne Staggenborg, eds. 2002. *Methods of Social Movement Research*. Minneapolis, MN: University of Minnesota Press. This book includes chapters on the major methods of social movement research, written by experts in the field.

McAdam, Doug, John D. McCarthy, and Mayer N. Zald. 1988. "Social Movements." pp. 695–737 in *Handbook of Sociology*, edited by J. S. Neil. Newbury Park, CA: Sage. This excellent review essay lays out important concepts and debates in the study of social movements.

Snow, David A., Sarah A. Soule, and Hanspeter Kriesi, eds. 2004. *The Blackwell Companion to Social Movements*. Malden, MA: Blackwell. This collection contains essays by well-known scholars on major theoretical issues and movements.

CHAPTER 4

The Protest Cycle of the 1960s

The year 1968 became known as "the year of the barricades," when turbulent demonstrations rocked many countries around the world, including France, Germany, Britain, Spain, Italy, Poland, Czechoslovakia, Mexico, and Japan, as well as the United States (Caute 1988; Fraser 1988; Marwick 1998). In France, students occupied an administration building at the Nanterre campus of the University of Paris on March 22, 1968, in response to the arrests of six members of the National Vietnam Committee; by May of that year, some 10 million students and workers were on strike. In Spain, students opposed the authoritarian government of General Francisco Franco, which closed down several universities; despite repression from the state, students joined with workers in a massive protest movement against the government. In the United States, students at Columbia University protested military recruitment on campus and occupied buildings, shutting down the university. Massive protests were held in Chicago at the site of the Democratic National Convention in August 1968, resulting in violent police response and the infamous arrests and subsequent trial of the Chicago Seven.

The world was experiencing a major wave of protest that would have aftershocks for decades to come. The Vietnam War was an important stimulus for the insurgency, both in the United States and elsewhere, but the cycle of protest of the 1960s was more than a protest against the war and American imperialism. The protest wave consisted of numerous social movements with international appeal, including student, antiwar, women's, gay and lesbian, and environmental movements. The American civil rights movement, which began in the 1950s, helped to provoke the protest cycle by providing a model of effective collective action and a vision of freedom and equality that was emulated by movements worldwide.

This chapter begins by examining some arguments about the origins, decline, and consequences of the protest cycle of the 1960s. I then look at the American civil rights movement and the New Left student and antiwar movements that arose around the world in the 1960s and their influence on other movements of the time. A number of social movements that survived the decline of the mass movements of the protest cycle, including ethnic protests, the women's movement, the gay and lesbian movement, and the environmental movement, are an important legacy of the 1960s. The left-wing movements of the 1960s also provoked right-wing countermovements that, as we will see in Chapter 8, are another important legacy of the sixties protest cycle.

THE RISE, DECLINE, AND SIGNIFICANCE
OF THE PROTEST CYCLE

Why did so many people around the world take to the streets in the 1960s? What happened to that protest and what are the lasting consequences of the protest cycle? These are important questions that have occupied numerous social theorists. Many have pointed to large-scale changes such as the economic booms taking place in many Western countries, shifts in capitalism based on technological advances, and the dramatic expansion of higher education, which helped to nourish a youth culture (Fraser 1988: 2–3). However, no single structural explanation can account for the variations in protest found in different countries. Sidney Tarrow (1989: 4) argues that, although the 1960s protest cycle "originated in the general structural problems of advanced capitalism, its forms were conditioned by the particular political institutions and opportunities of each country and social sector." The actors who mobilized and the course and outcomes of their protest differed greatly across nations, and numerous studies detail protests in France, Italy, Germany, the United States, Canada, and elsewhere (e.g., della Porta 1995; Gitlin 1987; Kriesi et al. 1995; Levitt 1984; Tarrow 1989; Touraine 1971).

While recognizing that the course of protest varies from country to country, social movement scholars have nevertheless developed some theoretical ideas about the common features of protest cycles and the factors that lead to their rise and decline. Tarrow (1998: 142) characterizes a **protest cycle** or **cycle of contention** as

> a phase of heightened conflict across the social system: with a rapid diffusion of collective action from more mobilized to less mobilized sectors; a rapid pace of innovation in the forms of contention; the creation of new or transformed collective action frames; a combination of organized and unorganized participation; and sequences of intensified information flow and interaction between challengers and authorities.

During a cycle of contention, collective action spreads to many different groups beyond those initiating the cycle. Because so many new actors are mobilized and so many activists interact with one another, they commonly devise innovative tactics and new collective action frames. Innovations in repertoires of collective action and new collective action frames are widely diffused, allowing new groups to mobilize, including opponents of some of the initial movements. During the 1960s, it was not only progressive social movements that mobilized, but also right-wing opponents and groups that felt threatened by their demands and actions. As we will see in Chapter 8, the New Right, like the New Left, has roots in the 1960s.

Explanations of the rise of protest cycles have focused on **political opportu-nities** for protest. A protest cycle occurs "when the costs of collective action are so low and the incentives are so great that even individuals or groups that would normally not engage in protest feel encouraged to do so" (Tarrow 1989: 8). Political opportunities and constraints such as increased access to political parti-cipation, realignments of power, splits among elites, the availability of allies and decreases in state repression (Tarrow 1998: 76) make protest attractive because of the resources available and the increased chances of success. In the case of the civil rights movement, Piven and Cloward (1977) argue that the increased size and instability of the black vote, related to large-scale changes such as economic modernization and urbanization, forced the Democratic Party to become more receptive to civil rights in the 1950s. Such opportunities are most likely to occur in democratic systems, though some theorists have extended the model to nondemo-cratic or semiauthoritarian contexts, particularly where there is some movement toward democratization. For example, Paul Almeida (2003, 2008) shows how liberalization of the military regime in El Salvador in the 1960s increased institu-tional access and permitted electoral reforms, allowing for the development of civic organizations; when the reforms were later reversed, activists could use the organizational structures created during the period of political opportunity to mobilize in the face of threats.

Movements that arise early in a protest cycle, when successful, provide evidence to other potential challengers that elites are vulnerable and that protest is worthwhile. These "early risers" (Tarrow 1989, 1998) are also important in creating master frames that inspire protest and can be adapted by other move-ments (Snow and Benford 1992), and highly visible models of protest tactics, which are often diffused by mass media. For example, the civil rights movement was an early riser in the protest cycle of the 1960s; it created a master "rights" frame, developed new tactics, and demonstrated to a variety of groups that nonviolent protest tactics could be used effectively. In some instances, the demands of early movements threaten the interests of other contenders, leading to the mobilization of countermovements. Thus, the protest cycle spreads through a variety of processes, as new contenders imitate early movements and extend or react to their demands (Tarrow 1998: 145).

In explaining how protest cycles diffuse, McAdam (1995: 219) distinguishes between **initiator movements** "that signal or otherwise set in motion an identifiable protest cycle" and **spinoff movements** "that, in varying degrees, draw their impetus and inspiration from the original initiator movement." He argues that political opportunities are critical to the emergence of the early riser or initiator movements, but that expanding political opportunities do not explain the rise of later, spinoff movements. In fact, later movements may be at a political disadvantage in that governments are already preoccupied with the demands of earlier movements and less receptive to new movements. Moreover, some movements appear during periods of declining political opportunity. For example, the gay rights movement flourished after 1969, when Richard Nixon took office, "marking the end of a long period of liberal Democratic dominance in presidential politics" (McAdam 1995: 225). Instead of being the result of political opportunities, spinoff movements may arise from the organizational, ideological, and cultural bases created by earlier movements. Networks created by one movement are often used as mobilizing structures by other movements. Collective action frames developed by early movements help to create new consciousness for other movements. And long-lived movements such as the women's movement create communities that spawn subsequent collective action and help to maintain movements after a protest cycle declines (Staggenborg 1998). During slow periods in between visible movement campaigns, collective identities are maintained within the submerged networks of cultural groups, institutional spaces, and other elements of movement communities. As McAdam (1995: 230) notes, "enduring movements such as feminism never really die, but rather are characterized by periods of relative activity and inactivity."

While individual movements maintain themselves in various forms, periods of intense protest activity by multiple movements do not last forever. Cycles of protest decline because they eventually "produce counter-movements, violence, and political backlash, new repressive strategies, and thence demobilization" (Tarrow 1989: 9). Tarrow (1998: 147–150) identifies three sets of processes involved in the decline of protest cycles: (1) Activists simply become exhausted, but not all activists drop out at an equal rate. Those who are more extreme in their beliefs, and less likely to compromise with authorities, are most likely to remain active despite exhaustion. Moderates are more likely to scale back their participation, and as they do so the movement may become more polarized between those who are willing to compromise and those who are not. (2) Splits between moderates and radicals lead to two tendencies. On the one hand, radicals may become more violent in their behavior while, on the other hand, moderates turn to more institutionalized actions. (3) Governmental authorities selectively repress some movement actions and facilitate others. When governments encourage the actions of moderates and repress those of radicals, they are likely to push the latter to further extremism while shrinking the movement as moderates turn to institutionalized action.

Despite the decline of intense periods of collective action, protest cycles continue to influence subsequent collective action in various ways. Many leaders and other participants who become active during a protest cycle remain involved in new social movements both inside and outside of institutions after the protest wave subsides. Tactics created during the protest cycle continue to be used by movements that persist or form after the cycle declines. For example, many activists, including gays and lesbians and environmentalists, continued to employ variants of the sit-in tactic devised by the civil rights movement. Master frames and new cultural understandings endure, influencing new generations of activists. Organizational bases created during the protest cycle often remain as submerged networks, which can be mobilized for subsequent collective action. And opponents aroused during the cycle of contention may also endure as countermovements or submerged networks. Many opponents have adopted movement tactics, as in the case of antiabortionists who have staged sit-ins at abortion clinics. In some cases, countermovements keep particular movements alive beyond the decline of a protest cycle as the two opposing movements continue to do battle (Meyer and Staggenborg 1996).

THE AMERICAN CIVIL RIGHTS MOVEMENT

The American civil rights movement provides an example of an initiator movement during the 1960s cycle of protest that has had a lasting influence on social movements worldwide. The civil rights movement played an important role in the rise of the New Left and the diffusion of protest in the 1960s. The movement has been studied extensively by historians and social scientists (e.g., Andrews 2004; Branch 1988; Carson 1981; Fairclough 1987; Garrow 1986; Luders 2006; McAdam 1988, 1999; Meier and Rudwick 1973; Morris 1984), and here I provide only a very brief account that highlights key factors in the origins and impact of the movement and the protest cycle.

Large-scale socioeconomic and political changes, including both international and domestic pressures, were critical to the emergence of the civil rights movement in the United States (Jenkins et al. 2003; McAdam 1999; Skrentny 1998). Internationally, the Cold War exerted a strong influence on American policy in the post–World War II era, and civil rights violations at home left the American government vulnerable to international criticism that its record on human rights was no better than that of the Soviet Union. With the establishment in 1946 of the United Nations Commission on Human Rights and the subsequent creation of its Subcommission on the Prevention of Discrimination and Protection of Minorities, the U.S. record was liable to challenge (Skrentny 1998: 256). This concern prompted some American officials to support various civil rights measures, resulting in domestic tensions between the federal government and the political elite in the American South, which was committed to racial segregation. Socioeconomic changes in the United States, including the decline of cotton as a cash crop and the large-scale migration of southern blacks to urban centers, also facilitated the emergence of the civil rights movement (McAdam 1999; Morris 1984). Many blacks moved to northern industrial states, where they had a national electoral impact, causing both major political parties to become concerned about the black vote and creating political opportunities for blacks. Blacks also migrated to southern cities, where their concentrated numbers allowed them to support their own institutions and organizations and where the black vote also became a potential political force.

These political opportunities fuelled perceptions that change was possible, and organizational shifts related to these opportunities helped to mobilize the black community. Significantly, urban black churches, unlike rural ones, were able to support their own ministers. Although not all black ministers committed their churches to the movement, a sizable number of the new urban ministers were educated middle-class devotees to a radical theology stressing social activism, and these ministers became key leaders of the civil rights movement (Fairclough 1987;

Morris 1984). The black church provided critical support to the emerging civil rights movement, including leadership, meeting places, and numerous cultural resources. Culturally, civil rights leaders were able to build on the participatory tradition of the black church, together with its theological emphasis on freedom, justice, and liberation (Morris 1984, 2000). Ministers who became leaders of the civil rights movement adapted the traditions of the black church to draw members into participation in the movement, and they also used their social networks to share information about strategies and tactics. Thus, preexisting organizational and cultural bases, together with large-scale changes, were key factors in the origins of the movement.

Based on perceptions of political opportunities, organizational resources, and cultural understandings, the civil rights movement developed a repertoire of strategies and tactics that was critical to its growth, success, and influence on other social movements. In framing movement concerns and devising tactics, movement leaders and their allies deliberately took advantage of global concerns about human rights (Skrentny 1998) in addition to drawing on themes of freedom and justice in the tradition of the black church (Morris 2000). Movement tactics, including bus boycotts, freedom rides, sit-ins, and community-wide protests, mobilized participants, produced victories, and helped to spread the ideas of the movement by creating dramatic confrontations (McAdam 1983, 1996). Worldwide media coverage showed images of heroic, nonviolent protestors facing police brutality and racist resistance, in some instances forcing federal intervention and resulting in movement victories. Tactics such as the sit-in have since become part of the contemporary repertoire of collective action (Morris 1981).

Movement tactics were critical to the ability of the civil rights movement to win many important victories, though there were also tactical problems that led to defeats and limitations of the movement. Some scholars have compared local civil rights campaigns to explain movement outcomes. Luders (2006) demonstrates that civil rights campaigns were most successful when they targeted vulnerable economic targets such as downtown businesses and other consumer-related industries. In his study comparing outcomes of the civil rights movement over time in different counties in Mississippi, Andrews (2004) demonstrates the importance of leadership, indigenous resources, and local organizations as well as the extent of state repression and countermovement activity in affecting movement outcomes. These and other studies show that both the strategies and tactics of the movement and the actions of movement targets and opponents matter; movements need to choose their targets carefully so as to exploit political, economic, and cultural opportunities.

The civil rights movement left a legacy of organizational structures, tactical models, and collective action frames. A number of scholars note that the themes of human rights, freedom, and social justice employed by the civil rights movement became part of a master frame adopted by women's, gay and lesbian rights, and ethnic and nationalist movements around the world. There is, however, some disagreement about what elements are most central to this frame. Several scholars emphasize the importance of the "rights" frame that was created by the civil rights movement and subsequently adopted by other movements (Snow and Benford 1992; Tarrow 1998). Morris (2000) disputes the characterization of the central frame of the movement as one of "rights" growing out of legal court challenges and instead emphasizes the "freedom and justice" frame rooted in the traditions of the black church. But both types of themes seem to have been important in influencing other social movements, and the rights theme draws on global concerns about human rights as well as legal efforts to secure civil rights.

The civil rights movement was exceptionally influential for other social movements because its activists promoted a global vision of human rights. As Gay Seidman notes, a number of civil rights movement leaders were involved in framing issues in global terms, creating linkages with activists in other countries, and speaking to international audiences about global issues of justice and freedom as well as issues specific to the United States. Many participants in the civil rights movement "viewed their struggle in terms of an international campaign to end racial inequality globally" and connected their movement to larger issues such as Pan-Africanism and decolonization (Seidman 2000: 345–346). Indeed, the philosophy and tactics of the civil rights movement were influenced by Mahatma Gandhi, who began his career fighting nonviolently for the rights of workers and "colored" peoples in South Africa and then India and who was a central figure in the Indian independence movement. Key leaders of the civil rights movement studied Gandhi's tactics and became convinced that the method of nonviolence could be applied in the United States. After the American civil rights movement "perfected and modernized nonviolent direct action," the tactics of nonviolent direct action "spread to other movements internationally" (Morris 1999: 529).

In addition to the influence of its ideological frames and tactical models, the civil rights movement was important in mobilizing students, who were critical to the international movements of the 1960s. In 1960, large numbers of black students participated in waves of sit-ins that galvanized the civil rights movement and stimulated increased participation by white and black students in the northern United States. Black students founded the Student Nonviolent Coordinating Committee (SNCC) and organized numerous campaigns, including Freedom Summer, which brought hundreds of northern white students to Mississippi in 1964 to register black voters and fight for civil rights in the state. The project had a huge impact on both the civil rights movement and the American student movement. For many black activists in SNCC, Freedom Summer ended in disillusionment owing to racial tensions on the project and to a lack of immediate success in influencing American politics (McAdam 1988). Some turned away from nonviolent protest and became committed to the emerging "black power" movement, which emphasized black pride, strength, and identity rather than racial integration (Bush 1999; Van Deburg 1992). For many white volunteers, Freedom Summer was a life-changing experience, and many of them returned in groups to their university campuses to become leaders in the emerging student movement (McAdam 1986, 1988).

THE RISE OF NEW LEFT STUDENT AND
ANTIWAR MOVEMENTS

In the 1960s, students were at the center of protests around the world (Caute 1988; Fraser 1988; Owram 1996). The large student cohorts of the 1960s developed "an entirely new student consciousness," which led them to focus on their condition as students and on transformation of the larger society (Ricard 1994: 114). Their concerns varied in different national contexts but included reforms of the university, calls for free speech, demands on governments, support for civil rights, and protests against the Vietnam War. Student movements emerged in several Western countries in the 1950s in response to issues such as the Cold War, nuclear threats, colonialism, and racism as part of a New Left. The New Left consisted of the radical movements of the 1960s, which dissociated themselves from existing Communist and democratic socialist parties and failures of the Old Left (Caute 1988: 33–38; Owram 1996: 226–233), and attempted to create a new kind of politics that would criticize capitalism and advocate meaningful forms of democracy. In Britain, the New Left was closely associated with the Campaign for Nuclear Disarmament, which mobilized many students through its youth wing. In Canada, students first mobilized around the antinuclear issue in 1959, developing a view of "the common welfare over partial interests, of humanity over politics" that would become central to the larger university movement of the 1960s (Levitt 1984: 40–41). In France, massive mobilizations of students began during the Algerian War, which lasted from 1954 to 1962, to support the Algerian National Liberation Front. In the United States, students began organizing on campuses in the late 1950s to support the civil rights movement and to protest U.S. Cold War policies. In many countries, a postwar boom in student enrollments put university students in a position of strength and also created grievances as to the dehumanizing nature of the "multiversity" and its role in producing workers for the capitalist elite.

At the University of California at Berkeley, what became known as the Free Speech Movement erupted in September 1964 when the university administration attempted to ban on-campus organizing and fundraising for off-campus political causes (Heirich 1968). Students who had been organizing on campus in support of the civil rights movement, some of whom had recently returned to campus after participating in the Freedom Summer project in Mississippi, led a protest against the policy. Highlights of the protest included the spontaneous surrounding of a police car to prevent an arrested student from being carried off, a student strike, and use of the sit-in, a tactic learned from the civil rights movement, to occupy the administration building. By January 1965, after the arrests of over 800 students, the university relented and agreed to allow organizing and fundraising for outside causes on campus once again. The Free Speech Movement gave a huge boost to the student movement, both in the United States and internationally.

Student concerns about the nature of the university were linked to their concerns about the nature of society. In complaining about student alienation, overcrowded and irrelevant courses, distant professors, and university bureau-cracy, students were also critiquing the large corporations and meaningless work of capitalist society (Levitt 1984: 33). While protesting against university restric-tions on their freedoms and demanding greater student involvement in university governance, students connected their struggles to larger issues of civil rights, racism, and democracy. In the United States, Students for a Democratic Society (SDS) used the slogan "A Free University in a Free Society" to connect the Berkeley movement to these larger concerns (Sale 1973: 168). In Canada, the Student Union for Peace Action (SUPA) worked with disadvantaged communities and cham-pioned Native rights in addition to organizing on campuses (Owram 1996: 221). In Britain, students protested government policy in the colony of Rhodesia (later Zimbabwe) and, in 1967, 100,000 students demonstrated in protest of the govern-ment's plan to raise foreign student fees, a move that particularly affected Third World students and was considered racist by the student movement (Fraser 1988: 109). In Italy, students in overcrowded universities protested lack of access to higher education for the working class as well as antiquated curricula, examination methods, and university hierarchies (Caute 1988: 77). While students organized around their own grievances, they also questioned the policies of governments and the nature of the larger societies in which they lived.

The Vietnam War became an important focus of student protest in many countries. In the United States, student concern about the war increased greatly after the war escalated and the draft was enlarged in 1965. SDS held a national protest against the war in Washington in April 1965 and, at Berkeley, the Vietnam Day Committee emerged out of the Free Speech Movement and sponsored a massive teach-in about the war in May 1965. Throughout the country, SDS and the New Left expanded as concerns about the war mounted. In Britain, teach-ins about the war were held at the London School of Economics and at Oxford in the summer of 1965 in support of the American antiwar movement (Caute 1988: 23). In Canada, a teach-in on Vietnam was held at the University of Toronto in October 1965, and, following the event, student antiwar activists began raising the issue of Canada's complicity in the war through armament sales and other actions (Kostash 1980: 46–48). In West Germany, the first major anti–Vietnam War demonstrations were held in Berlin in 1966, and opposition to the war was linked to antiauthoritarianism and concerns about German society (Fraser 1988: 101–107). As demonstrations against the war spread to many countries, including France, Italy, and Japan, student movements linked criticisms of American imperi-alism to critiques of their own societies and the need for greater democracy.

Movement activity in the United States clearly influenced activists in other countries, even as movements in each country had their own particular concerns. Both mass media and personal contacts among individuals and organizations in different countries are important to the international diffusion of protest (McAdam and Rucht 1993). In West Germany, for example, a student New Left organization called the Sozialistischer Deutscher Studentenbund (SDS) arose in the early 1960s at the same time as the American SDS was organizing. In the mid-1960s, writings of American New Leftists and descriptions of American tactics were published in the journal of the German SDS. Several activists from West Germany visited the United States, some as exchange students, and returned home to organize demonstrations in support of the Black Panthers and against the Vietnam War. The German New Left adopted tactics such as sit-ins and teach-ins, styles of dress, and their own versions of slogans from the American New Left and black power movements. For example, activists in Berlin turned the black power cry "burn, baby, burn" into "burn, warehouse, burn" to inspire fire bombings of warehouses and other symbols of capitalism in Germany (McAdam and Rucht 1993: 69).

LEGACIES OF THE PROTEST CYCLE OF THE 1960s

The civil rights, New Left, and antiwar movements mobilized large numbers of participants for a period of intense collective action. By the late 1960s, however, these movements began to disintegrate for a variety of reasons, including internal weaknesses in movement organizations, an escalation of violence by radical factions, backlash from right-wing groups, and repression by governments (Caute 1988; Gitlin 1980; Oberschall 1978). Nevertheless, the protest cycle of the sixties had an enduring influence, both in spawning new social movements that survived beyond that period and in challenging the dominant culture. As Fraser (1988: 317) argues, "one of the major effects of the student rebellion has been a generalized disrespect for arbitrary and exploitive authority among the 1968 and succeeding generations in the West, a lack of deference toward institutions and values that demean people and a concomitant awareness of people's rights." Women, gays and lesbians, animal rights activists, disabled people, environmentalists, and many others were inspired to question authority and organize during and after the 1960s.

Among the movements that continued to advocate for new rights after the 1960s were numerous ethnic and nationalist movements. Although such movements often originated prior to the 1960s, many grew in strength and changed in character along with the protest cycle. In some instances, government affirmative action policies provided incentives for new groups to organize around their ethnic identities. In the United States, a variety of ethnic groups such as American Indians, Latinos, and Asian Americans were inspired by the successes of African-Americans and encouraged by new government policies; as African-Americans developed a new collective identity and a new rhetoric of black pride, other ethnic groups followed suit (Nagel 1994: 166). The American Indian Movement, for example, experienced a resurgence of activity as a result of the precedent of the civil rights movement and opportunities created by new government policies and programs (Nagel 1996: 121). As ethnic identification became a source of status rather than stigma in the 1960s and 1970s, American Indians organized around the goal of "red power" in an effort to regain their cultural heritage as well as to settle various land claims (Nagel 1996: 124–125). At the same time as various ethnic groups organized to gain civil rights, however, white ethnic mobilization also occurred in response to affirmative action and deseg-regation efforts in the 1960s and 1970s, resulting in backlash movements such as antibusing movements (Nagel 1994: 158).

The protest cycle of the 1960s provided organizational bases, communications networks, and experiences that created new skills and new consciousness among activists. In the case of the women's movement, discussed in Chapter 5, women who were active in the civil rights movement and the New Left began to think about their oppression as women as a result of their new consciousness about the oppression of other groups, and they also developed grievances about their treatment in other movements. Women easily applied organizing skills gained in earlier movements to the new feminist movement. Gay and lesbian move-ments, the subject of Chapter 6, similarly expanded their consciousness and their organizational bases as a result of their experiences in New Left and other movements of the 1960s. As described in Chapter 7, the protest cycle of the 1960s also inspired a new wave of the environmental movement as activists applied frames and tactics learned in previous movements to the urgent problem of saving the environment. These and other movements survived the decline of the protest cycle of the 1960s, and their ongoing activism and accomplishments are an important legacy of the period. However, not all of the movements of the 1960s were left-wing or progressive movements such as the women's, gay and lesbian, and environmental movements; right-wing movements also picked up steam in the 1960s, as Chapter 8 discusses. Subsequent movements, such as the global justice movement discussed in Chapter 9, continue to draw on the frames and tactics of the protest cycle.

CONCLUSION

The protest cycle of the 1960s mobilized large numbers of activists in many countries for numerous causes. Early movements, including the civil rights and antinuclear movements, created collective action frames and tactical models that inspired massive New Left, student, and antiwar movements around the world. These movements generated change and conflict, and helped create new and lasting social movements, including the women's movement, gay and lesbian movement, and environmental movement. Although the cycle of protest of the sixties declined, a number of movements survived, continuing to perpe-tuate the values, organizational forms, and strategies of the 1960s protests. Many activists from the movements of the sixties continued their activism in other social movements for decades to come. In some instances, the movements of the sixties also created countermovements, as we will see in examining the ongoing efforts of feminists and other activists. The following chapters examine the origins, organization and strategies, and outcomes of several ongoing social movements.

DISCUSSION QUESTIONS

1. Why do numerous social movements emerge during a cycle of contention?
2. Why did the protest cycle of the 1960s decline? How did some movements survive beyond its decline?
3. How has the protest cycle of the 1960s influenced the social movements of today?

SUGGESTED READINGS

McAdam, Doug. 1995. "'Initiator' and 'Spin-off' Movements: Diffusion Processes in Protest Cycles." in *Repertoires and Cycles of Collective Action*, edited by M. Traugott. Durham, NC: Duke University Press. This article uses a political process model to analyze how movements that come early in a protest cycle influence later ones.

Morris, Aldon D. 1984. *The Origins of the Civil Rights Movement: Black Communities Organizing for Change.* New York: Free Press. This excellent book on the civil rights movement demonstrates the critical role of indigenous resources and local organizations, including the black church, in the mobilization of the movement.

Tarrow, Sidney. 1989. *Democracy and Disorder: Protest and Politics in Italy, 1965–1975.* Oxford: Oxford University Press. This book examines a cycle of protest in Italy, which ended in both institutionalization and violence in the mid-1970s.

CHAPTER 5

The Women's Movement

The "second wave" of the women's movement that emerged in many countries during the protest cycle of the 1960s mobilized large numbers of activists and created many social changes. By the late 1970s, however, feminism was already being declared "dead" by some observers, and young women were soon being described by journalists and commentators as the "post-feminist" generation (Hawkesworth 2004). Scholars and movement sympathizers also began to assess the fate of the mass women's movement as feminist activism became less visible (e.g., Epstein 2001; Reger 2005; Staggenborg and Taylor 2005). Although many organizations and activities of the women's movement declined after the early 1970s, there is evidence of continued growth: the formation of new types of movement organizations; the rise of feminism within institutions and increased support for feminism by organizations outside the movement; feminist participation and influence in other social movements; the development of feminist culture and collective identity; the creation of new collective action campaigns; and the expansion of the international women's movement. Perceptions of the women's movement depend in part on our conception of a social movement; if we understand social movements only as publicly visible contentious politics, we miss much of this ongoing feminist activity.

This chapter examines how the women's movement has grown and survived since the late 1960s and early 1970s, particularly in the United States. We begin by looking at the origins of the contemporary movement in the "first wave" of the movement and in the protest cycle of the 1960s. We then consider some areas of feminist activity that originated with the second wave and that remain highly important today, notably reproductive rights and violence against women. Other forms of ongoing feminist activity, including what has been called the "third wave" of the women's movement and the global women's movement, are also examined. This survey, while by no means comprehensive, provides a basis for a final discussion in the chapter of the important theoretical factors involved in understanding how the women's movement has endured over time and why it continues to be an important social movement, despite some decline and much opposition to movement goals.

ORIGINS OF THE SECOND WAVE

Women's movements emerged in many Western countries in the nineteenth century as large-scale changes associated with industrialization changed women's roles in the family (Buechler 1990). More middle-class women began to pursue higher education, and many women became involved in various social reforms, including temperance and abolition movements. Women gained valuable political experience through their work in such movements, and they also came to feel sharply the limits of their political influence as women. Consequently, many women became participants in the first wave of the women's movement, which advocated women's suffrage, education, property and custody rights, and other reforms. Although strongest in the West, incipient women's movements emerged in countries around the world and, by the 1920s, women had won the vote in many countries (Chafetz and Dworkin 1986). After suffrage was won, women's movements typically became less visible, though various groups survived the decline of the movement's first wave.

In the United States, many women who were active in the abolition cause and in other nineteenth-century moral reform work became active in a feminist movement that fought for women's rights to education, employment, public speaking, and marriage and property rights—and, by the 1870s, women's suffrage. The battle for women's suffrage was a long one; it involved the use of organizational structures and collective action frames capable of mobilizing large numbers of women. Some educated middle-class women advocated women's suffrage on the grounds of freedom and equality, and they created organizations such as the National American Women's Suffrage Association (NAWSA), which worked tirelessly for suffrage at both state and federal levels. A much larger number of women came to support suffrage as a result of their experiences in the temperance movement, led by the Women's Christian Temperance Union (WCTU), which organized women by building on the religious culture of the time to encourage women to go beyond their homes to reform their society (Giele 1995: 64–65). To extend women's power in the home to the public sphere, using what they saw as women's moral superiority to improve men, temperance activists came to realize that they needed to vote to have an impact. Despite its conservative gender ideology, the temperance movement prompted large numbers of women to engage in the public sphere and expanded the suffrage movement greatly (Giele 1995: 93). Through their work in temperance and suffrage organizations, many women learned new skills and became active political participants.

After the battle for women's suffrage was finally won in the United States in 1920, there was a visible decline in the women's movement, but many women continued to use their political skills in organizations such as the League of Women Voters, which replaced the NAWSA, and many worked on reforms related to issues such as child labor and infant and maternity care through various women's groups. Peace organizations, including the Women's International League for Peace and Freedom, founded in 1915, also helped to link the first and second waves of the women's movement by mobilizing women for international peace activism. In the United States, a new women's peace organization called Women's Strike for Peace was founded in 1961, and many of its activists also became receptive to the message of the women's movement later in the 1960s (Swerdlow 1993).

One militant suffrage organization, the National Women's Party (NWP), remained intact after the passage of suffrage and adopted the strategy of pushing for an Equal Rights Amendment (ERA) to the Constitution in order to achieve legal equality for women. Rupp and Taylor (1987) show how the NWP helped to maintain the U.S. women's movement in the years between the suffrage victory and the 1960s. Focusing on the period from 1945 to the 1960s, when the women's movement was often considered defunct, they explain how the NWP survived as an "elite-sustained" organization that lacked a mass movement base. Indeed, the League of Women Voters and other women's groups associated with the Women's Bureau of the Department of Labor actively opposed the ERA, which they thought would eliminate protective labor legislation for women. The NWP persisted in its campaign for the ERA, however, and remained isolated from other women's groups. Nevertheless, the NWP functioned as an "abeyance organization," which attracted intensely committed feminists and kept the movement alive until its "rebirth" in the 1960s (Taylor 1989). As we will see in Chapter 8, the ERA campaign generated strong opposition and ultimately failed, but it nevertheless played a key role in mobilizing the contemporary women's movement.

Although women's movements never disappeared after the first wave, they did not become highly visible again until a second wave of the women's movement emerged, primarily in Western countries in the 1960s. Large-scale socioeconomic and political changes, organizational factors, and related changes in women's consciousness were all critical to this revitalization of the women's movement. Increases in women's labor force participation and higher education, a decline in the birth rate, and increased divorce rates in many Western countries created new interests and grievances among women. Employment discrimination, for instance, became a major issue for the new women's movement. As Jo Freeman (1975: 15–17) argues, middle-class women with professional aspirations, in particular, felt an increased sense of *relative deprivation*; although the ideological justifications for male dominance were eroding, women felt deprived when they compared themselves to their male peers. At the same time that women felt these grievances, they also found *organizational vehicles* through which to organize a variety of different types of feminist groups. These included liberal women's organizations, some of which had their origins in the first wave, radical feminist groups connected to the New Left, and feminist groups arising out of various nationalist and ethnic movements (Roth 2004; Springer 2005).

Political opportunities and preexisting organizational structures, including networks created by the civil rights movement and the New Left, were critical to the emergence of the contemporary U.S. women's movement. In *Inviting Women's Rebellion*, Ann Costain (1992) argues that electoral realignments made political parties and government officials receptive to women as a constituency even before the women's movement organized to lobby for change. Shake-ups of electoral coalitions, caused in part by the civil rights movement and the desertion of southern Democrats from their party, resulted in efforts by the Democratic and Republican parties to court new voters in order to forge an electoral majority. While urban black voters became increasingly important, women also represented a large bloc of votes. Consequently, Presidents Eisenhower and Kennedy each made reference to sex discrimination in their speeches without prompting from the women's movement, and in the early 1960s more bills dealing with women's concerns began to be introduced into Congress. In 1961, President Kennedy established the President's Commission on the Status of Women, which spawned state-level commissions on the status of women. When the 1964 Civil Rights Act was passed, Title VII prohibited discrimination on the basis of "sex" as well as race, ethnicity, and religion.[1]

Political opportunities combined with organizational and ideological bases to support the rise of the contemporary women's movement. Two distinct branches emerged in the United States, including an "older" or "women's rights" branch founded largely by professional women concerned about employment issues and a "younger" or "women's liberation" branch made up of students and other young women concerned about a wide range of issues including women's health and sexuality (Carden 1974; Freeman 1975; Hole and Levine 1971). The older branch, formed earlier and including somewhat older women, spawned organizations such as the National Organization for Women (NOW), which was formed in 1966. These groups were organized in a traditionally formal manner—with elected officers, bylaws, boards of directors, and parliamentary procedure—based on the experiences of their founders in conventional voluntary associations and political parties. The state commissions on the status of women were an important mobilizing structure for the older branch, as many of its activists met one another and discussed their grievances through the state commissions. In contrast, the younger branch created informal organizations based on ideas about participatory democracy learned from the civil rights movement and the New Left. These earlier movements provided an organizational base and communications network for younger feminists. A number of independent feminist groups formed, including small consciousness-raising groups, which allowed women to discuss their personal experiences in political terms. Many young women were attracted to these groups due to experiences of sexism and changes in consciousness resulting from their work in the earlier movements (Evans 1979; Freeman 1975). Although many of the women who became active in such groups were white and middle class, working-class women and women of color also organized their own feminist movements through separate community networks, including black nationalist and Chicano movement networks (Roth 2004).

In other countries, radical branches of the new feminist movement also built on the organizational structures and ideologies provided by movements that came earlier in the protest cycle of the 1960s, while liberal feminists often had connections to pre-sixties women's organizations and peace movements. In Canada, women already active in groups such as Voice of Women, a women's peace movement organization, pushed the government to create a Royal Commission on the Status of Women, which held cross-country hearings that provided a communications network for the new women's movement. As in the United States, students and other young women who first became politically active in the Canadian student movement and in leftist politics began to organize independent feminist organizations, beginning with the Toronto Women's Liberation Movement in 1967. Women commonly encountered sexism in the New Left, and they initially attempted to challenge organizations such as the German SDS and the American SDS (Fraser 1988: 304) before forming their own organizations. In France, young women involved in the May 1968 protests discussed the contradictions between the New Left rhetoric of equality and their experiences as women in the movement, and formed a new women's liberation group, the Mouvement de Libération des Femmes (Duchen 1994). Owing to the women's movement, which survived the 1960s, New Left ideals and organizational forms also endured, influencing other social movements from the 1970s to the present.

Although the New Left and other preexisting social movements provided tactical models and mobilizing structures for the new women's movement, they were not the only places where contemporary feminism took root. In *Finding the Movement*, Anne Enke (2007) argues that we cannot truly understand the second wave of the women's movement by looking for feminism only in obvious places such as self-professed feminist organizations. In a study of the cultural origins of the women's movement in several U.S. cities, Enke looks at how feminism emerged in a variety of different places, including commercial spaces such as bars and civic spaces such as public parks. One of the stories she tells is that of the Motown Soul Sisters, a Detroit softball team that laid claim to male-dominated civic spaces and played an aggressive game of softball, defying race and gender norms in the 1960s and early 1970s. Following the Soul Sisters' example, many activists with explicitly lesbian and feminist identities organized around the use of civic athletic spaces, challenging race, class, and gender exclusion in the public parks. As this example shows, a broad-based movement such as the women's movement emerges in many different venues and affects many different elements of culture.

MOBILIZING ISSUES OF THE SECOND WAVE

To get a new movement off the ground, activists need to organize around issues that people care about deeply enough to want to join in collective action. This means tapping into genuine grievances, framing issues in ways that makes potential participants excited about the possibilities for change, and providing ways for people to become involved in movement campaigns. Grievances, frames, and campaigns were key ingredients in the mobilization of the modern feminist movement, which emerged out of the protest cycle of the 1960s as a new and creative force for change facing a world of gender relations that was very different from that of today. Women lacked access to many educational and occupational opportunities; they had difficulty obtaining birth control information, much less safe and legal abortions; problems such as rape and wife battering were not widely acknowledged; and a great deal of sexism existed in everyday life. These grievances provided the early movement with many unifying issues and stimulated the formation of numerous organizations that engaged in a wide range of activities.

The goals of the new women's movement included political and legal ones, such as antidiscriminatory legislation. They also included broader cultural objectives in that the movement was fundamentally redefining gender relations and challenging cultural attitudes and values as well as seeking to change laws and gain economic opportunities and political power for women. The idea that "the personal is political" was a central collective action frame for the second-wave movement, which raised issues related to sexuality, domestic violence, and gender roles in the family that had previously been considered outside the political sphere (Evans 2003: 3). This insight, as we will see, would continue to influence third-wave feminists and the international women's movement after the heyday of the second wave.

To achieve its goals, the second-wave women's movement mounted numerous campaigns, and these campaigns helped to mobilize movement participants. Although not all collective action campaigns result in changed laws or other new advantages, they often affect movements by creating new networks, strengthening organizations, introducing new tactics, and changing political opportunities (Staggenborg and Lecomte 2009; Tilly 2008). In the following sections, I discuss a few of the important campaigns and issues that mobilized the U.S. women's movement.

The ERA Campaign

One of the most important campaigns of the 1970s and early 1980s in the American women's movement was the campaign for an Equal Rights Amendment. The ERA was passed by Congress in 1972 and sent to the states for ratification, but it was defeated a decade later on June 30, 1982, when the deadline for ratification expired, three states shy of the 38 needed for ratification. Although the ERA campaign ultimately failed to achieve its objective of a constitutional amendment in support of gender equality, the campaign united many women and greatly strengthened organizations such as NOW. As Chapter 8 details, it also aroused a powerful countermovement, which was part of the emerging New American Right. Although public opinion supported equal rights for women in the abstract, conservative opponents feared that the ERA would undermine traditional gender roles, allowing men to shirk their bread-winning role and forcing women to work outside the home. The ERA also became associated with the controversial abortion issue after the U.S. Supreme Court legalized abortion in 1973, even though some feminists tried to keep the issues separate. The countermovement organized an extensive campaign and managed to block passage in enough states to kill the ERA.

Feminists also mounted an extensive campaign to pass the ERA, but it was encumbered by an amendment process that makes it possible for "intense sizable minorities" to block constitutional ratification (Mansbridge 1986: 34). Nevertheless, the women's movement did benefit from the ERA campaign, which stimulated public discussion of women's issues and brought many women, both pro- and anti-ERA, into active political participation for the first time. In particular, the National Organization for Women, which led the campaign, saw its membership and finances increase greatly as a result of the long ERA battle. At both the national and chapter levels, the ERA campaign resulted in increased activity and membership growth for NOW (Barakso 2004; Mansbridge 1986; Reger and Staggenborg 2006). Many women were passionate about the ERA, leading them to contribute both time and money to the cause. Moreover, the campaign convinced NOW and other feminist groups to become involved in electoral politics, as activists realized that they could not convince many intransigent state and national legislators; they had to replace them. As a result of the ERA campaign, NOW gained legitimacy and became more established as a national political organization. In part as a result of the ERA campaign, more women began running for legislative offices, and feminist organizations began to play a stronger role in supporting feminist candidates and causes in the national political arena.

Women's Health and Reproductive Rights

Other important women's movement campaigns and tactics focused on women's health and reproductive rights, including abortion rights. Before the second wave of the women's movement, very little information was available to women regarding sexuality, contraception, childbirth, and abortion. Consequently, women who became active in the new feminist movement began educating themselves about their bodies and publishing research about such issues as contraception so that women could take some control of their sexual and reproductive lives. One important project resulted in *Our Bodies, Our Selves*, written by a group of women who began discussing sexuality in Bread and Roses, a women's liberation group in Boston. Calling themselves the Boston Women's Health Book Collective, the women decided to gather information about women's health, which they distributed as a pamphlet in 1969. The work was later expanded into a book, which provides information to women in a form that demystifies medical expertise and includes personal accounts by women that focus on sexual self-determination (Evans 2003: 48). The book was originally published independently, but the collective later signed with a mainstream publisher to distribute it much more widely. *Our Bodies, Our Selves* has been revised and updated over the years, translated into a number of languages, and used in many schools and health clinics, diffusing a feminist perspective on women's health and sexuality to a broad audience.

Such projects were part of a larger women's health movement that involved efforts to give women control over their bodies (Morgen 2002). Feminists critiqued traditional models of health care delivery, in which doctors simply told their patients what was best for them, in favor of a new model in which women were actively involved in making decisions about their own health care. Feminists developed many women's health centers and services that attempted to deliver health care in a manner that gave women more control over experiences such as childbirth and abortion. For example, the women's movement inspired a trend towards home births and alternative birthing centers and the use of midwives in childbirth. Abortion became a major issue for the women's movement of the 1960s, and numerous countries eventually reformed their abortion laws in response to pressures by feminists and other abortion-law reformers (Francome 1984).

Many feminists were involved in providing referrals to women for both legal and illegal abortions. In Chicago in 1969, a group of women connected to the Chicago Women's Liberation Union formed an abortion collective known as "Jane" (Kaplan 1995). They first developed a list of referrals to doctors who would do abortions and who were considered "safe" and then worked with an abortionist who turned out not to be a doctor. However, he taught the women how to perform abortions themselves, and the collective ended up providing abortions to hundreds of women, including poor women who couldn't afford to travel to states such as New York, where abortion was legalized in 1970. Jane developed a supportive and nonjudgmental health service that, like other feminist health projects, was sensitive to women's needs and tried to empower its clients to make informed decisions about their sexuality and reproduction. Jane became famous in feminist circles, particularly after seven of the women were arrested in 1972 and movement activists organized in support of them.

Feminists in North America and Western Europe supported many abortion-related demonstrations and service projects and lobbied for legalization of abortion along with other abortion reformers. In the United States, abortion rights activists worked at the state level to change abortion laws, and they also engaged in litigation, bringing many lawsuits and filing briefs; these efforts eventually resulted in the 1973 Supreme Court decision that legalized abortion throughout the country (Faux 1988). In addition to these institutionalized tactics, feminists campaigned for abortion rights with confrontational tactics such as "speak-outs" and other demonstrations (Staggenborg 1991). Campaigns for legal abortion mobilized large numbers of feminists in the United States and in countries around the world.

Because of their visibility and successes, abortion rights activists provoked a powerful countermovement opposed to changes in the abortion laws. The anti-abortion movement includes a variety of constituents, including liberal Catholics as well as more conservative fundamentalist Christians. However, some antiabortionists are part of a larger antifeminist movement opposed to various changes in gender relations championed by the women's movement. As we will see in Chapter 8, this antifeminist movement is in turn part of a larger conservative movement opposed to gay and lesbian rights as well as feminist goals, both of which are seen as threatening the "traditional family." In the United States, many opponents of the ERA also became active in the antiabortion movement. American antiabortionists worked to overturn the 1973 Supreme Court decision through the courts and the legislatures, and they also worked to limit access to abortion, sometimes successfully, by means such as laws eliminating state and federal funding of abortions for poor women.

Although antifeminist activity has been detrimental to the achievement of some feminist goals, including unfettered access to abortion, the opposition has also served to keep feminists mobilized. Abortion, in particular, has continued to serve as a mobilizing issue for feminists as new generations of women defend what many now consider a basic women's right. Numerous challenges to abortion rights have generated much feminist protest along with antiabortion activity. In the United States, abortion rights activists have continually responded to countermovement efforts to pass antiabortion bills in Congress as well as to many Supreme Court rulings on issues related to abortion and battles over Court appointments. On April 25, 2004, over a million abortion rights supporters gathered for the largest march on Washington DC in American history, the March to Save Women's Lives, which focused on abortion and other reproductive rights. Abortion remains an important issue for feminists and arouses a great deal of passion among both movement and countermovement activists.

Violence against Women

Violence against women is another issue of continuing importance that was addressed by the second wave of the women's movement. In North America and in Western Europe, the women's movement played a key role in bringing issues of rape and domestic violence to public attention and in changing public views, as well as the practices of police departments and courts. Before the second wave of the women's movement, rape victims were often considered somehow responsible for the crime owing to provocative dress or behavior, and rape trials were often humiliating experiences for the victims. Consequently, rape was not seen as a common occurrence because so few women reported it. Domestic violence, similarly, was not considered a serious and widespread crime until feminists changed public perceptions of the problem in the 1970s (Tierney 1982). Feminist writings, such as Susan Brownmiller's influential book *Against Our Will: Men, Women, and Rape* (1975), helped to spread a radical feminist analysis of rape and other violence against women as means by which women were kept "in their place" (Rebick 2005: 69).

In the early 1970s, feminists in countries such as Britain, Canada, and the United States began creating rape crisis lines and battered women's shelters or "transition houses." They also publicized the high incidence of violence against women and challenged police and hospital practices. In New York in 1971, for example, the Radical Feminists held a "speak-out" at which women spoke publicly of their rape experiences in an effort to turn feelings of shame among rape victims into anger and action. Feminists also questioned police and hospital treatment of rape victims and legal requirements such as the need for the woman to prove that she resisted the rape in order for her report to be credible (Rosen 2000: 182). In the late 1970s, feminists in cities across North America began holding annual "Take Back the Night" marches to publicize violence against women. In addition to creating new services and helping to change public discourse about rape and domestic violence, feminists helped to change laws, such as rape laws that failed to recognize rape within marriage and that permitted defense attorneys to question rape victims about their sexual histories.

Issues of violence against women, like reproductive rights, continued to mobilize women after the 1970s. Pornography, which first became a feminist issue in the 1970s, was the focus of much activism in the 1980s connected to concerns about violence against women. A group called Women Against Violence Against Women formed in Vancouver in 1982 and soon became active in a number of North American cities as feminists in Canada and the United States became concerned about the expanding pornography industry. Canadian feminists made the film *Not a Love Story*, which was released by the National Film Board of Canada in 1981 and shown all over North America. Although the issue of pornography created division among feminists, with some organizing against the censorship that they thought resulted from campaigns against pornography, feminists did create a new consciousness about pornography as a form of violence against women. Activists battling against pornography also worked on raising consciousness about sexual harassment. For example, law professor Catharine MacKinnon, a well-known feminist active on the issue of pornography in North America, publicized the problem with her 1979 book *Sexual Harassment of Working Women*. Once feminists succeeded in drawing public attention to the issue, they were able to convince government agencies and workplaces to implement sexual harassment policies.

Thus, the women's movement brought a number of issues to public attention and created new ways of looking at behaviors that previously were socially acceptable or not addressed publicly. Issues such as reproductive rights and violence against women would continue to be important for third-wave feminists and for the growing international women's movement.

FEMINIST SURVIVAL AND THE EMERGENCE OF THE THIRD WAVE

The women's movement made great progress in a number of areas, and its successes contributed to a decline in grievances among women and a feeling among many young women today that feminism is no longer so necessary. Because the goals of the women's movement were so far-reaching, however, and because the movement was targeting many different "structures of authority" (Snow 2004), the women's movement of the 1960s never really died, but instead spread into many different cultural and institutional structures and arenas. Feminists have been active on numerous issues, such as employment and pay equity, child care, abortion, and lesbian rights. Although the women's movement has changed since the highly visible years of the second wave, a feminist collective identity continues to be shared and developed by new cohorts of feminists, and important ideas and issues developed by second-wave feminists continue to stimulate activity in a variety of arenas.

After the women's movement became less visible in the early 1970s with the decline in the larger protest cycle, some observers felt that the movement was becoming more focused on internal cultural activities rather than externally targeted political actions (e.g., Echols 1989). Cultural feminist groups and events did proliferate in the 1970s and 1980s, but, as we have seen, the movement remained very active on issues such as abortion and pornography. In the 1980s, feminists in a number of countries faced conservative political regimes— exemplified by the governments of Margaret Thatcher in Britain, Ronald Reagan in the United States, and Brian Mulroney in Canada. As "new conservatives advanced a pro-achievement, pro-individualist position that ceded little room to competing traditions of collective action, social protest, and progressive political engagement," feminists and other progressive activists were put on the defensive (Bashevkin 1998: 14). Faced with antifeminist countermovements and governments hostile to many feminist goals, women's movements often had to defend existing gains, such as abortion rights, and to fight cutbacks in funding for women's groups and services. Despite the lack of political opportunities for pushing feminist goals, however, feminists took advantage of opportunities to mobilize support and to push for new advantages wherever possible. After the defeat of the ERA in 1982, many feminists in the United States became convinced that they had to become more involved in electoral politics and they founded new organizations to support these activities. For example, EMILY's List was founded in 1985 as a political action committee devoted to the election of feminist candidates and became highly effective in raising money and influencing election outcomes.

While feminists continued to fight in the political sphere despite conservative times, changes in the political climate affected the collective identities of new generations of activists recruited to the movement. An enduring feminist collective identity helps to maintain the movement but also continues to evolve as new generations of women join and change the women's movement. In a study of feminist generations in Columbus, Ohio, Nancy Whittier (1995) found that different cohorts of feminists shared somewhat distinct collective identities based on their experiences and the political context when they joined the movement. Women who joined the movement during the protest cycle of the 1960s were influenced by the New Left and the sense that revolutionary changes were possible, and radical feminist identities reflected the fervor of the era. As American feminists experienced the defeat of the ERA and feminists worldwide saw the spread of neoliberal policies, new cohorts became less optimistic about institutional change. Thus, the collective identity of feminists who joined the movement in the conservative climate of the 1980s shifted, and there was "an increasing focus on personal growth and transformation" through means such as self-help groups and feminist spirituality (Whittier 1995: 196). The collective identity of the movement continued to shift in the 1990s, creating something of a "generation gap" between second- and third-wave feminists, but also sustaining the movement.

Beginning in the mid-1990s, a number of anthologies were published by young women who declared themselves different types of feminists from second-wave feminists (e.g., Baumgardner and Richards 2000; Findlen 2001 [1995]; Heywood and Drake 1997; Mitchell et al. 2001; Walker 1995). Some of the authors claimed to be part of a third wave of activism that was already under way, while others called for a third wave (Reger 2005: xvii). This new "wave" of feminist activity, which began in the 1980s, was not so much a visible new burst of movement activity (as the second wave had been) as an assertion of feminist identity among young women. Feminism had not died out in the 1980s—it was relevant and important to many women—but young feminists were declaring their generational and ideological differences from the second wave (Henry 2004). North American women born after the early 1960s took many gains of the women's movement for granted and felt less need for a collective orientation to feminism. Self-declared third-wavers did not reject feminism, but they wanted to recast feminism on their own terms.

For some third-wavers, those terms were more individualized and personal than collective and overtly political. Arguing for an inclusive type of feminism, a number of feminist writers in the 1990s rejected what they saw as the dogmatic approach of the second wave and argued that women could define feminism for themselves (Henry 2005). Whereas second-wavers declared that "sisterhood is powerful," third-wavers challenged the idea that women have similar interests, focusing instead on diversity and the need to include women of color, transgendered people, poor women, and others in the feminist movement. Third-wavers also argued that their brand of feminism is distinguished from second-wave feminism by its orientation to sexuality, which emphasizes "women's pleasure and power over their victimization" (Henry 2004: 22). But despite such claims, there are clearly important continuities between the second and third waves. Many second-wave feminists, including women of color, have also worked for a diverse movement (Henry 2005: 89) and for a positive approach to women's sexuality (Gilmore 2005). And issues such as abortion, rape, and lesbian rights, which were central to the second wave, remain critical to young feminists of the third wave.

Although there is much continuity between the second and third waves of the women's movement, the third wave has generated new organizations and activities, including many cultural activities that have a political intent. For example, a group of art activists calling themselves the Guerrilla Girls organized in 1985 to protest an exhibition by New York's Museum of Modern Art that included only a small number of female artists. They donned gorilla masks and took on the names of dead women artists, making posters and using humor "to convey information, provoke discussion and to show that feminists can be funny" (www.guerrillagirls. com). Since 1985, the Guerrilla Girls have written books, engaged in street theater, and developed various projects dealing with art, popular culture, and discrimination. Another example of third-wave activism is the Riot Grrrls, a network of young women in the alternative rock music scene that started in Olympia, Washington, in 1991 and quickly spread across North America through band tours, zines (self-published journals), word of mouth, and the Internet. In 1992 there was a Riot Grrrl Convention in Washington DC with workshops on a number of topics including sexuality, rape, racism, and domestic violence (Evans 2003: 216).

The Vagina Monologues, which started as a one-woman play by Eve Ensler, is another cultural and political activity that has engaged the energies of young feminists (Reger and Story 2005). The play consists of a series of monologues based on interviews with hundreds of women, celebrating women's sexuality and dealing with issues such as rape, body image, menstruation, and the genocide of Natives in North America. In 1997, Ensler created V-Day, a nonprofit organization with the goal of stopping violence against women by acting as "a catalyst that promotes creative events to increase awareness, raise money and revitalize the spirit of existing anti-violence organizations" (www.vday.org). In 1999, V-Day began the College Initiative to encourage colleges and universities to perform the *Monologues* as a benefit for local organizations fighting violence against women. Since then, feminist students at hundreds of colleges and universities in North America and around the world have performed the *Monologues*, as have hundreds of community groups. In addition to performing the *Monologues*, V-Day groups have held workshops, shown films, and carried out various campaigns opposing violence against women and building networks in Latin America, Africa, the Middle East, and Asia as well as in Europe and North America.

To express their ideas and spread feminist views, third-wave feminists have published books, developed Web sites, and created zines, which often build on the notion of the personal as political (see grrrlzines.net). In this regard, third-wavers are similar to second-wave feminists. Both have recognized that women's movement activities often are unreported in the mass media and that, when the mass media do cover movement issues and activities, women are often portrayed in stereotypical ways and movement issues lack serious coverage (Goddu 1999). Second-wave feminists responded to this problem through various means, such as the development early in the movement of an informal rule of speaking only to female reporters and the use of feminist newsletters to spread word of the movement (Freeman 1975; Tuchman 1978). Third-wave feminists have avoided reliance on mass media by organizing through the Internet and developing internal movement publications such as zines.

Thus, young feminists have continued to engage in innovative collective action, and many issues of concern, including violence against women and abortion rights, provide clear connections between the second and third waves of the women's movement. Many young feminists are also active in other social movements, including the environmental, gay and lesbian rights, antiracist, and global justice movements, bringing a feminist perspective to those movements. And young feminists have joined with more seasoned activists in expanding the global women's movement.

THE GLOBAL WOMEN'S MOVEMENT

Although the international women's movement dates back to the nineteenth century (Rupp 1997), in recent decades the global women's movement has expanded significantly. Not all women's groups within the international women's movement are feminist, but they are becoming increasingly so. Ferree and Mueller (2004: 577) distinguish between *women's movements*, which they define as "mobilizations based on appeals to women as a *constituency* and thus an organizational strategy" and *feminism*, which has "the *goal* of challenging and changing women's subordination to men." They note that many women's movements start out concerned about issues such as peace or social justice and later become explicitly feminist, while some feminist movements later expand their goals to include other issues such as racism and colonialism. Both dynamics are important to the expanding global women's movement.

The expansion of the global women's movement can be traced to the creation of an organizational infrastructure that aided the formation of transnational women's networks (Antrobus 2004; Keck and Sikkink 1998; Moghadam 2005; Rupp 1997). Owing to the efforts of first-wave feminists involved in transnational women's organizations such as the Women's International League for Peace and Freedom early in the twentieth century, the United Nations established offices to deal with women's issues early in its history. In response to women's groups, the UN declared 1975 International Women's Year, and worldwide conferences were held under UN sponsorship as a result. In 1975, the first official UN women's conference was held in Mexico City, using the themes of equality, development, and peace. Although this first conference focused on issues such as literacy, education, and health rather than violence against women, sexuality, and sexual orientation, these more controversial issues "were to appear in subsequent meetings as women found the confidence and power to advance them" (Antrobus 2004: 42). Most importantly, the 1975 conference resulted in a call to the UN General Assembly to declare 1975–1985 the Decade for Women, resulting in a mid-year conference in Copenhagen in 1980 and an end-of-the-decade conference in Nairobi in 1985. On the recommendation of the Nairobi conference, a fourth UN World Conference on Women was held in Beijing in 1995. With resources from the UN, activists met to follow up on the plans for action formulated at the conferences and to plan for subsequent conferences, in the process creating a strong global network of activists. Most significantly, this network included activists from the global South as well as the North, and leaders emerged from developing countries as well as from the developed world. Feminist leadership also came from UN personnel and government delegations, and the UN conferences provided an opportunity for women to interact with government officials and to develop resolutions and challenge governments (Antrobus 2004: 61).

With each conference, and with the expansion of international women's networks, more and more issues were added to the movement agenda. Feminism was increasingly recognized as relevant to women around the world, rather than only to privileged women from the West, and the feminist movement was broadening its concerns in response to the increased participation of women from developing countries. Although there were important divisions among women from the North and the South, there were also efforts to overcome the divisions. As Keck and Sikkink argue, one of the concerns that first helped to create unity was "violence against women," a category used to include a wide range of issues such as rape and domestic battery, female genital mutilation, female sexual slavery, dowry death in India, and torture and rape of political prisoners in Latin America. Bringing together these various issues "implied rethinking the boundaries between public and private" and considering activities carried on in households as well as public and state violations of women's rights (Keck and Sikkink 1998: 173). The issue of violence against women resonated with many women from around the world, and it underlined the continued relevance of the focus on the personal as political by the second wave of the women's movement. The international women's movement successfully used opportunities such as the UN Conference on Human Rights in 1993 to campaign for recognition of women's rights as human rights and to place the issue of violence against women on the human rights agenda. These efforts resulted in concrete achievements, such as adoption in 1993 of the Declaration on the Elimination of Violence Against Women by the UN General Assembly as well as the strengthening of regional women's human rights networks (Antrobus 2004: 91–94).

International women's networks have also been active on issues of sexual and reproductive rights, but the issues are complicated and sometimes divisive. Women's groups have opposed forced family planning methods and they have argued against blaming poor women's fertility, rather than economic inequality, for environmental and economic problems in the global South. At the same time, women's groups have argued in favor of safe, accessible women's health programs for all women. A network of feminists in developing countries known as DAWN (Development Alternatives with Women for a New Era), formed in 1984, has argued that women's health should be addressed in the context of socioeconomic, cultural, and political conditions (Antrobus 2004; Mayo 2005). Feminists have clashed with the Vatican and Islamic fundamentalists over abortion and contraception, and an ongoing countermovement, fuelled by the spread of religious fundamentalism, opposes many efforts of the international women's health movement. Activists from the American Christian Right have become involved in the UN process in recent years in an effort to counter feminist domination in that arena (Butler 2006).

Along with issues of violence against women and reproductive rights, the global women's movement has focused on economic issues in a way that emphasizes connections between the personal and the political. Feminists have critiqued policies associated with neoliberalism, the economic policy championed by countries such as the United States and Britain that became prominent in the 1980s. Neoliberal economic strategies rely on trade and free-market mechanisms, rather than investment in social services and education, to promote economic growth. Developing countries seeking loans and international aid were forced to scale back government services and focus on debt reduction in order to receive assistance from the International Monetary Fund (IMF), the World Bank, and, later, the World Trade Organization (WTO), which was formed in 1995. Women in both developed and developing countries were affected by neoliberal economic policies, and the international women's movement was spurred by their concerns. Feminists in global women's networks developed analyses of how women's unpaid labor was required to compensate for cutbacks in government services and how these economic policies affected the everyday lives of poor women. DAWN, in particular, has drawn on the skills of academic feminists to conduct research, prepare policy papers, and conduct workshops at international conferences (Mayo 2005: 139–152). Whereas second-wave feminists had conceived of the "personal as political" primarily in terms of individual experiences, international feminists were expanding this insight to connect macro-level economic policies to women's everyday lives (Antrobus 2004: 45).

MAINTENANCE AND GROWTH OF THE WOMEN'S MOVEMENT

As the above description of ongoing activities shows, feminism is far from dead; the women's movement has maintained itself into the twenty-first century and even expanded in some areas. Factors identified by theories of social movements help explain the origins and ongoing activities of the women's movement. The grievances emphasized by collective behavior theorists combined with the preexisting organizational structures, resources, and political opportunities emphasized by resource mobilization and political process theorists to fuel the modern movement. Once important gains were achieved, it was natural for the movement to lose some of its urgency and visibility, but feminist issues and campaigns—and, in some cases, specific events—have continued to attract new generations of women. New commitments to an evolving collective identity, emphasized by new social movement theory, along with ongoing mobilizing structures and political opportunities, have kept the movement alive. Internationally, grievances created by neoliberal policies, and mobilizing structures and resources provided by the UN and other international organizations, have expanded the global women's movement. Enduring issues, and collective action frames such as "the personal is political," have proved relevant to broad constituencies of women. Opposition to the movement from antifeminist countermovements and governments made it difficult for the movement to achieve some of its goals, but also mobilized feminists to defend against threats to women's rights.

While existing theories of social movements help to explain the maintenance and growth of the women's movement, the trajectory of the movement suggests a need to go beyond theories of social movements that focus primarily on the public face of movements in interaction with the state (Staggenborg and Taylor 2005). Although contentious politics are critical to social movements, so are the submerged networks emphasized by new social movement theorists. To explain the maintenance and development of a movement such as the women's movement, we need to look for social movement activity in a variety of venues rather than only in publicly visible protests targeted at states. And, although it is convenient to talk about "waves" of the women's movement and "cycles of protest" generally, we need to recognize that many social movements continue even when periods of heightened protest subside and the activities of particular movements become less visible. In the case of the women's movement, ideologically structured action (Zald 2000) and collective challenges to authority (Snow 2004) have continued to maintain the movement. Moreover, the movement is still capable of large-scale collective action campaigns even though it does not continually engage in contentious politics.

Much ideologically structured action in support of feminism occurs within institutions. Indeed, scholars have shown that movement activity within institutions occurs at various stages of movement development, aiding the emergence, maintenance, and growth of movements. Before the public emergence of the second wave of the women's movement in North America, women working within government agencies, civil liberties organizations, foundations, churches, unions, and traditional women's organizations such as the YWCA helped to push for women's rights and spread feminist ideas to members of their organizations and the larger public (Adamson et al. 1988; Hartmann 1998). Once the contemporary women's movement was under way in the late 1960s and early 1970s, feminists created footholds within established institutions. In a study of feminism within the U.S. military and the American Catholic Church, Mary Katzenstein (1998: 19) found that "feminists have created organizational habitats (formal groups and informal networks) within which feminists (mostly women) share stories, develop strategies, and find mutual support." In universities, feminists have established organizational habitats such as Women's Studies departments and research centers, which continue to develop feminist discourse and disseminate movement ideas to new generations of students. Often, activists inside institutions work with outsiders to promote changes, and organizational habitats may serve as mobilizing structures for the larger movement. In the international women's movement, feminists within the United Nations and national governments have worked with feminists in networks such as DAWN (Mayo 2005). Thus, feminist activism within institutions has helped the women's movement to maintain itself and to develop in new arenas.

Feminist activism within other social movements is another means by which the movement has survived and spread. As some second-wave organizations declined and women's movement activity became less intense in the 1970s and 1980s, many feminists put their energies into peace, antinuclear power, environmental, gay and lesbian, disability rights, antiracism, and ethnic and community movements, to name a few (Epstein 1991; Meyer and Whittier 1994). Through their participation in other social movements, feminists helped to keep alive the participatory democratic tradition championed by movements of the 1960s, and they helped to maintain and spread a feminist collective identity. For example, Connell (1990) found that feminist pressures in the Australian environmental movement led men in the movement to reexamine their ideas about masculinity and to engage in collective projects. Feminist participants, including young women, have influenced a wide variety of movements, including the recent global justice movement.

Feminists have also been heavily involved in cultural and service activities, which are other means by which a movement remains alive. For example, feminists continue to be active in battered women's shelters, rape crisis lines, women's centers, feminist book stores, spirituality groups, theatrical performances, women's music festivals, writers' groups, and presses. During times when there are few active campaigns, such activities maintain feminist networks and collective identity. Third-wave feminists have participated in a wide range of cultural and political activities around issues such as sexual harassment, sexuality, body image, eating disorders, violence, racism, and sexism in popular culture (Reger 2005). Third-wave feminists have been particularly concerned to connect issues of sexism with interlocking oppressions of race, class, and sexuality in cultural and political projects.

In addition to ongoing cultural and service activities, the women's movement also maintains explicitly political organizations and campaigns. The European Women's Lobby, an umbrella organization of some 4,000 women's associations in the European Union, coordinates lobbying efforts and campaigns among European and international feminist organizations (www.womenlobby.org). Worldwide, feminist networks continue to expand, and coalitions continue to organize collective action. In 1995, an international coalition was formed at the World Conference on Women in Beijing to stage a World March of Women in 2000. After successful demonstrations were held around the world in 2000, focusing on the issues of poverty and violence against women, the coalition continued to build a global collective identity among women, and in 2005 the coalition staged another campaign in which a Women's Global Charter for Humanity was relayed around the world (Dufour and Giraud 2007). In the United States, the National Organization for Women continues to maintain many active chapters and a large national membership (Barakso 2004). NOW and other U.S. feminist organizations have successfully organized large-scale collective actions from time to time, including the March for Women's Lives in 2004, which brought over a million women to Washington DC in the largest march on Washington in U.S. history. These national and international campaigns build on grassroots feminist action and help to stimulate local involvement in the women's movement (Staggenborg and Taylor 2005).

CONCLUSION

Despite the decline of the cycle of protest of the 1960s, the women's movement remains a vital social movement. This chapter points to some important reasons for the continued survival and growth of the movement. The second wave of the women's movement organized around critical issues, including reproductive rights and violence against women, that remain relevant to women around the world. Along with these grievances and collective action frames, preexisting organizational structures and political opportunities helped to mobilize the movement, and ongoing mobilizing structures, new opportunities and frames, and an evolving feminist identity have maintained the movement. While issues such as abortion have generated much conflict, countermovement activity has also maintained feminist abortion rights activities. Issues of violence against women have united women's movements around the world. An extensive international women's movement has developed, and feminism is increasingly viewed as important to women in developing as well as developed countries. Feminist frames, such as the idea that "the personal is political," have been adapted to new issues, linking macro-level economic policies, for example, to women's everyday lives. The women's movement has targeted many different systems of authority, and the movement has become institutionalized in many different arenas. Internationally, feminists have worked within the United Nations, national governments, and many organizations and agencies to advance movement goals. Feminists have also worked through a variety of other social movements, spreading feminist ideas and creating coalitions. The women's movement continues to spawn many cultural activities and collective action campaigns, attracting new generations of women to the movement.

NOTE

1. The congressman who chaired the House Rules Committee apparently proposed adding "sex" as a way of making the legislation seem ridiculous, but female legislators backed the amendment as a serious goal (Rosen 2000: 70–74). Because the legislation was designed to deal with racial discrimination, with sex an afterthought, the Equal Employment Opportunity Commission (EEOC), which was set up to enforce Title VII, failed to take sex discrimination seriously. This became a major grievance for politically active women and spurred creation of the National Organization for Women in 1966.

DISCUSSION QUESTIONS

1. How and why might women's movements turn into feminist movements?
2. To what extent has the women's movement declined since the years of the "second wave"? What explains the endurance or decline of the movement?
3. What are the challenges involved in continued expansion and development of the global women's movement?

SUGGESTED READINGS

Buechler, Steven M. 1990. *Women's Movements in the United States*. New Brunswick, NJ: Rutgers University Press. This book provides a comparison of suffrage and second-wave women's movements.

Ferree, Myra Marx, and Carol McClurg Mueller. 2004. "Feminism and the Women's Movement: A Global Perspective." pp. 576–607 in *The Blackwell Companion to Social Movements*, edited by D. A. Snow, S. A. Soule, and H. Kriesi. Oxford: Blackwell. This essay provides a historical and transnational perspective on the women's movement.

Staggenborg, Suzanne, and Verta Taylor. 2005. "Whatever Happened to the Women's Movement?" *Mobilization* 10(1):37–52. This article analyzes the transformation of the women's movement, arguing that the movement survives in various cultural and political forms.

CHAPTER 6

The Gay and Lesbian Movement

Since the emergence of a "gay liberation" movement out of the social movements of the 1960s, movements to improve the lives of gay men, lesbians, bisexuals, and transgendered persons[1] have made enormous strides in many countries, particularly in the Western world (Adam 1995). Gay and lesbian activists have battled against discrimination in areas such as employment and housing. They have also fought for recognition of same-sex relationships, including rights to partner benefits, custody and adoption of children, and marriage or civil unions. Activists have responded to violence against gays and lesbians, and they have battled against the deep-rooted stigma attached to homosexuality. Gays and lesbians have also confronted the AIDS epidemic, targeting both medical practices and governments. In all of these battles, the gay and lesbian movement has met with harsh opposition from an antigay countermovement.

Focusing primarily on North America, but also making some comparisons to other countries and regions, this chapter examines some of these struggles to normalize same-sex relationships and to achieve equal rights for gays and lesbians. We begin with a discussion of the origins of the contemporary gay and lesbian rights movement in the context of the 1960s protest cycle and then examine important battles and results of the movement. I attempt to explain how these struggles and their outcomes are influenced by political and cultural opportunities as well as by movement organization and strategy.

ORIGINS OF THE GAY AND LESBIAN MOVEMENT

The contemporary gay and lesbian movement mobilized in the late 1960s and, like the modern women's movement, survived the decline of other sixties movements. World War II provided opportunities for many gay men and lesbians to meet one another in the armed services, in the war industries, and in the growing gay subcultures of cities, where greater freedom to socialize in places such as bars existed during wartime (D'Emilio 1983; Kennedy and Davis 1993). Networks formed during the war helped to support urban gay subcultures after the war, and gays and lesbians formed some organizations in Western Europe and North America before the 1960s, including the Mattachine Society in Los Angeles in 1951. McCarthyism and the Cold War created a repressive political climate in

North America and Western Europe, with the result that early "homophile" organizations took a cautious, assimilationist approach (Adam 1995: 69). However, public consciousness about homosexuality began to shift with publications such as the Kinsey studies on sexual behavior, which reported in the late 1940s and early 1950s that homosexual acts were fairly common. In Britain in 1954, the government initiated a Committee on Homosexual Offences and Prostitution, which recommended the decriminalization of consensual homosexual acts between men who were at least 21 years of age (Engel 2001: 71). In the 1960s, support for the civil rights of homosexuals broadened, as organizations such as the American Civil Liberties Union "accepted the principle of a basic right to private consensual sex" (Engel 2001: 37). Homophile organizations founded before the 1960s, including the Mattachine Society, provided organizational bases for the movement in a number of countries (Adam 1995).

The modern gay rights movement is often dated from the Stonewall Rebellion of 1969, when gay patrons at the Stonewall Inn in New York City rioted in response to a police raid on the bar. McAdam (1995) views the gay rights movement as a "spinoff" movement that came late in the protest cycle of the 1960s, and suggests that, at least in the United States, there were no obvious political opportunities that affected the emergence of the gay rights movement; after Richard Nixon was elected president in 1968, the political climate became hostile for progressive social movements. In a comparison of the gay and lesbian movement in the United States and Britain, however, Engel (2001) shows how features of political institutions in the two countries, which are more stable elements of the political opportunity structure,[2] did affect the emergence and outcomes of the movement in each country. In particular, the separation of powers in the U.S. system of government provides multiple points of access but also multiple veto points for social movements, while the British parliamentary system allows a receptive ruling party to take action and an unsympathetic government to avoid action despite public opinion and interest group lobbying. In Canada, interestingly, the 1982 Charter of Rights and Freedoms created new opportunities for the gay rights movement to employ legal strategies, but the movement took off in the early 1970s *before* the objective change in political opportunity. In her study *Lesbian and Gay Rights in Canada* (1999) Miriam Smith shows that, influenced by the American civil rights movement, the Canadian movement used litigation and the language of equality in a broad way to develop political consciousness and generate public discussion of homosexuality using the rights frame. Once the Charter opened up greater legal opportunities, the movement was able to make important strides, putting Canada far ahead of the United States and many other countries in establishing gay and lesbian rights.

Regardless of political opportunities, the protest cycle of the 1960s clearly had an important impact on the development of a gay liberation movement. Many activists who became involved in the gay liberation movement were first active in other social movements, including the civil rights movement and New Left. They were radicalized by these experiences and ready to apply the new collective action frames and tactics to gay liberation (Adam 1995; Warner 2002). The militancy of other movements of the 1960s helped to overcome the previously cautious approach of gay groups and led to new rhetoric and tactics, such as the emphasis on gay pride and the use of "sip-ins" to assert the right of gays to go to bars without harassment by police (Adam 1995: 74–78). Before the Stonewall Rebellion occurred, other incidents of street violence had followed police raids on gay bars, but these earlier incidents occurred before an extensive protest environment had developed (Duberman 1993). By the time of the Stonewall raid, a movement subculture was present, ready to support the protestors and to inspire the formation of gay liberation fronts across North America and Western Europe.

Shifts in collective identity, emphasized by new social movement theory, were critical to the origins of the new gay and lesbian movement. Many gay liberationists had adopted a flexible leftist ideology from the New Left, and they were able to expand this ideology to create a new "gay identity" and new collective action frames around "gay liberation" and other themes (Valocchi 1999, 2001). Collective action frames from the 1960s emphasizing both "rights" and "liberation" were important to the spread of gay and lesbian movements. Although these frames represented different perspectives, which sometimes created divisions between activists advocating the radical idea of liberation and those employing the more mainstream idea of rights, the ideas coexisted and liberationists often used civil rights frames strategically. As Warner (2002: 70) explains, "civil rights were simple to understand" and the movement used civil rights battles as a way of attracting gays and lesbians to the movement and fighting homophobia even if, for liberationists, these struggles were never an end in themselves.

GAY AND LESBIAN LIBERATION

The gay liberation movement spawned by the New Left raised issues of gender and sexuality, and connected the struggle for gay liberation to other social movements. From 1969 to about 1972, a number of gay liberation groups formed in North America, Western Europe, Australia, and New Zealand. Like the women's liberation movement, gay liberationists formed consciousness-raising groups, which produced "immense anger, joy, pride, and a boiling over of new ideas" (Adam 1995: 83). Gay liberationists did not conceive of themselves as a minority group seeking civil rights; rather, they were challenging conventional notions of sexuality. In the liberationist analysis, homosexuality was seen as "a natural and normal alternative sexuality that must be liberated from oppression imposed by the church, state, and medical institutions, rigid gender-role socialization, and the supremacy of the nuclear family" (Warner 2002: 64). Many of the early groups called themselves gay liberation fronts in solidarity with revolutionary movements of the 1960s, such as the Vietnamese National Liberation Front, and they saw the gay liberation struggle as part of a larger movement against numerous forms of oppression. To tackle oppression on many fronts, gay liberationists felt they had to be militant and highly visible, "coming out" in many arenas.

Activists engaged in a variety of confrontational tactics aimed at challenging authorities and educating the public. In the United States, the 1969 Stonewall Rebellion was a critical event that inspired a great deal of movement activity. Because activists considered the Stonewall Rebellion worthy of commemoration, they worked to ensure that the event was commemorated each year, eventually with gay pride parades in cities across North America (Armstrong and Crage 2006). In the year following Stonewall, gay liberation groups picketed a wide variety of institutions associated with the oppression of gay people, such as the *Village Voice* for refusing to print the word "gay," airlines for their discriminatory employment practices, and Macy's department store for its entrapment of gay men by police in its washrooms (Adam 1995: 85). Activists staged a number of demonstrations at the sites of professional meetings to protest against the medical definition of homosexuality as a social pathology, and in 1973, as a result of gay protests, the American Psychiatric Association voted to change its official diagnostic manual so that homosexuality was no longer classified as a psychiatric disorder (Kutchins and Kirk 1997).

In other countries, such as Canada and Great Britain, the Stonewall Rebellion was not such an immediate event, but it was highly symbolic and resulted in much publicity and widely disseminated movement literature, stimulating the growth of gay liberation fronts (Warner 2002: 66). Gay liberation activists around the world were influenced by the movements of the 1960s, but protests in particular countries took on unique characteristics and organizations formed in response to local and national events. In Britain, gay liberationists tended to be "far more concerned with personal liberation and cultural development" than with political goals because consensual homosexual relations had been legalized in England and Wales in 1967 (Engel 2001: 85). For a short time, British activists promoted a unique gender-bending "radical drag" that included fashions such as the mixing of dresses and beards (Adam 1995: 90; Engel 2001: 85). In Canada, gay liberation groups formed in Montreal, Vancouver, and Toronto, and a national gay liberation journal, *The Body Politic*, began publishing in Toronto in 1971 (Warner 2002: 66–69). In Mexico City, a Frente de Liberación Homosexual was organized in 1971 in response to the firing of several gay employees at a Sears store, and in Argentina a Frente de Liberación Homosexual formed in 1973 in response to political changes after the end of a dictatorship (Adam 1995: 95–96).

Gay liberationists engaged in a range of militant and visible actions aimed at challenging the mainstream culture and constructing a positive collective identity for gays and lesbians. Movement frames and strategies were affected by ideological positions and network connections to the New Left, and gay liberation organizations helped activists to connect issues of sexuality to larger political goals. Participants were attracted to gay liberation organizations because they provided one of the few spaces at the time where gay men and lesbians could come out of the closet and openly express their sexuality and because they offered a vision of social change relevant to the times (Lent 2003: 44). As an activist in the Gay Liberation Front (GLF) in London explained:

The GLF made us aware of our sexuality as a political issue. So I could then see the links to other struggles. I wouldn't put it in the same terms today but then the idea was that gay lib would operate as part of social and structural revolution which was the wave of the future. In 1970 we really believed that the whole world was going to crash down and that revolution was on the cards. We wanted sexual revolution to be part of that. (Lent 2003: 38–39)

Early gay liberation organizations tended to be very short-lived, however, as they often lacked sustaining organizational structures. They were also torn apart by internal conflicts, such as ideological debates and conflicts over sexism. Because gay liberation groups tended to be preoccupied with issues affecting gay men, lesbians in the early 1970s began withdrawing from gay liberation groups and forming autonomous organizations in many countries (Adam 1995: 99). Whereas gay men enjoyed many of the privileges of other men, lesbians suffered from the discrimination that affected all women, and they were drawn in large numbers to the women's movement. Lesbian feminists created many alternative institutions, such as women's bookstores, presses, music festivals, and theatres that became part of "cultural feminism" after the early years of the women's liberation movement (Echols 1989).

The gay liberation movement did not end with the decline of its early organizations, but it did change its strategies. Gay liberationists had wanted to overcome set categories of gender and sexuality, but the goal of liberating sexuality conflicted with the need to create a lesbian and gay identity for political purposes (Smith 1999: 45). Ironically, liberationists ended up helping to create gay communities and a gay identity (Epstein 1999: 42). While lesbians created women's communities, gay male culture in major cities came to be organized around gay services, restaurants, bars, bathhouses, and other community organizations and businesses. Armstrong (2002) argues that gay activism in San Francisco underwent an important transformation with the decline of the New Left; the movement became focused on gay pride and identity, but in a way that promoted the acceptance of sexual and political diversity, including the pursuit of equal rights as one way of expressing gay identity and protecting individual differences. In San Francisco and other cities, the number of gay and lesbian cultural and political organizations expanded dramatically in the 1970s, creating a strong basis for the ongoing movement. Gay liberationists remained involved in spreading gay culture in the major cities of North America and Western Europe and continued their involvement in new political organizations founded after the early 1970s. Successor organizations to the GLF groups abandoned their attempts to link gay rights to a larger revolutionary movement, however, and focused on activism surrounding specific gay issues, particularly civil rights, as a strategy for building a movement and providing opportunities for visible collective actions such as demonstrations (Warner 2002: 68–70).

STRUGGLES FOR EQUAL RIGHTS

Gay and lesbian activists have made great gains in liberal democracies by presenting themselves as a quasi-ethnic group and framing their demands in terms of civil rights. Gay rights activists built national organizations, such as the National Gay and Lesbian Task Force (NGLTF) in the United States, as well as local and regional groups, to engage in legislative, judicial, and electoral campaigns. They also pressured businesses, churches, professional associations, and other organizations to adopt nondiscriminatory policies. And, as gay and lesbian movement culture and political campaigns became increasingly visible, an antigay countermovement mobilized in response.

Beginning in the 1970s, gay and lesbian activists waged campaigns to outlaw discrimination in areas such as housing, employment, and government services through local and state legislation, ballot initiatives, referendums, and attempts to add sexual orientation to municipal, state or provincial, and national human rights charters. Gay and lesbian rights groups also filed lawsuits to support individuals against discrimination and to attempt to overturn legislation, such as sodomy laws, that permitted police harassment and arrests of sexual minorities. In response, an antigay countermovement organized in the United States in the late 1970s, employing the conservative master frame of protection of the "traditional family." In 1977, an antigay rights organization called Save Our Children spearheaded a successful campaign in Dade County, Florida, to repeal a new civil rights ordinance that prohibited discrimination on the basis of sexual orientation. The antigay rights campaign was headed by former Miss America and evangelist singer Anita Bryant, who went on a speaking tour in the United States and Canada following the countermovement victory in Dade County and helped to defeat gay rights ordinances in several other U.S. cities, including St Paul, Minnesota, Wichita, Kansas, and Eugene, Oregon (Adam 1995). Bryant was invited to Canada by Ken Campbell, a Christian minister from Milton, Ontario, who campaigned with Bryant against human rights legislation for gays and lesbians on the grounds that homosexuals recruited children and undermined families (Warner 2002: 136). In Canada and Australia during this period, police raids against gay bars also intensified, creating a climate of antigay repression (Adam 1995: 124–127).

The rise of a countermovement often helps to increase movement mobilization, and the gay and lesbian rights movement rallied in response to the threats. In Canada, the Anita Bryant crusade "provided unprecedented opportunity" for gays and lesbians to organize a Coalition to Stop Anita Bryant, to gain a huge amount of media exposure, and to galvanize gay and lesbian communities in cities across the country where Bryant spoke (Warner 2002: 136–137). Anita Bryant was at the time the national spokesperson for Florida orange growers, and gay and lesbian activists in North America launched a boycott of Florida oranges to protest her role as a crusader against gay rights. In response to the controversy, Bryant was dismissed from her job with the orange growers, while gay and lesbian groups flourished as they battled the countermovement. In California, where Harvey Milk was elected as the first openly gay city supervisor in San Francisco in 1977, the movement organized to defeat an antigay rights initiative sponsored by state senator John Briggs, known as the Briggs Initiative, which would have outlawed the employment of gay and lesbian teachers and prohibited positive discussion of homosexuality in the schools. The campaign featured public debates between Harvey Milk and John Briggs and resulted in a strong show of support for gays and lesbians by unions and ethnic group leaders. When Harvey Milk, along with San Francisco mayor George Moscone, was murdered in 1978 and his killer was convicted only of manslaughter, the movement responded with rage, rather than retreating in the face of repression as gays and lesbians had done in earlier periods (Adam 1995: 114).

Since the 1970s, gay and lesbian rights groups have made great strides in achieving antidiscrimination measures, although they have also continued to provoke opposition. In the United States, a study of gay and antigay rights efforts between 1974 and 1994 found that gay rights advocates were more successful overall than their opponents and increasingly so over time (Werum and Winders 2001). Most battles were fought at the state and local levels, rather than the federal level, and gay rights supporters were particularly successful in passing local ordinances prohibiting discrimination and in using the state legislatures and courts to secure rights. Antigay activists were most successful with ballot initiatives and referendums, which allowed them to arouse public fears about gay rights. As we will see in Chapter 8, antigay campaigns contributed greatly to the mobilization of the larger New American Right.

Movement strategies have varied, depending on the state of the opposition as well as the state of the movement. In a study comparing campaigns for gay and lesbian rights ordinances in several locations in the United States, Mary Bernstein (1997) found that activists made different choices as to whether to celebrate or suppress their differences from the majority, depending on the structure of movement organizations, their access to the polity, and the nature of the opposition. In New York City in 1971, gay activists attempted to add "sexual orientation" to the city's human rights ordinance using theatrical tactics borrowed from the repertoire of the sixties, such as infiltrations of meetings in order to "zap" or bombard public officials with questions about police raids and discriminatory policies. Activists in Eugene and Portland, Oregon, also waged campaigns for antidiscrimination laws in the 1970s, but they chose very different strategies, discouraging mass participation in favor of private meetings with elected officials.

Bernstein argues that these sharply different strategies can be explained by the needs of New York activists to build participatory organizations, their lack of a strong infrastructure, and their lack of access to political authorities. Whereas New York activists were trying to build a movement, Oregon activists had more resources and business connections to elected officials. In Vermont in the 1980s, activists also enjoyed positive relations with government officials, and they engaged in strategies aimed at educating public officials about the need for policy change. In places where opponents became more organized, however, strategies shifted. After a virulent countermovement formed in Oregon, and hate crimes against gays and lesbians increased dramatically in the late 1980s and early 1990s, the movement became divided. Some activists focused on abstract principles of equality, stressing the similarity of gays and lesbians to other citizens, while groups such as Queer Nation and Bigot Busters became more militant in confronting the dominant society and stressing an alternative collective identity (Bernstein 1997: 555).

As gay and lesbian movements became more widespread and activists became more confident, they responded boldly to opposition. In 1991, for example, the Cracker Barrel restaurant chain issued a policy against the employment of "homosexuals" and then fired a number of gay and lesbian employees in locales in the United States that lacked gay rights ordinances prohibiting discrimination (Raeburn 2004: 43). In response, movement activists quickly held demonstrations and sit-ins at Cracker Barrel restaurants and called for a boycott of the chain. Consequently, shareholders rebelled against the discriminatory policy, the national media gave extensive coverage to the story, and the company eventually rescinded the policy. The incident helped to publicize gay and lesbian employee grievances and resulted in a great deal of moral outrage, which helped to further mobilize the movement (Raeburn 2004: 45). Thus, opposition can actually help a movement by arousing emotions and stimulating strategic responses.

At the federal level in the United States, lesbian and gay rights advocates have had a more difficult time, both in the courts and in Congress (Engel 2001; Rayside 1998; Rimmerman 2002). During the conservative Reagan era of the 1980s and the one-term George H.W. Bush administration of the late eighties and early nineties, there was little national opportunity for progress, and the Christian Right continued to thrive. After the election of President Bill Clinton in 1992, the friendlier Democratic administration provided more political opportunity to the movement, but issues such as the proposed end of the military ban on gays and lesbians also helped the right to mobilize strong opposition. Consequently, the movement failed to win a full lifting of the military ban on homosexuals—instead, a "don't ask, don't tell" policy was instituted in the American military—and passage of the Employment Discrimination Act in 1996 was blocked in Congress, while a federal Defense of Marriage Act that prohibited same-sex marriages was passed in the same year. Following the lead of the American civil rights movement, gay rights activists tried to use the courts to establish civil rights, but progress was slow. Although many American states quietly dropped laws prohibiting sodomy, a challenge to Georgia's sodomy law by a man who was arrested for having consensual sex with another man in his own home failed when the U.S. Supreme Court in the 1986 *Bowers v. Hardwick* case refused to grant protection to sexual minorities (Pierceson 2005: 23). It was not until 2003 that the Supreme Court in *Lawrence v. Texas* finally overturned 14 remaining state sodomy laws in a case that provided strong impetus to the antigay rights movement.

In other countries, gay and lesbian activists also struggled for and won changes in human rights laws and other civil liberties measures. In Canada, activists took advantage of the new political opportunity that came about after the equality rights provisions of the Charter of Rights and Freedoms came into effect in 1985, greatly expanding the role of the courts and allowing movements to use litigation to bring about legal change. Between 1986 and 1999, despite opposition from antigay rights forces, the movement succeeded in getting the federal government, all provinces, and one territory to amend their human rights laws to prohibit discrimination on the grounds of sexual orientation (Warner 2002: 197). In Europe in 1984, the European Parliament adopted a comprehensive position on the civil rights of gays and lesbians, and a number of European countries, including France, Denmark, Sweden, Norway, and the Netherlands, passed antidiscrimination and antihate crime legislation in the 1980s and early 1990s. In New Zealand, a national human rights law was passed in 1993, despite an intensive antigay campaign by religious conservatives when male homosexual relations were decriminalized in the mid-1980s (Adam 1995: 132–133). In countries other than advanced capitalist ones, in regions such as Latin America, Asia, and Africa, gay and lesbian groups have organized, but they often face a great deal of state repression and societal condemnation (Adam 1995: 165–176). International organizations, such as the International Lesbian and Gay Association, have formed to assist in the promotion of human rights worldwide.

AIDS ACTIVISM AND QUEER POLITICS

The AIDS crisis that began in the early 1980s profoundly affected the gay and lesbian movement in both negative and positive ways. Most obviously, AIDS led to the deaths of many gay activists and leaders. The spread of the disease also prompted increased opposition from the right in countries such as the United States, Canada, and Britain. On both sides of the Atlantic, gays were attacked for engaging in unnatural and dangerous behavior that resulted in the "gay plague." In the United States, conservative politicians and religious leaders spoke about AIDS as "the cost of violating traditional values" and as "an awful retribution" (Engel 2001: 50). In 1987, Congress passed the Helms Amendment to the AIDS appropriation bill, which prohibited the use of federal money for any educational materials that "promote or encourage, directly or indirectly, homosexual activities" (Rimmerman 2002: 94). In Britain, the Conservative government introduced Clause 28 to the 1988 Local Government Bill, which did not restrict spending as the Helms Amendment did, but sought to prevent local authorities from intentionally "promoting homosexuality" or teaching in schools "the acceptability of homosexuality as a pretended family relationship." The threat of Clause 28 in Britain had a similar effect to the Stonewall Rebellion, resulting in an unprecedented new wave of protest that included several marches in London and Manchester of 10,000–30,000 protestors (Engel 2001: 92–93).

In North America and Europe, the AIDS epidemic and opposition from the political right sparked renewed mobilization and new strategies in the gay and lesbian movement. Owing to the crisis, increased numbers of gay people came out of the closet and gay visibility in the mass media increased dramatically. The AIDS movement spawned a large number of service organizations to assist people with AIDS, creating new forms of gay community. Many lesbians who had been disillusioned by the earlier gay movement were appalled by right-wing opposition and evidence of homophobia as well as government inaction, and they returned to work with gay men (Engel 2001: 48–49). AIDS movements developed both national lobbies to influence government policies and new grassroots organizations that engaged in a new round of direct-action tactics. The AIDS Coalition to Unleash Power (ACT UP) was organized in New York in 1987 and soon spread to cities across the United States, Canada, Europe, and Australia. Returning to the street theatre employed by countercultural movements of the sixties and the gay liberation groups of the early seventies, ACT UP and similar groups engaged in tactics intended to raise public consciousness about AIDS and to challenge the stigma attached to homosexuality (Gamson 1989). They staged "die-ins" where activists drew police-style chalk outlines around one another's bodies, likening AIDS deaths to murders and shifting responsibility away from the victims of AIDS. The pink triangle, which was the emblem used by the Nazis to mark homosexuals, was reclaimed by AIDS activists and used along with the slogan "silence = death" as an indictment of homophobia and indifference to gay deaths.

ACT UP converted feelings of grief into anger, resulting in a period of militancy that helped to create a new "queer" identity (Gould 2002). By the mid-1990s, the AIDS movement had made progress, and some of the anger that fuelled ACT UP subsided. ACT UP chapters were often short-lived and in some cities ACT UP was never particularly strong compared to local groups of AIDS activists (Brown 1997). Nevertheless, grassroots AIDS activism by ACT UP and other radical groups helped to renew liberationist challenges. Queer Nation was founded in New York in 1990 by ACT UP activists and others who wanted to go beyond the AIDS issue and address concerns such as homophobia and gay bashing. Bisexual and transgender politics, which had often been left out of gay and lesbian movements, became part of the queer agenda, as activists challenged the idea of a fixed sexual identity and the assimilationist approach of trying to "fit in" to mainstream society (Epstein 1999: 61).

Queer Nation groups formed in a number of cities in North America, and they engaged in tactics intended to raise consciousness about homophobia and heterosexism. For example, same-sex couples held "kiss-ins" in places like shopping malls and straight bars. Like ACT UP, Queer Nation groups tended to be short-lived, but they left a legacy of activism and consciousness in gay communities. Queer Nation Toronto, for example, was founded in 1990 and lasted for about two years, attracting some 200 activists. The group put up posters in downtown Toronto with messages like "Queers are Here, Get Used to It" and held demonstrations against the religious right, antiabortionists, and the war in Iraq as well as gay bashings. Queer Nation tried to be inclusive of all sexual orientations and to work in coalition with antiracists, feminists, peace activists, and others. However, groups such as Queer Nation Toronto found themselves lacking the processes and strategies needed to resolve differences and effect change, and they often succumbed to internal conflict over problems such as how to deal with racism and sexism as they attempted to create inclusive organizations (Warner 2002:

259–260). Queer activism nevertheless helped to expand the boundaries of gay and lesbian organizing, pushing for greater inclusion of bisexual and transgendered people and raising more awareness of racial and cultural diversity in gay communities. The movement also reclaimed and popularized the use of the term "queer" and helped to launch the academic field of "queer theory" (Warner 2002: 262).

RELATIONSHIP RECOGNITION AND SAME-SEX MARRIAGE

As part of campaigns to secure equal rights, gay men and lesbians began pressuring governments, unions, and employers to provide benefits to same-sex partners and recognize same-sex relationships. Issues of relationship recognition became increasingly important in the 1980s and 1990s, and same-sex marriage became legal in a handful of countries after the turn of the century. European countries led the way in same-sex partnership recognition, with Denmark becoming the first country to allow the registration of partnerships in 1989. Since then, a number of other countries have allowed same-sex registered partnerships or civil unions, including France, Germany, and Britain. The Netherlands became the first country to allow same-sex marriage in 2001, followed by Belgium in 2003, Canada and Spain in 2005, South Africa in 2006, Norway in 2008, and Sweden in 2009.

In Canada, the enactment of Section 15 of the Charter of Rights and Freedoms in 1985 provided a major political opportunity for lesbian and gay rights advocates, who were then able to challenge the country's marriage laws through the courts. In 2004, the Supreme Court of Canada cleared the way for federal legislation on same-sex marriage, and in 2005 the federal government followed the lead of the courts and passed a bill allowing same-sex marriage throughout the country. Although there was controversy over this momentous change in Canada, same-sex marriage was the culmination of years of equality-seeking by gay and lesbian activists that resulted in laws against discrimination and protections for same-sex relations and parenting rights (Smith 2005: 225). In the United States, in contrast, laws still permit discrimination against gays and lesbians in many states, and same-sex marriage remains highly controversial. Several U.S. states have legalized same-sex civil unions, beginning with Vermont in 2000 following a court ruling. The state of Massachusetts became the first state to permit same-sex marriages following a Supreme Court of Massachusetts ruling in 2004. Connecticut was the second state to allow civil unions in 2005 and, after a court ruling, legalized same-sex marriage in 2008. In 2009, the same-sex marriage movement won a string of victories as Iowa, Maine, New Hampshire, and Vermont legalized same-sex marriage. However, Maine repealed its new law allowing same-sex marriage in a November, 2009 referendum, joining many other states that have passed laws banning same-sex marriage. In California, same-sex marriage was banned through a ballot initiative (Proposition 22) in 2000 and then banned again through a voter initiative to amend the state constitution (Proposition 8), which passed in November 2008, after the state Supreme Court had permitted same-sex marriage earlier that year. Proposition 8 was challenged in the courts but was upheld by the California Supreme Court in May 2009.

Movement/countermovement dynamics strongly influenced the strategies of both sides in the conflict over same-sex marriage in the United States. In the early 1990s, few gay and lesbian groups focused on marriage rights, in part because there was disagreement within the movement over the desirability of marriage, which many saw as a conservative institution, and in part because activists knew that the issue would provoke strong opposition (Fetner 2008: 111). However, some same-sex couples were filing lawsuits over marriage licensing discrimination, and in 1993 the issue gained a great deal of media attention when it looked like the Hawaii Supreme Court would legalize same-sex marriage until the state legislature stepped in to limit marriage to opposite-sex couples. Seeing the same-sex marriage issue as a highly symbolic one that would mobilize a great deal of support, the religious right then launched a massive campaign to prohibit same-sex marriage across the United States. This campaign in turn produced a strong response from the gay and lesbian movement, which put aside internal differences on the issue in the face of opposition and began to organize extensively around the battle for marriage rights (Fetner 2008: 112; Pinello 2006). Public same-sex weddings became a strategy of the gay and lesbian movement meant to protest marriage discrimination (Taylor et al. 2009). In 2004, when Mayor Gavin Newsom permitted same-sex marriages in San Francisco, thousands of gay and lesbian couples lined up to be married, in part as a coordinated strategy to make same-sex partnerships visible in the mass media.

Both sides in the battle over same-sex marriage organized in response to the strategies and victories of their opponents. In an analysis of which states were most likely to ban gay marriage, Sarah Soule finds that both citizen ideology and interest group activity had an influence and, surprisingly, that states were more likely to ban gay marriage if they had previously passed some type of gay-friendly legislation. These findings point to the role of interactions between movement and countermovement; movement groups play a key role in making gains, but their victories provoke countermovement retaliation. Thus, Soule finds that "same-sex marriage bans represent a backlash against policy gains made by gays and lesbians" (Soule 2004: 472). Although Soule's analysis was published before the most recent events in California, it is clearly applicable. Prior to the 2000 ban, California had enacted domestic partnership legislation. Prior to the 2008 ban, the decision of San Francisco's mayor to issue marriage licenses to same-sex couples led to the court case that temporarily legalized same-sex marriage in the state, provoking strong countermovement reaction. Proposition 8 in turn outraged and disappointed gay rights activists, leading to large protests, as well as litigation, against the measure (McKinley 2008).

In a comparison of the United States and Canada, Miriam Smith argues that differences in political institutions in the two countries are also important in explaining outcomes on same-sex marriage. In Canadian federalism, criminal law is controlled by the federal government, and sodomy was legalized as part of law reforms in 1969. In the United States, battles against criminal laws prohibiting sodomy had to be fought in various states until the 2003 Supreme Court ruling struck down remaining sodomy laws. While conflict over the legality of homosexuality in the United States helped to reinforce religious and moral opposition to gay rights, the debate over same-sex marriage in Canada was framed in terms of human rights. Moreover, the Canadian parliamentary system made it easier for the Liberal Party to push forward the change despite opposition, whereas in the United States the division of powers makes it easier for opponents to resist change (Smith 2005: 226).

Despite political obstacles in the United States, new developments in gay and lesbian communities created further pressure for same-sex marriage. As a result of the AIDS epidemic, many gay couples were suddenly faced with issues such as control over medical decisions, needs for health insurance, and funeral arrangements, resulting in a greater need for relationship recognition (Chauncey 2004: 96). Around the same time, a lesbian "baby boom" was taking place in many major cities, as lesbians began to live openly and to have children, creating another impetus for legal protections for gay and lesbian families (Chauncey 2004: 105). In addition to these practical concerns, "the freedom to marry, including the right to choose one's partner in marriage, has come to be regarded as a fundamental civil right and a powerful symbol of full equality and citizenship" (Chauncey 2004: 165; see also Hull 2006).

Besides campaigns for same-sex marriage, battles for partnership recognition have also been waged in the private sector, as lesbian and gay employee networks have lobbied employers to provide same-sex benefits. Raeburn (2004) finds a dramatic increase in the provision of same-sex benefits by major corporations in the United States in the 1990s in response to pressures from gay, lesbian, and bisexual employees. Employees who joined together in networks to pressure employers to provide same-sex benefits were often active in the larger gay and lesbian rights movement, and they received a great deal of support from the movement, including extensive research on employer practices posted on Web sites and national conferences on workplace organizing that allowed activists to exchange information and mobilize support (Raeburn 2004: 85). Once some corporations began to adopt benefits, others were motivated to do so in order to compete for top employees.

INFLUENCES ON MOVEMENT STRATEGIES AND OUTCOMES

Gay and lesbian movements have clearly made important gains, and they also continue to face strong obstacles. Movement strategies have played an important role in changing political and cultural climates and creating new opportunities for gay and lesbian rights. The strategies employed by activists are in turn influenced by political and cultural opportunities, as well as by the organization and resources of the movement, and they have varied across time and place. Frequently, gay and lesbian activists have focused on achieving equality through means such as antidiscrimination legislation, emphasizing similarities between themselves and other citizens. However, even when pursuing seemingly "assimilationist" strategies such as litigation to achieve equal rights, activists were often at the same time trying to build a movement and a collective identity (Smith 1998). Movements can "deploy" identity for different strategic purposes (Bernstein 1997). In some instances, activists aim to empower constituents with a sense of collective identity and to create a shared community before they can engage in more instrumental action. In other instances, the goal is to transform the values, categories, and practices of mainstream culture rather than to win specific policy changes, and activists may focus on developing community and collective identity among gays and lesbians by emphasizing their uniqueness and differences from the mainstream culture.

Extreme repression of a movement, such as occurred during the McCarthy era, can lead to cautious tactics and difficulty in mobilizing support, but with the development of supportive cultural and political organizations and a positive collective identity, movements can defend themselves against opponents (Adam 1995: 115). By the end of the 1970s, when an antigay countermovement emerged, the gay and lesbian movement had created this type of infrastructure and identity in North American cities (Armstrong 2002). Although the countermovement has created obstacles for the gay and lesbian movement, such as opposition to same-sex marriage in the United States, it has also stimulated movement organization and strategies. Threats, as well as opportunities, have helped to mobilize the movement and to shape its frames and tactics.

Cross-national comparisons point to the importance of political and cultural opportunities in accounting for variations in movement strategies and outcomes. Despite many similarities between the United States and Canada, differences in the political institutions of the two countries help to account for the much greater success of the gay and lesbian movement in achieving human rights and relation-ship recognition in Canada (Pierceson 2005; Smith 2005). Before the adoption of the Charter of Rights and Freedoms, there was little opportunity for Canadian activists to engage in the type of rights-seeking litigation used by movements in the United States, notably the civil rights movement. Nevertheless, Canadian activists, influenced in part by the American civil rights movement, used court cases in the pre-Charter era to raise public consciousness and to create collective identity, and then took advantage of the new political opportunity presented by the Charter to use litigation more instrumentally (Smith 1999). Supportive rulings by the courts then helped to spread an "equal rights" frame, which further influenced public opinion in Canada in favor of gay rights (Matthews 2005). The parliamentary system and party discipline in Canada made it possible for sympathetic elites to pass gay-friendly legislation, despite remaining opposition to policies such as same-sex marriage. In the United States, some court rulings have been favorable to the movement, but the separation of powers in the American federalist system has provided more opportunities for opponents to block nondiscriminatory reforms.

In comparing the British and American gay and lesbian movements, Engel (2001) finds that variations in strategies and outcomes are related to both political institutions and cultural differences in the two countries. In Britain, interest groups tend to focus on the executive because there is no judicial review and the prime minister, in a majority government, can exert party discipline and control legislation in Britain's parliamentary system. Consequently, under sympathetic governments, British gay and lesbian activists have achieved much greater national-level success in reforming laws related to sexual orientation than have American activists. In the United States, however, activists have enjoyed greater success in mobilizing, in part because the American federal system, with its separation of powers, provides more targets for movements and interest groups. At the same time that American federalism creates more points of access for the movement, however, it also has more veto points and more possibilities of conflict with the antigay countermovement in different venues and at different levels of government. These differences in political institutions have structured the tactics of the movements in the two countries (Engel 2001: 120). The cohesion and centralization of the British parliamentary system has encouraged focused campaigns and a targeting of resources at the executive when the ruling party is sympathetic. Alternatively, when the party in power is not so sympathetic, the European Court of Human Rights now offers a political opportunity for the movement as an alternative venue to the British Parliament as this Pan-European forum has established precedents sympathetic to gays and lesbians (Engel 2001: 115). In the United States, lack of party discipline and decentralization have encouraged more grassroots activism and a wider range of strategies, including many direct-action tactics as well as institutional strategies.

Cultural factors are also critical to movement strategies, and cultural outcomes, as well as political ones, are an important consequence of social movements. The political culture in the United States encouraged the gay and lesbian movement to frame issues in terms of "rights" and to present itself as a quasi-ethnic group. In contrast, the British political culture encouraged a framing of the issue in terms of conscience and the acceptability of private behavior, although membership in the European Union has resulted in greater acceptance of a human rights frame (Engel 2001: 135–137). In the United States, the greater religiosity of the population compared to that of Britain has created more institutionalized homophobia and more need for the movement to counter the frames of the Christian right (Engel 2001: 147–150). In Canada, where there is less influence from religious conservatives, a culture of political liberalism made the courts receptive to the equal rights claims of the gay and lesbian rights movement (Pierceson 2005). Thus, movements make different strategic framing decisions and experience different outcomes, depending on the cultural contexts in which they operate.

Just as movements are influenced by larger cultural contexts, they also help to change the dominant culture. One of the accomplishments of the gay and lesbian movement is the creation of new forms of culture and discourse regarding sexual orientation. In addition to targeting the state, gay and lesbian activists have greatly expanded the cultural spaces available to them, such as social clubs, bars, churches, commercial services, and mass media (Engel 2001: 126). This expanded cultural "field" of gay-friendly organizations (Armstrong 2002) helps to maintain the movement and to spread the acceptance and inclusion of gay culture within the larger society. As the nature of gay and lesbian organizations changes, so do the strategies of the movement. Whereas early gay liberation groups shared the values and networks of the New Left and operated in a culture in which gay sexuality was strongly repressed, by the late 1980s and 1990s, gay men and lesbians could come out to an extensive cultural and commercial arena, and the movement became more open to a variety of gay lifestyles (Lent 2003: 45–46).

CONCLUSION

The gay and lesbian movement has created a great deal of cultural and political change since the birth of gay liberation in the late 1960s. This chapter illustrates the role of a number of factors emphasized by social movement theorists in shaping the strategies and outcomes of the movement. The movements of the 1960s created a climate of social and political change that inspired gay liberation groups, which built on the networks and ideology of the New Left. Developing in the counter-culture of the 1960s, the early movement began to create its own internal culture and collective identity. As the cycle of protest of the 1960s declined, gay and lesbian culture continued to expand, and many groups began to pursue civil rights strategies. By the late 1970s, an antigay countermovement had organized in response, but this development served to further mobilize the movement, as did homophobia and threats in the wake of the AIDS epidemic. Cultural and political opportunities, including political institutions and cultural values, have resulted in varying degrees of support for gay and lesbian rights in different countries. But with major social changes such as the spread of same-sex marriage, it is clear that the movement has had a profound cultural impact.

NOTES

1. Like a number of other scholars (e.g., Adam 1995; Armstrong 2002; Engel 2001; Raeburn 2004; Rayside 1998; Smith 1999), I use "gay and lesbian movement" to refer to efforts to advance the rights of sexual minorities, even though it would be more accurate to talk of *movements* (Epstein 1999), which may include gay, lesbian, bisexual, and transgendered activists. Although the term "queer" provides a convenient label to include bisexuals and transgendered persons as well as gay men and lesbians, it also tends to refer to a more specific brand of action that departs from the gay and lesbian identity-based activism that became dominant in the 1970s and remains important (cf. Armstrong 2002: xix; Engel 2001: xii–xiii).

2. Gamson and Meyer (1996) distinguish between "volatile" aspects of political opportunity, such as shifting political alliances, and "stable" aspects, such as judicial and legislative capacity and independence.

DISCUSSION QUESTIONS

1. How did public opinion on homosexuality change, and what role did changes in public opinion play in advancing gay and lesbian rights?
2. What have "liberationist" and "equal rights" strategies each contributed to the movement and its successes?
3. How do we explain differences in movement outcomes in comparing countries such as the United States, Britain, and Canada?

SUGGESTED READINGS

Adam, Barry D. 1995. *The Rise of a Gay and Lesbian Movement*, Revised Edition. New York: Twayne Publishers. This book is an excellent introduction to the origins and development of the movement through the early 1990s.

Armstrong, Elizabeth A. 2002. *Forging Gay Identities: Organizing Sexuality in San Francisco, 1950–1994*. Chicago: University of Chicago Press. Examining the gay community in San Francisco, this study shows how a gay identity movement arose by looking at the organizational and cultural expansion of the movement.

Engel, Stephen M. 2001. *The Unfinished Revolution: Social Movement Theory and the Gay and Lesbian Movement*. Cambridge: Cambridge University Press. This comparative study of gay and lesbian movements in the United States and Britain employs political process theory and usefully expands the approach with its analysis of cultural factors.

CHAPTER 7

The Environmental Movement

Environmental problems are extremely complex, long term, and critical to the future of our planet and its species. The environmental movement, which originated in a number of countries in the nineteenth century, is faced with the difficulties of maintaining effective campaigns of action over many decades. Maintaining a vital environmental movement involves keeping activists involved, influencing public opinion and holding public attention, creating lasting organizations, and devising collective action campaigns that have a real impact on environmental problems. The stakes are extremely high: beyond long-standing problems of pollution and habitat destruction, global warming is now causing the oceans to warm and the glaciers to melt at an alarming rate, with consequences such as increased hurricanes, floods, a potentially catastrophic rise in sea levels, droughts, and accelerated loss of species. Environmentalists face enormous challenges in tackling the causes of such devastation and, despite the urgency of the issues, difficulties in motivating individuals, industries, and governments to participate in bringing about the radical changes necessary.

In this chapter, we examine some of the problems involved in sustaining an influential environmental movement, concentrating on the movement in North America. We begin with a discussion of the origins of the contemporary movement in the 1960s and then turn to questions of individual and public interest in the environment: the extent to which environmentalism is backed by public opinion; how active participants are recruited from among those members of the public who believe in the goals of the movement; and how participation is maintained. Next, we examine some debates on the direction of the environmental movement and consider a selection of organizations and campaigns: Greenpeace and such media-focused efforts as antiwhaling campaigns; green lobbies and consumer-based boycotts; and antilogging and anti-roads direct-action campaigns.

ORIGINS OF THE ENVIRONMENTAL MOVEMENT

Although the protest cycle of the 1960s gave impetus to new types of environmental organizations and activities, the environmental movement originated much earlier. Conservation movements emerged in a number of countries in the nineteenth century to promote national parks, wilderness preservation, resource management, and the exploration of nature (Lowe and Goyder 1983: 15–17). In Europe, Australia, and North America, campaigns were initiated to connect environmental concerns such as sewage disposal and clean air and water with public health (Rootes 2004: 612). In the United States, organizations such as the Sierra Club, the National Audubon Society, and the Izaak Walton League formed in the late nineteenth and early twentieth centuries. Women active in Progressive Era organizations supported the conservation movement by lobbying for clean air and water, pure food, and public parks. In the early 1960s, activists in the women's peace movement raised environmental issues in connection with their concerns about atmospheric testing of nuclear weapons (Rome 2003: 534–536). Women's Strike for Peace created public awareness of the environmental effects of the nuclear arms race by organizing events and collecting children's baby teeth to dramatize the issue of high levels of strontium 90, a by-product of radiation, in milk (Swerdlow 1993). With the publication of such landmark works as Rachel Carson's *Silent Spring* (1962), which focused attention on pollution from pesticides, the concerns of the environmental movement broadened, and many women became part of a network that championed Carson's work and led campaigns for conservation (Rome 2003: 536–537).

Although the earliest environmental groups in the United States were regionally based and narrowly focused on particular concerns, many of these organizations expanded their missions and their memberships greatly. A number of established conservation organizations such as the Sierra Club, exhibiting extraordinary longevity, served as mobilizing structures for new groups formed in "the environmental era" of the 1960s (Bosso 2005). New political opportunities, such as increased access to the courts and the right to file "class action" suits, led to organizational and tactical changes, including the creation of legal defense funds, such as the Sierra Club Legal Defense Fund, which was founded in 1971 and became Earthjustice in 1997. Most established conservation organizations created lobbying offices in Washington DC, and many expanded their memberships greatly through direct-mail appeals, bringing new, nationwide dues-paying members into the environmental movement (Bosso 2005: 39–41).

The cycle of protest of the 1960s led to a major new wave of environmentalism, with a number of new environmental organizations, such as Friends of the Earth and Greenpeace, forming in the late 1960s and early 1970s. As in the case of the women's movement, however, the earlier "wave" of the movement provided a foundation for the new wave. Established conservation organizations were important to the organizational expansion of the environmental movement, as "most of the organizations that emerged during the environmental era got critical early help from an older organization" (Bosso 2005: 45). Other social movements of the 1960s were also key, providing activists, tactics, and energy to the environmental movement. Many New Left activists, like women's peace activists, became concerned with the issue of nuclear arms in the 1950s and early 1960s, which helped make them receptive to environmental issues. The counterculture of the 1960s created and supported "back to the land" rural communes and natural food restaurants as well as street theatre on environmental issues. For example, activists in New York held a "soot-in" at the Consolidated Edison building, at which they sprayed black mist and passed out darkened flowers (Rome 2003: 544). By the late 1960s, activists in political groups such as SDS were increasingly connecting the degradation of the environment to capitalism and the Vietnam War. Student antiwar activists formed eco-action groups on a number of North American campuses. An activist at Berkeley in 1969 started "Earth Read-Out," a radical report on environmental issues that appeared in many underground newspapers. Anti–Vietnam War activists accused the U.S. government of "ecocide" for use of chemical defoliants and bombs that devastated the landscape of Vietnam (Rome 2003: 544–547).

Environmental activists who came out of the protest movements of the 1960s adopted many of the direct-action tactics used by the civil rights, antiwar, and women's movements. In the United States, massive demonstrations were held on the first Earth Day in 1970, which was envisioned as a nationwide "teach-in" modeled on the teach-ins held by anti–Vietnam War activists, and campus activists made connections between military activity and chemical pollution (Sale 1993: 24). The influence of sixties tactics continued in later decades, with huge celebrations of the twentieth anniversary of Earth Day in 1990 in the United States and many other countries. "Redwood Summer," influenced by the 1964 "Freedom Summer," was also organized in 1990 to protest logging in the old-growth forests of northern California (Devall 1992: 59). Greenpeace, which was founded in 1971 and quickly became an international organization, is perhaps the environmental organization best known for its use of media-oriented direct-action tactics. The founders of Greenpeace were Canadian and American peace activists and journalists involved in the protest movements of the 1960s, who originally organized as a committee of the Canadian branch of the Sierra Club (Dale 1996: 16). The political context of the student New Left and anti–Vietnam War protest was critical to Greenpeace's first action in 1971, when activists sailed an old fishing boat from Vancouver to the site of a planned U.S. nuclear test on the island of Amchitka in the Aleutian Islands. Because the U.S. test, which would occur underground, could create tidal waves on Canada's west coast, the Greenpeace organizers called themselves the "Don't Make a Wave Committee" in reference to the tidal wave threat. Although the Greenpeace campaign was framed to appeal to mainstream Canadian nationalism, it was also calculated to build on previous peace movement and student protests against U.S. military tests. Exploiting both Canadian patriotism and anti-U.S. sentiment created by the Vietnam War, Greenpeace took off during a period of expanded activism generated by the movements of the 1960s.

In addition to inspiring direct action by Greenpeace and other environmental organizations, students and other activists in the movements of the sixties also supported other forms of environmentalism. In West Germany, activists from the student movement became involved in environmental issues and in 1979 founded the Green Party, which became the most successful environmental party in

Western Europe. The German Green Party attempted to be a different type of political party, incorporating ideas about participatory democracy into its structure and rotating its members of parliament (McKenzie 2002: 58). Thus, the cycle of protest of the 1960s helped to spawn an enduring environmental movement that has influenced the laws and policies of many countries, despite the numerous difficulties the movement encounters in achieving its goals.

PUBLIC SUPPORT FOR ENVIRONMENTALISM

Public interest in the environment and membership in environmental organizations have ebbed and flowed over the years, as has media attention to environmental issues. Anthony Downs (1972) argues that there is an "issue attention cycle" whereby the public becomes alarmed about a problem and very concerned with its amelioration. Once the public comes to realize the cost of significant progress, however, enthusiasm for solutions to the problem dampens. Eventually, a decline in public interest is followed by a "post-problem phase" during which the problem may sporadically recapture public interest. In 1972 Downs wrote that the public was already starting to realize the enormity of the social and financial costs involved in cleaning up the environment. Between 1965 and 1970, numerous environmental groups formed in North America and there was a great sense of urgency about environmental issues (McKenzie 2002: 89). On April 22, 1970, massive demonstrations were held across the United States on what organizers called Earth Day, stimulating public and media interest in environmentalism. After extensive media attention to the environment in the early 1970s, however, media coverage of environmental issues dropped off dramatically by the late 1970s (Steinhart 1987).

Media attention is one factor that affects public concerns and, although there have been periods of heightened media attention to the environment since the early seventies, the movement has struggled to maintain ongoing, serious coverage of environmental problems. Media coverage of environmental issues tends to focus on dramatic events, such as oil spills and nuclear power accidents. For example, the 1989 *Exxon Valdez* oil spill in Alaska and the confrontation over logging in British Columbia in the 1990s were major stories (Hacket and Gruneau 2000: 169). As Downs (1972) suggests, coverage also tends to go in cycles. For example, one study shows that coverage of global warming by the *New York Times* and the *Washington Post* increased dramatically in the late 1980s, but declined in the 1990s (McComas and Shanahan 1999). Systematic, ongoing coverage that does not involve major crises or movement-created drama is generally lacking in the North American media, which have difficulty sustaining interest in idea-based issues, and this has important consequences for public attention to environmental issues.

The extent of public concern about the environment also depends on competition from other concerns, such as economic problems. During periods of economic recession and high unemployment, environmental concerns tend to be less salient than economic ones, meaning that they take on less immediate personal importance for members of the public. New social movement theorists have argued that support for environmental protection is associated with "postmaterialist" values, which focus on quality of life and self-expression, rather than "materialist" values, which emphasize economic and physical security (Inglehart 1990, 1995). Some countries, such as the Scandinavian countries and the Netherlands, score high on measures of postmaterialism and also have high levels of support for environmentalism. Within countries, individuals with postmaterialist values are more likely to support environmentalism and to join environmental groups (Inglehart 1995: 57).

The postmaterialist-values explanation suggests that citizens of affluent countries are likely to be more concerned with environmental protection than citizens of poorer nations. However, this conclusion does not appear to be supported by multinational survey data, which shows high levels of concern for the environment in poor countries (Dunlap and York 2008). One explanation for this is that environmental concerns are based on "essentially materialist concerns with safety and security" as well as postmaterialist values (Rootes 2004: 618). Support for environmentalism is linked to objective problems such as water and air pollution as well as postmaterialism, and high levels of support for environmental protection exist in low-income developing countries where these problems are most severe as well as in developed countries that score high on postmaterialism (Inglehart 1995). But Dunlap and York (2008) question the utility of a distinction between materialist and postmaterialist values; they find that people in poor countries care about global as well as local environmental problems and that there is evidence that people in poorer countries may be even *more* concerned about the environment than those in richer countries. They conclude that environmentalism has become a worldwide movement that is not dependent on postmaterialist values or national affluence.

It is clear that public support for environmentalism has risen to strikingly high levels worldwide. The 1990–1993 World Values Survey (WVS) found that on average 96 percent of people in over 40 countries approved of the ecology movement. Ten years later, another World Values Survey in a larger number of countries, together with other global surveys, again found very high levels of environmental concern (Leiserowitz et al. 2005). And support for environmentalism remains high even when it is seen as costly. For example, 65 percent of the combined global sample in the 1990–1993 World Values Survey said they would agree to a tax increase if the money went towards preventing environmental pollution (Inglehart 1995: 59). In the 1999–2001 WVS, 52 percent of respondents worldwide agreed that environmental protection should take priority over economic growth and job creation. Moreover, Dunlap and York (2008) found in their analysis of this most recent WVS that people in poor countries were even more willing to make sacrifices for the environment than those in affluent countries. In another global survey in 2000, 69 percent of the sample said that environmental laws and regulations in their countries were not strong enough. However, despite

Table 7.1 Percentage of Global Public Calling Environmental Problems "Very Serious"

Water Pollution	72%
Rainforests	70%
Natural Resource Depletion	69%
Air Pollution	69%
Ozone Layer	67%
Species Loss	67%
Climate Change	56%

Data from 2000 Environics International Survey, adapted from Leiserowitz et al. (2005).

the willingness of substantial numbers of people around the world to pay more for less-polluting cars, few support higher gasoline prices (Leiserowitz et al. 2005: 26). Thus, there are high levels of public support for environmentalism, but it is not clear how willing people are to sacrifice lifestyles based on high levels of consumption and conveniences such as automobiles. Table 7.1 provides a picture of global concern regarding particular environmental issues.

On the all-important issue of global warming, it appears that significant numbers of people are waking up to the urgency of the problem, but the environment still competes with other issues for public attention. In the United States, Gallup polls show increasing awareness of global warming, with 58 percent of Americans believing in 2006 that global warming has already begun, but only 36 percent worrying "a great deal" about the problem (Saad 2006: 20). Yet a Zogby postelection survey of voters in November 2006 found that, although the war in Iraq was the main preoccupation of voters, 58 percent of them wanted their government to make it a priority to combat global warming (Zogby International 2006). As Americans later became preoccupied with the economy, however, a 2009 poll conducted by the Pew Research Center found that global warming had fallen to last place among 20 voter concerns and that only 30 percent of voters considered global warming a top priority compared to 35 percent in 2008 (Revkin 2009). Thus, the environmental movement is faced with the challenge of maintaining interest in environmental problems even as other issues become pressing for the public. Environmental organizations and campaigns must also mobilize participants in order to convert the base of public support for environmentalism into the major changes necessary for limiting the impacts of the global warming crisis and other environmental problems.

PARTICIPATION IN THE ENVIRONMENTAL MOVEMENT

Attitudinal support for the environmental movement does not necessarily translate into environmentally conscious behavior or support for environmental organizations. Because environmental protections are a public good, and because individual contributions to the reversal of large-scale environmental degradation are not likely to make a dent in the problem, the movement is, not surprisingly, faced with a free-rider problem. Many more people believe in environmental goals than actively support the movement, and recent surveys suggest that only 10–13 percent of the worldwide public supports the movement by donating to environmental organizations, writing letters, and signing petitions (Leiserowitz et al. 2005: 28–29). Table 7.2 shows environmental group membership in

Table 7.2 Environmental Group Membership

NATION	1981	1990	1999
Netherlands	11.4	23.8	45.1
United States	5.1	8.3	15.9
Denmark	5.4	12.5	13.2
Venezuela			11.9
Sweden	6.7	10.6	11.7
Greece			11.0
Belgium	3.1	6.6	10.5
Uganda			9.7
Austria		2.9	9.6
Philippines			8.2
Canada	4.9	7.6	8.1
India			7.0
South Korea	2.7	2.0	6.2
Finland	0.7	5.4	4.8
Mexico	3.2	2.8	4.7
Iceland	4.5	4.8	4.6
Italy	1.7	3.3	3.8
South Africa	3.1		3.8
Ireland	2.7	2.3	3.2
Japan	0.7	1.1	3.2
Chile		1.6	3.1
West Germany	3.3	4.6	2.8
Argentina	1.1	0.2	2.2
France	1.5	2.3	2.1
Spain	2.4	1.4	1.9
Hungary		1.4	1.9
United Kingdom	5.0	5.0	1.5
China		1.0	1.2
Russia		1.7	0.7
Turkey			0.2

Percent of World Value Survey respondents from selected countries who report being members of environmental groups, adapted from Dalton (2005).

selected countries for the years 1981, 1990, and 1999. Global surveys also show differences in richer and poorer societies with regard to behaviors such as recycling and selection of "green" products. For example, one survey found that among respondents from high-income countries 67 percent reported buying "green" products and 75 percent reported recycling, compared to only 30 percent of respondents from low-income countries who reported buying green and 27 percent who reported recycling. However, such results may reflect the lack of facilities and markets in lower-income countries, and it is unlikely that surveys adequately represent the very poor, "who are most likely to reuse and recycle as part of survival" in low-income countries (Leiserowitz et al. 2005: 28). Moreover, residents of wealthier countries engage in high levels of consumption and use large amounts of energy. And, as environmental activism becomes more common in many poor countries and as international environmental organizations work to spread environmental values around the world (Wapner 2002), multinational survey evidence shows that activism is viewed favorably by residents of poor countries (Dunlap and York 2008: 542).

Despite gaps between attitudes and behavior, and variations over time and place in levels of support, environmental organizations have attracted members and contributions, even at times when environmental concerns are low in saliency because people are preoccupied with other concerns such as the economy or terrorism. During the 1980s, for example, support for environmentalism among Americans remained high, but economic issues were far more salient. When Ronald Reagan was elected president in 1980, "there was no evidence that environmental protection was a salient issue to more than a very small percentage of the general public" (Mitchell 1984: 54). Nevertheless, threats to environmental progress by the Reagan administration elicited a great deal of financial support for national environmental groups. During the 1980s, a number of large American environmental organizations, such as the Wilderness Society, the Sierra Club, Defenders of Wildlife, and Friends of the Earth, experienced dramatic growth (Mitchell et al. 1992: 15). Worldwide, membership in environmental groups more than doubled in the 1980s and 1990s (Dalton 2005). In 1990, celebrations of the twentieth anniversary of Earth Day were held in 140 countries, attended by an estimated 200 million people (McKenzie 2002: 65).

Although such extensive participation in the environmental movement is not always in evidence, many people have attended movement events and joined environmental organizations over the years in part because "public bads" such as toxic dumps and air and water pollution are powerful motivators (Mitchell 1979). As collective behavior theorists argue, environmental degradation creates grievances, which help to motivate collective action—though grievances in themselves are not enough to sustain a social movement. Another reason for ongoing mobilization is that many national and international environmental organizations, such as the Natural Resources Defense Council and the World Wildlife Fund, are professionalized organizations with paid staff. As resource mobilization theorists have suggested, such groups make the free-rider problem less significant because they provide easy, low-risk ways for individuals to participate. For example, many people join environmental organizations by contributing money in response to direct-mail solicitations.

There are also, of course, more active ways to participate in the environmental movement, and social movement theorists have looked at the types of organizational bases and ideological commitments that affect participation beyond financial contributions. Active participation can take numerous forms, including relatively low-cost and low-risk behaviors such as attending legal rallies, writing letters, and signing petitions as well as more costly and riskier activities such as joining illegal blockades, participating in "tree sits," and setting up protest camps. In predicting who will participate in which types of activities, social movement analysts have explored the role of various types of individual attributes, such as ideological commitments, and structural variables, such as network connections and organizational affiliations. For example, in a study of relatively low-cost, low-risk participation in the British Columbia Wilderness Preservation Movement, David Tindall (2002) finds that people are most likely to continue to participate if they have numerous network ties within the movement that provide them with information about movement events and issues and encourage identification with the movement. In contrast to research on high-risk activism (McAdam 1986), Tindall found that weak, rather than strong, network ties and only minimal ideological support were conducive to low- to moderate-risk activism, such as attending nonviolent demonstrations and meetings, signing petitions, or participating in information campaigns.

In a study of several environmental groups in California, Paul Lichterman (1996) looks at how political communities are developed and maintained. He found two types of foundations for community in the environmental groups that he studied: "communitarian" and "personalized" commitments. In an anti–toxic waste group located in an African-American community, for example, participation was based on preexisting racial and religious community ties; members of the group were mostly black, church-going citizens who were already integrated into a larger community. By participating in the environmental group, they were acting as good citizens of their community seeking particular goals, and they willingly allowed community leaders to direct their participation in a traditionally organized group. In contrast, Lichterman found that members of a group associated with the U.S. Green movement, which organized in the 1980s to promote "green values" through Green electoral parties as well as other means, did not have ties to a preexisting community. They were acting as individuals with a "personalized commitment" to values they wanted to put into action. Their participation was not strictly instrumental, and the groups they joined tended to spend a great deal of time discussing ideology and creating structures that allowed for extensive participation and the development of collective identity. Although participants were developing their identities as activists and seeking self-fulfillment, Lichterman argues that this type of "personalism" was not simply therapeutic and did not detract from public-spirited action. Rather, individuals with personalized orientations were developing long-term commitments to political activism that would help to sustain certain types of participatory groups such as the Greens.

This sort of value orientation to political activism clearly underlies many environmental activities. In addition to community-based local groups and national environmental organizations, the movement includes many grassroots organizations that mobilize individuals motivated by a desire to act on their personal values and activist identities. Such individuals often remain active in various groups for many years, even a lifetime. An example of the type of group supported by such activists is Earth First!, which was founded in the United States in 1980 by activists seeking to create an environmental movement based on strong commitments to the value of nature (Brulle 2000: 198). Earth First! became known in North America for its radical environmental values and use of direct-action tactics by highly committed activists. An Earth First! group launched in the UK in 1991 became heavily involved in the British anti-roads movement and attracted activists looking for personal empowerment and committed to social justice (Wall 1999). In Canada, Earth First! and other grassroots groups have carried out radical environmental protest in a similar activist tradition, such as the Clayoquot Sound protests against logging in British Columbia in the 1990s.

DEBATES ON THE DIRECTION
OF THE ENVIRONMENTAL MOVEMENT

Because contributions to environmental groups vary with changes in political opportunities and other socioeconomic shifts, the environmental movement has not enjoyed continuous growth and stability. Environmental movements in different countries have experienced periods of upsurge and decline, depending on local and national as well as international factors (Rootes 2004). These movements have also had varying amounts of success in influencing public policies, and serious environmental problems such as global warming remain urgent. Consequently, there have been many debates over the organization, strategies, and effectiveness of the environmental movement. One important theme in these debates is the impact of **institutionalization**, which generally refers to the tendency of movement organizations that survive over many years to develop bureaucratic structures, rely on professional staff, and cultivate relations with government officials and other elites. Environmental movements in most developed countries are highly institutionalized, based on indicators such as size, income, formalization of organizational structures, number and professionalization of employees, and relations with government and other established actors (Rootes 2004: 624). The strategic choices of environmental movements are also a prime subject of debate, involving questions about the importance of direct-action tactics versus institutional ones, the use of media-oriented tactics, efforts to influence and work with corporate elites, and other issues.

In an influential study of the decline of American environmentalism, *Losing Ground*, Mark Dowie reports that between 1990 and 1994, membership in the Sierra Club fell from 630,000 to 500,000; membership in Greenpeace dropped from 2.5 million to 800,000; and the National Wildlife Federation laid off 100 staff (Dowie 1995: 175). The economic recession of the early 1990s was one factor, but Dowie notes that the crisis for environmental organizations outlasted the economic recession. The election of the Clinton-Gore administration was another factor; because Vice President Al Gore was an environmentalist, many people apparently believed that financial contributions to environmental organizations were less important during this period. Dowie also notes a problem with "list fatigue" in that mailing lists were being overused by national environmental groups, and direct-mail solicitation ceases to work when the same people keep getting the same type of appeals from various groups. In addition, other issues such as AIDS and homelessness were competing with the environment for donors. But Dowie argues that mainstream environmental groups also had themselves to blame for their decline; they became overly institutionalized and coopted by government and corporate elites. Nevertheless, he is encouraged by new forms of environmental activism, such as multiracial struggles for environmental justice and grassroots direct-action campaigns.

In a study of the organizational evolution of the American environmental movement, Christopher Bosso notes that, despite its shortcomings, "the organized vanguard of national environmental advocacy in the United States *has survived*. Moreover, as even Dowie admits, it has made a difference, although how much of a difference is a matter of debate" (2005: 6). Bosso reports that, despite the dips in membership in the 1990s cited by Dowie, in 2003 the Sierra Club boasted a membership of 736,000, while the National Audubon Society had 550,000 members and the National Wildlife Federation had 650,000 members. These organizations, along with others such as Greenpeace and the Nature Conservancy, have become "permanent fixtures in national politics" because they have adapted to changing political and economic conditions (Bosso 2005: 7–9). Bosso describes how established environmental organizations such as the Sierra Club changed their organizational structures to meet new demands, and older organizations facilitated the emergence of new ones, which often occupied particular advocacy niches such as land conservancy or clean water. In maintaining themselves, Bosso argues, national environmental organizations have sustained an environmental presence in American politics, which has helped to sustain policy gains and spread environmental values (Bosso 2005: 153).

Studies of environmentalism in other countries have also noted positive as well as negative effects of institutionalization (Rootes 1999). In a report on the Canadian environmental movement, Jeremy Wilson (2001: 60–61) notes that many of the large national organizations in Canada, such as the Sierra Club and the David Suzuki Foundation, have managed to create opportunities for volunteer participation despite their bureaucratic structures. In addition, these large organizations continue to cover a range of issues, and numerous smaller local and regional organizations also thrive alongside the national groups in Canada. Moreover, Wilson, like Bosso, notes that there are distinct advantages to institutionalization, including organizational stability and access to government insiders and other decision makers. In their analysis of the German environmental movement, Rucht and Roose (1999, 2001) similarly argue that institutionalization helps the movement to gain influence in established politics (e.g., through the Green Party) and that other types of groups also flourish in the decentralized German environmental movement.

Related to concerns about the effects of institutionalization, observers have also debated the effectiveness of movement strategies. In another widely debated critique of mainstream American environmentalism, Shellenberger and Nordhaus, in their 2004 essay "The Death of Environmentalism," claim that the movement has become overly narrow in its strategies and objectives, acting as a "special interest" that lobbies for limited legislative proposals but fails to supply the vision needed to address the global warming crisis and other major issues. They argue that environmentalists need to frame issues in new ways to create new alliances. For example, an overall vision for creating jobs in new types of energy industries, rather than a focus on isolated technological fixes, could unite environmentalists, workers, and businesses. Instead of looking for the "short-term policy payoff," environmentalists need to offer "alternative vision and values" to support long-term strategies such as "big investments into clean energy, transportation and efficiency" (Shellenberger and Nordhaus 2004: 25–26; see also Nordhaus and Shellenberger 2007). The "Death of Environmentalism" thesis sparked much debate, including rebuttals to Shellenberger and Nordhaus's contention that the movement is declining and public support is fading (e.g., Dunlap 2006).

Although there is general agreement among environmentalists that pressing problems such as global warming require new strategies, many doubt that a reframing of the issues will lead to solutions to major problems. Brulle and Jenkins (2006: 84) point to the power dynamics and financial costs involved in addressing global warming; beyond changing values, the movement has to figure out how to deal with "the inevitable economic trade-offs" and "the strong vested interests and sunk costs in the existing carbon-intensive economy." Thus, the environmental movement faces huge obstacles in developing effective strategies and tactics. In fact, the dramatic change needed "in the way the world produces and consumes energy far outstrips the capacity of environmental groups" (Bryner 2008: 330).

However, the movement has made progress in introducing new frames and discourse that have created some cultural changes as well as new political coalitions (Brick and Cawley 2008). For example, the "climate change" frame for the global warming phenomenon has helped people to understand that a variety of events such as heat waves, hurricanes, and flooding are related, and environmental Web sites have shown people how to calculate their "carbon footprints" and to change everyday behaviors to reduce them (Brick and Cawley 2008: 213). Some new coalitions between environmentalists and business leaders are also emerging, as shareholders concerned about the financial implications of climate change force some companies to address the issue (Bryner 2008: 331). And, although the federal government during the George W. Bush administration failed to take leadership on climate change, there has been more action at the state and local levels in the United States (Bryner 2008: 332). Hundreds of cities in the United States and around the world participate in the Cities for Climate Protection campaign aimed at reducing greenhouse-gas emissions (www.iclei.org). In the United States, connections to international environmental organizations encouraged participation in the program, offsetting a deficit in national government change agencies, which were associated with participation in other countries such as Canada and Australia (Vasi 2007). Both nationally and internationally, numerous environmental organizations provide educational materials and support to a growing climate protection movement (Moser 2007).

Environmental activists and organizations have waged a wide variety of campaigns and employed various strategies and tactics aimed at dealing with many different issues and problems. The following discussion of a small number of these campaigns and tactics points to some of the organizational and strategic dilemmas facing the environmental movement. The efforts of Greenpeace, one of the most successful international environmental organizations, to harness the power of the mass media reveal that movement organizations can exert some control over media frames, but at a cost. The use of consumer boycotts shows the promise, but also the complexities, of green consumption. The antilogging movement in Canada and the anti-roads movement in Great Britain show the potential of direct-action campaigns for influencing public policy and mobilizing not only activists, but also opponents.

GREENPEACE AND THE MASS MEDIA

Greenpeace was founded in Vancouver in 1971 by Canadian and American activists, including some experienced journalists, who determined to create an international organization capable of manipulating the increasingly global mass media. Despite its beginnings as "a rag-tag collection of long-haired, bearded men" (Dale 1996: 1), Greenpeace became a powerful, multinational movement organization through the use of its trademark strategy of creating dramatic events that generate sympathetic media coverage and large numbers of supporters (Brown and May 1991; Weyler 2004). Initially calling themselves the "Don't Make a Wave Committee," the group got its start with a campaign to stop a U.S. military nuclear test at Amchitka in the Aleutian Islands (see Hunter 2004 for a detailed account). Led by media-savvy activists, the campaign exploited anti-U.S. sentiment in Canada by emphasizing the threat of tidal waves on Canada's west coast from the nuclear test. The activists bravely sailed an old fishing boat to the test site, thereby creating a "David-versus-Goliath spectacle of ordinary people defying a morally bankrupt and intellectually unsound enterprise" (Dale 1996: 18). The campaign provoked an enormous amount of opposition to the nuclear test among the Canadian public and an equally large amount of media coverage. Although the test proceeded as planned, the U.S. military later announced that it would cease nuclear testing in the North Pacific, allowing Greenpeace to claim victory.

In choosing a strategy of nonviolent direct action, Greenpeace leaders were influenced by their political ideology, and they framed the issue in terms of the need for organizations and individuals to stand up to corrupt and unjust governments and corporations (Carmin and Balser 2002: 379). Through direct action, Greenpeace aimed to create dramatic confrontations that would generate media coverage and direct public attention to environmental issues. The Amchitka campaign proved highly successful in this regard, but in adopting this strategy Greenpeace was already limiting its public presentation of the issues. To win the favor of the media and the mainstream public, the group had chosen to appeal to Canadian patriotism and to avoid more radical and controversial issues such as Canada's participation in the Vietnam War effort through the sale of war materials to the United States (Dale 1996: 20). Nevertheless, Greenpeace's media-oriented direct-action strategy did allow the group to avoid compromising its ideals in the political arena (Carmin and Balser 2002: 381).

Greenpeace continued sailing ships to confront opponents, including whaling vessels. The organization's first big breakthrough came in 1975 when its ship confronted a Soviet whaling fleet in San Francisco Bay and a Greenpeace photographer captured Soviet whalers plunging a harpoon into the back of a sperm whale. The close-up of "blood and gore as the huge creature died" was irresistible to the mass media and "allowed Greenpeace to use the image to change the way millions of people thought about whales" (Cassidy 1992: 169). Greenpeace activists, who took great risks, came across as "a noble and brave group of crusaders up against a heartless and barbaric band of murderers" (Dale 1996: 150). Once again, however, the Greenpeace strategy required a certain type of frame, in this case blood and conflict, to attract media coverage. In two later antiwhaling campaigns, efforts at diplomacy and temporary success in stopping the whale hunts were not newsworthy (Cassidy 1992: 170–171; Dale 1996: 151).

As a result of all the media attention, Greenpeace became very "hot" as an organization and grew rapidly. Greenpeace eventually developed into an organization with the kind of professional expertise among its staff that allowed it to engage in all of the "preparation, training and research" that goes into putting on sophisticated "media events" (Eyerman and Jamison 1989: 107). This expansion and professionalization came at a cost, however; as Greenpeace transformed from a small group of activists into a large, respected organization, the group placed "new emphasis on organizational structure, merchandising, and cash flow" (Cassidy 1992: 170). Greenpeace did develop an effective media strategy, which involved providing "emotionally charged images to counter the effects of negative framing by the mass media" (Cassidy 1992: 171). Whereas many movement organizations are stymied by undesirable media frames, Greenpeace gets around this problem by providing images that send a powerful message regardless of how the mass media frame the story. To hone this strategy, the organization invested enormous resources and acquired the technological expertise to meet the production needs of television (Dale 1996). Greenpeace learned to create an event, film it, and deliver a video news release designed to allow news editors to select short video clips with great ease. In this way, Greenpeace was able to get air time for important environmental issues. In 1993, for example, Greenpeace created international publicity about Russian dumping of nuclear waste in the Sea of Japan by catching the polluters in the act and beaming back live pictures with sophisticated equipment on board the Greenpeace ship (Dale 1996: 110).

Although Greenpeace has enjoyed great success, its media strategy has some clear limitations. To maintain its media expertise, Greenpeace has had to develop a professionalized organization, making it difficult to encourage initiatives from rank-and-file activists, and some Greenpeace activists have become disenchanted with "the inflated attention they give to media coverage of their events" (Rucht 1995: 82). One problem is that many serious environmental concerns lack dramatic visuals and are difficult to address with a media-based strategy. Complex and long-term issues cannot be easily framed into the kind of stories with narrative structures that appeal to the mass media, and the content of Greenpeace communications had to be limited to "easily understood and accepted messages" (Eyerman and Jamison 1989: 108). Because it is extremely difficult for movements to present issues with any nuance through the mass media, another problem is that new constituents attracted through media presentations may have a different understanding of issues than older activists and leaders. For example, Greenpeace's antisealing campaigns in the 1970s used images of baby seals being clubbed, which attracted many animal rights sympathizers to Greenpeace (Dale 1996: 94). The successful antisealing campaigns resulted in a collapse of the seal-pelt markets, which devastated the Inuit economy in Canada. When Greenpeace tried to address these economic problems, arguing for a ban on sealing that exempted indigenous peoples, there was a great deal of conflict and many animal rights activists eventually left Greenpeace to form a new organization.

In conveying its messages to the public through the mass media, Greenpeace is limited by media features, such as the tight formats of television news programs and the need to frame messages in ways that appeal to mass audiences. Some Greenpeace leaders have recognized the need to branch out in terms of strategies in order to address complicated environmental issues. The organization has offices in both the global North and the South, and staff in regions such as Latin America have helped to develop the organization's thinking about problems that cannot be addressed easily with media-oriented tactics. Consequently, Greenpeace has developed a greater understanding of the relationship between environmental degradation and globalized trade, and the need to address disparities between developed and developing countries in solving environmental problems. Nevertheless, Greenpeace is structured to engage in dramatic tactics and remains reliant on media attention to generate support. Following its decline in membership in the early 1990s, Greenpeace revived itself using its classic tactics in an antinuclear testing campaign against France in 1995—10 years after French agents sank Greenpeace's *Rainbow Warrior* in New Zealand, provoking international outrage. After France announced its intent to end the global moratorium on nuclear testing by resuming its test program in the South Pacific, Greenpeace deployed its ship and generated headlines to mobilize world opinion against the French. France went ahead with the test, but agreed to a moratorium on further testing, and the campaign "rocketed Greenpeace back to superstar status" (Dale 1996: 206). Although it is rarely possible for Greenpeace to generate this level of attention, the organization has difficulty departing from the strategies that have brought it so much success.

GREEN LOBBIES AND CONSUMER BOYCOTTS

Like Greenpeace, other large environmental organizations also have problems devising effective strategies and tactics. In the United States, large national organizations, such as the Sierra Club, the World Wildlife Fund, and the Nature Conservancy, lobby the federal and state governments, while a variety of local and regional groups employ diverse strategies. Lobbying strategies tend to be largely futile during periods when the national government is hostile to movement initiatives, as was the case during the Reagan–Bush years of the 1980s and early 1990s and during the George W. Bush administration of 2001–2009. Corporate lobbies have countered the efforts of environmentalists by opposing environmental regulations and increasing political donations to congressional candidates (Beder 2002: 34). Moreover, even when environmental policies are passed into law, it is often difficult to get them implemented so as to have a real impact (McCloskey 1992). Consequently, it has been very difficult for American environmental organizations to influence public policy, and there is a great need for coalition work among environmental groups to pool resources and carry out effective strategies.

Green lobbies have played an important role in putting issues on the public agenda and they do enjoy strong public support. Michael McCloskey, a long-time activist, suggests that mainstream environmental groups can do a better job of tapping into high levels of public support by using their own strengths at gathering information. In particular, national environmental groups can use their research capabilities to provide information about various products and engage in market-place tactics such as boycotts, letter-writing campaigns, and protests at stock-holders' meetings—tactics that could be employed in coalition with grassroots groups. McCloskey gives the example of Alar, a chemical commonly used on apples, which was the subject of a television exposé by the Natural Resources Defense Council in the United States in 1989. Although the U.S. Environmental Protection Agency had debated the safety of Alar for years, no action was taken; after the NRDC exposé, however, consumers revolted and refused to buy Alar-treated apples, stores refused to sell them, and growers agreed to stop using Alar (McCloskey 1992: 86).

This kind of consumer power, in conjunction with the skills of national environmental organizations and the energies of grassroots activists, seems to hold great potential for the environmental movement. Insofar as the strategy of harnessing public concerns relies on the mass media, however, the movement risks oversimplification of issues. This can be seen in the case of a tuna boycott organized by environmental groups in the late 1980s to protect dolphins, which are often caught and killed in tuna-fishing nets because they swim with schools of tuna. Many environmental groups used the image of the dolphin as a very sympathetic sea mammal to get the public to boycott tuna so that they could force the international tuna industry to change its technology to use nets that allow dolphins to escape. In 1990, the major U.S. tuna companies announced that they would buy only "dolphin-safe" tuna, labelled accordingly. While most environmental organizations were thrilled with this outcome, "Greenpeace began to consider the social consequences of an international boycott of dolphin-caught tuna" (Dale 1996: 161). Greenpeace had learned from its earlier boycott of seal pelts that the issues were often more complex than simply saving an attractive animal, and the organization's Latin American bureaus also offered a different perspective on the tuna boycott. They argued that the U.S. companies were acting to protect themselves from foreign competition insofar as the industries of poorer countries did not have the technology to avoid killing dolphins and would be driven out of business by the boycott. Greenpeace wanted to try to address these economic problems and look for a long-range solution to the dolphin-tuna problem, but that position created public relations problems for Greenpeace as well as tensions with other environmental groups that wanted to declare victory (Dale 1996: 161–163).

As this example shows, there are no easy strategies for dealing with complicated environmental and socioeconomic problems. Many national environmental organizations in North America have been working with industries to promote "sustainable development" practices to save both energy and money. Critics argue, however, that industries want to define sustainable development on their own terms, and that they assume workers will bear much of the cost of greater efficiency in the form of loss of jobs (Adkin 1992: 138). Indeed, many businesses lobbied against ratification of the Kyoto Protocol to the United Nations Convention on Climate Change, warning that many jobs would be lost. Nevertheless, environmentalists have worked hard to form coalitions with labor unions and others and to address socioeconomic issues in both developed and developing countries. In Canada, where the Kyoto Protocol was ratified in 2002 with strong public approval, the David Suzuki Foundation collaborated with the Communications, Energy and Paperworkers Union to report on the economic benefits of Kyoto, effectively countering the "doom-and-gloom job-loss" framing by corporate lobbyists, and labor unions backed ratification together with "Just Transition" programs to assist displaced workers (Stewart 2003: 42). In the United States, Obach (2004) provides evidence that environmental protection can create jobs and that environmental organizations and labor unions do sometimes work together to advance mutual goals. Thus, green lobbies are pursuing a variety of strategies and coalitions as they attempt to tackle global warming and other complex problems.

GRASSROOTS ENVIRONMENTALISM AND DIRECT-ACTION CAMPAIGNS

While many large national environmental organizations have become highly institutionalized, grassroots environmental groups have also mobilized to expand the goals and tactics of the movement. Some of these local groups organized to oppose the siting of environmental hazards in their own neighborhoods—critics labelled them NIMBYs (not in my back yard)—but many developed into environmental justice groups with expanded understandings of the political and economic underpinnings of environmental problems (Szasz 1994: 80). In some instances, local environmental disasters served as critical events that helped to mobilize grassroots movements. Movement organizations then successfully framed issues in ways that appealed to local activists and devised direct-action tactics that allowed for grassroots participation.

In the United States, a toxic waste movement emerged in the late 1970s, based primarily in white working-class and middle-class communities and spurred by the saga of an abandoned chemical waste site and its devastating impact on a neighborhood community built atop the Love Canal, which had been a dumpsite for a chemical plant in Niagara Falls, New York. Racial and ethnic communities also mobilized around concerns such as toxic contamination and public health threats (Brulle and Pellow 2006). The environmental justice movement raised issues of racism and inequality, charging that the working poor and people of color typically pay the highest price for environmental pollution as industrial facilities and toxic waste dumps are often placed in poor and minority neighborhoods (Szasz 1994: 75). This branch of the movement continued to develop internationally, and in 1991 delegates from the United States, Canada, and Central America gathered in Washington DC for the first People of Color Environmental Leadership Summit (Dowie 1995: 151).

Radical environmentalists, who were motivated by ideology and an activist commitment rather than being connected to local communities and ethnic groups, also organized grassroots groups in the 1980s and 1990s. Many of these activists were influenced by the philosophy of "deep ecology," which emphasizes "ecocentrism" or human solidarity with nature and the rights of nature as opposed to a human-centered view of the world (Devall 1992: 52). Organizations inspired by the deep ecology philosophy, including Earth First! and the Rainforest Action Network, became active in North America, Europe, and Australia. Not all radical environmentalists consider themselves deep ecologists, but they advocate direct-action tactics as an alternative to institutionalized environmentalism and as a way to empower activists, and these tactics have attracted many participants. Some groups, such as the U.S. branch of Earth First!, have advocated controversial tactics such as tree-spiking to damage logging equipment, which critics argue can also endanger loggers.

Because of their visibility and apparent threat to the interests of groups such as loggers, miners, and farmers, radical environmental groups helped to provoke countermovement activity. Owing to the successes of grassroots environmental groups in mobilizing new supporters, opponents have mimicked their organizational forms. Some artificial grassroots coalitions, known as "astroturf" for the synthetic grass product, have been created for corporations by public relations firms to give the appearance of citizen support for antienvironmental positions (Beder 2002: 32). The Wise Use movement was created in 1988 when representatives of U.S. and Canadian groups, including interest groups such as the American Mining Congress and corporations such as Exxon and Macmillan Bloedel, came together to create an antienvironmental movement, known as Wise Use in the United States and the Share Movement in Canada (Beder 2002: 46). As Chapter 8 details, industry-backed Wise Use groups have framed issues, such as "jobs versus owls," in order to recruit to the countermovement rural dwellers, loggers, and other workers concerned about loss of jobs and land. By adopting the form of a social movement, antienvironmentalists are able to claim a greater legitimacy for opposition to environmental policies than industrial lobbies, and countermovement entrepreneurs can appeal to the fears of local activists by painting environmentalists as "the enemy" (Switzer 1997).

Opposition to social movements, particularly in the form of a countermovement, is often a sign of the movement's success (Meyer and Staggenborg 1996; Useem and Zald 1982). The emphasis on direct action helped to reinvigorate the grassroots environmental movement, resulting in some dramatic campaigns in the 1990s. In Canada, radical environmentalists worked in coalition with organizations such as Greenpeace to protect the forests of Clayoquot Sound, British Columbia. In the UK, Earth First! led a militant anti-roads movement, which involved many local communities in the environmental movement.

The Clayoquot Sound Protests

In 1993, after the provincial government of British Columbia announced that it would allow clear-cut logging in much of the old-growth forests of Clayoquot Sound on the west coast of Vancouver Island, one of the most dramatic direct-action campaigns in the history of the environmental movement was organized in British Columbia. As many as 12,000 protestors blocked access to a logging road and some 800 people were arrested in largely nonviolent protests. A local group called Friends of Clayoquot Sound, which had been fighting for preservation of the forests for over a decade, established a peace camp, which became a base for protestors involved in the blockades. The protests drew attention around the world, and numerous environmental organizations, including Greenpeace and the Sierra Club, became involved. A countermovement also mobilized; in the spring of 1994, some 20,000 forestry workers and their families lobbied the provincial legislature, and in July of that year thousands of people held a festival designed to celebrate "timber culture," which they felt was threatened by the protests (*Globe and Mail*, July 14, 1994).

Nevertheless, public opinion was strongly opposed to clear-cutting, and the campaign employed market-based tactics as well as direct action, using the resources of large international organizations as well as local groups. After Greenpeace threatened to boycott their products, two British paper companies cancelled contracts to buy pulp from the Canadian timber company MacMillan Bloedel. The British Columbia government eventually set stricter limits on logging in Clayoquot Sound, and the direct-action protests ended, but the struggle over clear-cutting continued. In a boycott campaign led by the Sierra Club and Greenpeace against Home Depot, the huge home improvement and building supplies retailer based in the United States, environmentalists deluged the company with postcards, sent an exhibit on the Great Bear Rainforest (located on the central mainland coast of British Columbia) to a shareholder meeting, and erected a Home Depot protest billboard over a clear-cut patch near Vancouver. The campaign resulted in a major victory when Home Depot, which has over 850 stores worldwide and sells 10 percent of the world's market supply of wood, announced in 1999 that it would phase out sales of wood from endangered forests by 2002 (Brooke 1999). Boycotts also forced timber companies to agree to more sustainable practices, although conflicts over logging in British Columbia continue. Overall, the movement campaign made important gains by building on favorable public opinion, using the resources of large environmental organizations, and harnessing the energies of grassroots activists with direct-action tactics.

The Anti-Roads Movement

Another dramatic direct-action campaign took place in the UK in the early 1990s, spearheaded by the Earth First! network founded there in 1991. As Derek Wall describes, protests against new roads and anti-car campaigns first occurred in the late 1960s and early 1970s, as local NIMBY activists fighting the loss of their neighborhoods to motorways joined with environmentalists who framed car use in terms of global environmental destruction (Wall 1999: 27). Activists in cities such as London and Manchester blocked roads to demand car-free streets and free public transportation with actions such as Reclaim the Streets parties held on busy roads and "bike-ins" by large numbers of cyclists. Some anti-car and anti-roads activity continued after the early 1970s, but radical activists in Britain became increasingly involved in antinuclear protests and peace campaigns, including the well-known women's peace camp at Greenham Common. In the 1980s a "green movement" was emerging in Britain and some anti-roads activity continued. Protest accelerated dramatically in the 1990s after the Conservative government issued a call for increased road construction in its 1989 White Paper *Roads for Prosperity* and after the founding of Earth First! (UK) in 1991 (Wall 1999: 29–37).

During the 1990s, anti-roads campaigns were mounted in a number of locations, involving thousands of activists and resulting in major reductions in the government's plans for road construction. The first major campaign took place in Twyford Down, near the city of Winchester, in protest of construction of the M3 motorway there. Inspired by the Greenham Common peace camp and similar tactics used by the Australian rain forest movement, activists created an anti-roads protest camp at Twyford that attracted large numbers of activists (Wall 1999: 67). Alliances were created between local activists and radical environmentalists from groups such as Earth First! (UK), and direct-action tactics such as digging and occupying tunnels, sitting in trees, and blockading roads were employed to raise the costs of road construction. Campaigns in other locations used similar tactics, and the "green network" in the UK expanded greatly, spreading strategies and a radical environmentalist collective identity. Reclaim the Streets parties were held in many cities, and the movement built on youth counterculture as well as environmental networks and memberships of large groups such as Friends of the Earth and Greenpeace. The movement faced great obstacles, including countermovement activity in favor of road construction and strong opposition from the government. Despite opposition and an initial lack of political opportunities and extensive resources, however, the movement was able to create divisions within the government (Doherty 1999: 284). The movement spawned effective alliances between local activists and radical networks and gained a great deal of media attention with its use of innovative direct-action tactics. Activists felt empowered by the protests, and an expanded network of radicalized green activists and a repertoire of direct-action tactics are among the movement's enduring outcomes (Wall 1999).

CONCLUSION

The modern environmental movement has endured for decades despite ebbs and flows in its organizational strength and activity. The movement's organizational and strategic diversity is one important reason for the continued salience of environmentalism. Large national organizations have created green lobbies in numerous countries. International organizations have spread to many countries and are capable of mounting both national and transnational campaigns. Greenpeace, in particular, is expert at generating media coverage. Local and regional groups, such as Friends of Clayoquot Sound and Earth First!, have demonstrated the potential of nonviolent direct action for the environmental movement. Networks of environmental activists and collective identities endure, even when particular organizations and campaigns decline. The movement has provoked significant countermovement activities, but these responses are an indicator of environmentalism's appeal, even though they are harmful to the movement cause.

Strong public support for environmentalism helps the movement to endure, creating financial support for movement organizations and political support for movement positions. Environmental problems are subject to issue attention cycles, but the movement continues to be relevant to the public because critical environmental problems are ongoing and local populations are often affected by environmental devastation. Public support creates the potential for greater use of market-based strategies but also the risk of developing only strategies that appeal to the mainstream public. Strategies that are difficult to convey through the mass media, and that involve slow and complicated solutions, may be difficult to sell to the public. Organizations that depend on donations from large numbers of people may fail to develop solutions that require lifestyle sacrifices on the part of the public. Moreover, even with public support to combat enormous problems such as global warming, economic interests and financial costs create major barriers. As Chapter 8 discusses, opposition to the movement from industry and an industry-backed countermovement has often stymied progress. Coalitions with labor unions and other groups are clearly necessary, as are international efforts to address the global scope of environmental problems. Many environmentalists are involved in such efforts, including the global justice movement, as we will see in Chapter 9.

DISCUSSION QUESTIONS

1. How can the environmental movement overcome the free-rider problem and get citizens to contribute to the movement and its goals, either through individual action such as recycling or through participation in collective action?
2. What are the strengths and weaknesses of Greenpeace's media-based strategy?
3. How might the environmental movement convert public concern about the environment into cultural changes and public policies that address major issues such as global warming?

SUGGESTED READINGS

Bosso, Christopher J. 2005. *Environment, Inc.: From Grassroots to Beltway*. Lawrence, KS: University Press of Kansas.

Brulle, Robert J. 2000. *Agency, Democracy, and Nature: The U.S. Environmental Movement from a Critical Theory Perspective*. Cambridge, MA: MIT Press. This book analyzes the major forms of environmentalism in the United States.

Rootes, Christopher. 2004. "Environmental Movements." pp. 608–640 in *The Blackwell Companion to Social Movements*, edited by D. A. Snow, S. A. Soule, and H. Kriesi. Malden, MA: Blackwell. This essay provides a comparative perspective, analyzing trends such as the institutionalization of environmental organizations in Western countries.

CHAPTER 8

The New American Right

The protest cycle of the 1960s is typically associated with progressive movements, including the civil rights, antiwar, women's, gay and lesbian, and environmental movements. However, conservative movements were also active during the decade, giving birth to a "New Right" that countered the "New Left." Although right-wing movements are active in many countries, the Right has been particularly influential in the United States, where movement supporters have moved into positions of power (Lindsay 2007; Micklethwait and Wooldridge 2004). This chapter will focus on what we can call the New American Right, which includes the New Right and its Christian Right allies.[1] A revitalized American Right emerged in the 1960s and became an important national political force in the 1970s, supporting Ronald Reagan for president in 1980 and continuing since then to influence the Republican Party. In addition to its elite patrons, the movement includes many grassroots activists, particularly evangelical participants in the Christian Right. The New American Right has acted as a countermovement to other movements considered in this book, exerting an extraordinary impact on American politics and culture.

In this chapter, we examine how conservative movements in the United States picked up steam in the 1960s, transforming into the New Right in the 1970s. We then look at some of the important issues around which the movement has mobilized. The New American Right was not simply a countermovement to the movements of the 1960s; it has roots in movements earlier in the twentieth century, and its own agenda extends beyond reactions to the progressive movements of the 1960s. However, the movement has opposed many of the initiatives of other social movements and, in particular, its opposition to feminist and gay rights issues played an important role in its growth and development. Thus, we examine New American Right campaigns against the women's movement, particularly abortion rights and the Equal Rights Amendment, against the gay and lesbian movement, and against some environmental concerns. After discussing these mobilizing issues, we consider briefly the question of the future of the New American Right in light of recent developments.

ORIGINS OF THE NEW RIGHT

Numerous right-wing movements have organized throughout the history of the United States, including extremist movements such as the racist Ku Klux Klan and anti-Catholic and anti-Semitic movements as well as more mainstream conservative movements (Allitt 2009; Blee 1991, 2002; Diamond 1995; Lipset and Raab 1978; Lowndes 2008; Martin 1996). Racist groups such as the segregationist White Citizens' Councils that organized in many southern states strongly opposed the civil rights movement of the 1950s and 1960s, and many participated in the 1968 third-party presidential campaign of George Wallace, which won nearly 10 million votes. However, racist activists failed to prevent civil rights victories, and the Americanist movement associated with the George Wallace campaigns eventually found its agenda coopted by the Republican Party, which used issues of race to recruit from the historically Democratic south (Diamond 1995: 144–149). After the 1960s, the Americanist movement and the ideology of racist nationalism continued through the Liberty Lobby, which subscribed to conspiracy theories and worked in coalition with the John Birch Society. In the 1980s the Liberty Lobby supported the political campaigns of Klansman David Duke and also promoted Holocaust revisionism. Racist and extremist movements in the United States continue to attract participants active in a variety of organizations and activities, including illegal and violent ones (Aho 1990; Blee 2002). The New Right, however, disassociated itself from blatant racism and violence, focusing instead on anticommunism and, increasingly, the traditional morality issues of the Christian Right (Diamond 1995: 142). Americanists also subscribed to anticommunist and traditionalist views, but, unlike the New Right, they were unwilling to make compromises and work within the political system. Consequently, the Americanist movement "moved further toward arcane and conspiratorial forms of racist ideology combined with tactics of lawbreaking and violence" while the New Right adopted a more "achievable agenda" (Diamond 1995: 160).

One very influential analysis of extremist right-wing movements saw them as part of a "radical right" (Bell 1963; Lipset and Raab 1978). In this analysis, which was later disputed and revised, participants in movements and organizations such as McCarthyism and the John Birch Society were thought to be motivated by "status anxiety," or the fear that one's social status is declining. For example, American-born whites who lack occupational mobility might blame immigrants or blacks for taking over their jobs or culture. The historian Richard Hofstadter ([1955] 1963: 77) suggested that the radical right appealed primarily to "the less educated members of the middle classes" who projected their worries about their social status onto the political arena. Lipset and Raab (1978: 29) saw extreme right movements as *backlash politics*, "defined as the reaction by groups which are declining in a felt sense of importance, influence, and power, as a result of secular endemic change in the society, to seek to reverse or stem the direction of change through political means." According to these theorists, right-wing extremism, which employed conspiracy theories and attacks on scapegoats such as racial minorities and supposed domestic communists, was an irrational response to real social changes.

Other scholars criticized this analysis of the radical right, and the "status politics" approach generally, on a number of grounds. In *Symbolic Crusade*, Joseph Gusfield (1986) uses the concept of status politics to explain the American temperance movement, but he revises the assumption of earlier theories that such conflicts are irrational. Instead, he argues that status politics involves battles over symbolic issues that can result in real changes in the distribution of status prestige. Another criticism, however, is that the focus on anxiety about social status is misguided; a variety of different types of people are attracted to right-wing campaigns for different reasons, not all of which involve status defense (Himmelstein 1990: 74). A number of studies show that participants in right-wing campaigns are concerned to defend their culture or way of life rather than to defend their social status (Bruce 1988: 16; Wallis 1979). For example, parents who object to school textbooks are concerned to protect their values; they correctly see textbooks that teach alternatives to their own values as competing with their efforts to pass down their beliefs to their children (Page and Clelland 1978). Thus, the concern is not with social status or prestige, but with cultural values and lifestyles, and the participants in such protests are not acting irrationally. Wilcox (1992) even argues that support for the religious Right can be seen as a rational choice, based on religious and political values and beliefs.

Another problem with the status politics analysis of the radical right, as Jerome Himmelstein (1990) argues, was that it neglected less marginal conservative groups, including those most closely tied to the Republican Party, while focusing on extreme types of right-wing activism. Moreover, the approach depicted the movement "not as a sustained organizational effort but as a series of discrete political eruptions" (Himmelstein 1990: 73). Contrary to characterizations of right-wing activists as marginal outsiders, the conservative movement actually mobilized many upper middle-class supporters and enjoyed some connections to political and economic power holders. Building on a number of different ideological and organizational foundations, the movement mobilized support from the Republican Party and from elements of the business community (Diamond 1995; Himmelstein 1990; Martin 1996; McGirr 2001). To understand the rise of the New Right, we need to examine how the movement organized and mobilized resources as well as what motivated participants. At the same time, as we will see, ideas about **status politics** and **cultural defense** remain helpful for understanding the mobilization of some right-wing activists and campaigns. Often, **symbolic politics** is involved, as issues such as abortion come to symbolize broader concerns such as changes in gender roles.

While the conservative movement of the 1950s and 1960s included the extreme racists and proponents of conspiracy theories described by analysts of the radical right, it also included intellectuals, college students, business entrepreneurs, and professionals, some of whom were drawn to organizations such as the John Birch Society while others sought more moderate groups (McGirr 2001).

Prior to the emergence of the New Right in the 1970s, several strands of the conservative movement unified in an ideological current known as "fusionism" (Diamond 1995: 29–36; Himmelstein 1990: 55–60). One element of this synthesis was *libertarianism*, which is concerned with the preservation of individual freedom and a "pristine capitalism" based on market and commodity relations and individual entrepreneurship (Himmelstein 1990: 47). Another element was *traditionalism*, concerned with the decline in moral order and community standards. A number of intellectuals, such as William F. Buckley Jr., the founder of the conservative journal *National Review*, debated the merits of libertarianism and traditionalism in their writings and also helped to synthesize the two positions. The synthesis was aided by a common anticommunism, which "provided a perspective from which both libertarians and traditionalists could see each other's points of view" (Diamond 1995: 31). Whereas libertarians saw little role for the state in the economy, they recognized the role of the state in preventing socialism. Traditionalists saw the importance of preserving capitalism as well as moral values and cherished institutions such as the family.

Young Americans for Freedom

Beyond the ideological and intellectual currents of conservatism, organizational structures also gave the movement shape in the 1960s. College campuses were one important site of mobilization for the conservative movement. While New Left activists were organizing through Students for a Democratic Society, New Right activists were joining Young Americans for Freedom (YAF), which was founded in 1960, the same year as SDS. Although most studies of student activists in the 1960s focus on their participation in left-wing movements, Rebecca Klatch (1999) in *A Generation Divided* compares activists in these two organizations. She shows that the generation of the 1960s produced passionate activists with conservative as well as progressive worldviews who developed political identities that they carried with them into their adult lives.

YAF tactics included anticommunist activities such as boycotts of corporations selling products to Eastern Europe, demonstrations in support of the Vietnam War and campus ROTCs, and involvement in electoral politics (Klatch 1999: 101). Both libertarians and traditionalists participated in YAF, but conflicts between the two ultimately led to the purging of libertarians from the organization. Tensions occurred as libertarians tended to support the counterculture of the 1960s, with some using marijuana and other drugs, while traditionalists opposed the counterculture. Conflicts also occurred because libertarians opposed the draft and, increasingly, the war itself, while traditionalists strongly supported U.S. involvement in Vietnam. Despite this internal strife, however, YAF survived as an organization, and many of its members continued their activism in the 1970s and beyond. Whereas libertarians typically became involved in libertarian organizations such as the Libertarian Party, many traditionalists became involved in the Republican Party, and many YAF activists became leaders of the New Right in the 1970s.

Local Community Networks and Organizations

In addition to movement organizations such as YAF, new and preexisting organizations in local communities also served as mobilizing structures for the conservative movement in the 1960s. In *Suburban Warriors*, Lisa McGirr (2001) examines the origins of the New American Right in Orange County, California, an area in which the movement thrived, contributing activists and strategies to the national movement. She describes participants in the Orange County Right as solidly middle-class people who, for the most part, were beneficiaries of the growing local economy with its new industries and expanding professional opportunities. Far from declining in social status, Orange County activists were relatively wealthy and upwardly mobile people who believed strongly in individual achievement, strict moral values, and free enterprise. Many had migrated to California from small towns in the South and Midwest, and they found that their beliefs clashed with the liberal culture of the state, with its progressive social movements and "an ever more cosmopolitan and multicultural Los Angeles." This "cultural clash led to easily heightened fears of communist subversion of the American way of life" (McGirr 2001: 92). Yet, McGirr finds, these conservatives were not battling "modernity"; they were people who enjoyed American consumer culture and who were taking advantage of individual and occupational opportunities, which they were anxious to preserve.

Such persons were mobilized in a variety of ways (McGirr 2001: 97–103). Books and literature by conservative authors, distributed through the social networks and organizations of suburban communities, were critical in educating middle-class people about the movement. Local businessmen founded organizations such as the Orange County School of Anti-Communism and the California Free Enterprise Association. Evangelical and Catholic churches were also important mobilizing structures as conservative religious leaders preached about the evils of communism and allowed their churches to be used by right-wing speakers and for the showing of anticommunist films. Aroused by McCarthyism in the 1950s, many evangelicals continued their anticommunist activities in the 1960s through organizations such as the Christian Anti-Communist Crusade, which conducted training seminars and large public rallies (Diamond 1995: 103; Martin 1996: 38–39).

Although televangelists and direct-mail campaigns played a role in the rise of the Christian Right, preexisting networks of conservative clergymen provided a critical mobilizing structure for the movement (Liebman 1983). Leaders of national organizations, such as the Moral Majority, recruited clergy from churches around the country, particularly independent Baptists. They were successful in doing so because a national network of fundamentalist clergy had been created through church-building activities and national conferences, alumni ties among those attending the small number of fundamentalist colleges, and work in the Christian schools movement. Owing to their "work in recruiting congregants through telephone chains and door-to-door visits," these local clergy possessed "a strong local resource base and extensive organizational experience" (Liebman 1983: 68). Building on the mobilizing structures provided by local churches, Christian Right leaders successfully established local chapters of the Moral Majority and other organizations throughout the country.

Electoral Politics and Political Opportunity

One of the key ways in which the New Right mobilized was through participation in electoral politics, most importantly Barry Goldwater's 1964 presidential campaign. The Republican Party became increasingly open to the Right, representing an important political opportunity for the movement. In Orange County, conservatives took over the California Republican Assembly (CRA) by flooding it with activists and building on the conservative networks created through churches and right-wing organizations (McGirr 2001: 117). Some of the activists who became involved in the CRA and the Goldwater campaign were members of the John Birch Society, which adhered to a conspiratorial theory as well as to the anticommunist, moralist, and laissez-faire economic views shared by many Republicans. However, the activists who mobilized through the CRA consisted of a broad range of conservatives who were by no means marginal outsiders: "They were solidly middle-class men and women, including housewives, ranchers, small businessmen, engineers, doctors, and dentists" (McGirr 2001: 118).

Through the mid-1960s, the "extremist" label associated with the John Birch Society dogged the conservative movement, providing "a constant reminder that its ideas lay outside the boundaries of respectable discourse." Yet the label also caused the movement's opponents to underestimate its appeal, when in fact the movement drew on "ideological inheritances with deep roots in American political culture to express concern with social, political, and cultural change in the 1960s" (McGirr 2001: 128–129). The movement in California mobilized large numbers of supporters for Goldwater, and the campaign helped to expand the conservative movement by attracting many new activists to the CRA. Goldwater appealed to religious conservatives who were worried about the political and cultural changes occurring in the 1960s. Conservatives were energized by his militant anticommunism, his concern about moral decline and the breakdown of the family, and his championing of "'property rights' over civil rights," which was particularly important in California owing to the state's recent passage of fair housing legislation (McGirr 2001: 132–133). Orange County activists helped Goldwater to win the California primary, a critical battle in the fight for the Republican nomination.

Although Goldwater was soundly defeated in the presidential election of 1964, the conservative movement had demonstrated its ability to control the Republican Party, and many grassroots activists were mobilized by the campaign. The Goldwater campaign provided a training ground for young activists in organizations such as YAF who became leaders of New Right organizations in the 1970s and 1980s. Although conservatives split their support between third-party challenger George Wallace and Republican candidate Richard Nixon in the 1968 election, by the 1970s the New Right had become influential within the Republican Party. Several features of this form of conservatism made it "new": it included new, well-funded organizations; it made inroads within the Republican Party; and it began forging alliances with conservative evangelical Christians (Diamond 1995: 128). In the 1980 elections, the New Right felt vindicated by Ronald Reagan's victory and also took credit for the defeat of a number of liberal veterans of Congress, including George McGovern.

The New Right continued its involvement in electoral politics in the 1990s and beyond, helping to elect the right-wing Republicans who took over the party, and also working at the state and local levels. After his failed presidential campaign in 1988, the television preacher Pat Robertson founded the Christian Coalition in 1989, hiring former College Republicans organizer Ralph Reed to direct the project. Under Reed's leadership, the Christian Coalition focused on developing local chapters and fielding candidates for city councils, school boards, and state legislatures. Focus on the Family, founded by Dr. James Dobson as a radio ministry in the 1970s, also expanded after the 1988 election, joining forces with the Family Research Council, a Washington-based think tank headed by Gary Bauer. Together, the two groups mobilized Dobson's radio listeners into a network of state-based think tanks, which organized grassroots activists to lobby state legislatures and became involved in local campaigns (Diamond 1995: 250; Hardisty 1999: 106–107). Thus, the New American Right developed a strong organizational infrastructure in both national politics and local communities.

Elite Support and Expanded Resources

The successful mobilization of the New Right in the 1970s depended on expanded funding, organizational infrastructure, and alliances (Diamond 1995: 131). The mobilization of corporate conservatism greatly increased the financial resources available to the movement. This elite support occurred not only in response to the hard economic times of the early 1970s. It was also a response to ideological concerns about the role of the state, and alarm that the U.S. position in the global economy was declining and that governmental regulations were limiting control by business within the political system (Diamond 1995: 132; Himmelstein 1990: 135). In the 1970s, big business began to assist the New Right through corporate political action committees (PACs), which made contributions to conservative candidates on the basis of their ideology (Himmelstein 1990: 141). Businesses also contributed to New Right PACs such as the National Conservative Political Action Committee (NCPAC) and the Committee for the Survival of a Free Congress (CSFC). In the 1970s, these PACs began to raise and spend large sums of money on congressional campaigns, with extensive funding from corporations such as the Coors beer company (Diamond 1995: 133). Big business also contributed to the New Right through the production of films and other educational materials for schools and "advocacy advertising," consisting of advertisements about topics such as tax reform rather than product advertisements (Himmelstein 1990: 144). Perhaps most importantly, big business contributed to the development of movement ideology through the funding of conservative think tanks such as the American Enterprise Institute and the Heritage Foundation. These policymaking organizations produced many high-level appointees in the Reagan administration and helped to make conservative ideology more influential in the world of business. Some 50 conservative think tanks, which employ large numbers of staff and interns and hold many debates and conferences each year, now operate across the United States as established structures for conservative ideology and action (Micklethwait and Wooldridge 2004: 157).

With increased funding from big business, the New Right thus expanded organizationally in terms of movement organizations, PACs, think tanks, and issue-oriented lobbies (Diamond 1995: 134–135). New Right leaders worked with existing conservative organizations, such as the National Right to Work Committee, which opposed labor unions, and they also created new organizations, such as Stop ERA (Himmelstein 1990: 82). The movement included many insiders in the Republican Party as it became involved in electoral politics to the extent that a "New Right-backed Congressional bloc became a coordinated *party faction*, one that would help usher in the Reagan revolution of 1980" (Diamond 1995: 135). Movement organizations expanded their memberships with the use of direct-mail appeals, as New Right leaders took their message directly to receptive individuals (Crawford 1980). Most importantly, movement entrepreneurs attracted many new constituents from the religious Right by appealing to social conservatives on a range of issues and channeling the energies of television evangelicals and other leaders into new Christian Right organizations such as Christian Voice and the Moral Majority (Himmelstein 1990: 83).

ISSUE CAMPAIGNS

The expansion of the New Right in the 1970s and 1980s depended, above all, on the passionate concerns of movement constituents about social and moral issues. While anticommunism continued to preoccupy conservatives, and libertarianism thrived as a movement with its own agenda, the New Right "devoted increased attention to fusionism's traditional morality component" (Diamond 1995: 123, 135). By organizing campaigns against the Equal Rights Amendment, abortion, pornography, drug use, school textbooks and curricula, gay rights, and other concerns, the New Right was able to mobilize Christian Right activists, who already had their own organizational infrastructure consisting of electronic ministries, superchurches, and a network of independent churches (Himmelstein 1990: 98; Martin 1996). These social and moral issues became increasingly salient to right-wing constituents as a result of the activities of left-wing movements of the 1960s and widespread cultural changes such as shifts in gender roles, rising divorce rates, and other changes in family life. Alarmed by threats to the "traditional family" and their cultural values and lifestyle, conservative Christians and other right-wing activists engaged in cultural defense, embarking on campaigns that sought to advance a "pro-family" position.

Although the New American Right was not simply a reaction to the progressive movements of the 1960s, the issues raised by these movements were critical in mobilizing new support for the movement. Abortion and homosexuality were probably the two issues that aroused the most passion and helped the most to mobilize activists and contributions for the New Right. However, there was also right-wing opposition to issues that might have been expected to create consensus, including the Equal Rights Amendment and environmental protection. In the following sections, I examine right-wing campaigns in reaction to the movements discussed in earlier chapters—the women's movement, gay and lesbian rights movement, and environmental movement.

Antifeminist Campaigns

One of the major themes of the New American Right is the threat to gender and family, and feminists are often portrayed as being responsible for increased divorce rates, abortion, lesbianism, and the "sexual revolution" (Hardisty 1999: 71). In reaction to feminist actions, right-wing activists have mounted a number of anti-feminist campaigns, including a successful campaign to defeat the Equal Rights Amendment (ERA), ongoing opposition to legal abortion, and efforts to promote conservative understandings of women's interests (Schreiber 2008). Many evangelical Christian women have been mobilized for these campaigns by organizations such as Concerned Women of America (CWA), which was founded in 1979 by Beverly LaHaye, the wife of Tim LaHaye, a well-known leader of the New Right who "accused feminists of destroying femininity and undermining men" (Durham 2000: 35). CWA is an explicitly Christian women's organization that has organized women through "prayer circles" of about seven women who meet "around the kitchen table" not only to engage in specific activities such as writing letters to legislators but also "to become emotionally and spiritually engaged" (Hardisty 1999: 80). CWA and other Christian Right organizations have successfully organized large numbers of women to oppose feminist initiatives.

The ERA Battle

The seemingly innocuous text of the Equal Rights Amendment declared that "equality of rights under the law" should not be denied on the basis of sex. When the ERA was passed by Congress in 1972, it enjoyed overwhelming support, including that of President Nixon, and 30 of the 38 states needed for ratification passed the ERA by early 1973. But despite early expectations that the ERA would be ratified easily, the feminist campaign for the ERA, as noted in Chapter 5, generated a powerful countermovement. The anti-ERA movement was led by New Right and Christian Right leaders and resulted in the creation of new organizations that mobilized large numbers of conservative activists. The most important leader of the anti-ERA campaign was Phyllis Schlafly, who had long been active in right-wing and Republican politics before founding Stop ERA (later called the Eagle Forum) in response to congressional passage of the ERA. Schlafly joined forces with other New Right leaders, such as Richard Viguerie, who pioneered the Right's use of direct-mail solicitations, and with Senator Sam

Ervin, the chief congressional opponent of the ERA, to mount a very effective campaign.

Stop ERA groups mobilized in the states and many anti-ERA leaders were drawn from right-wing organizations, including the John Birch Society (Mathews and De Hart 1990: 153). The anti-ERA campaign attracted participants who shared classic right-wing concerns about communism, "big government," and traditional morality (Arrington and Kyle 1978; Brady and Tedin 1976; Tedin et al. 1977) and the campaign was the first to mobilize large numbers of women for the New Right (Diamond 1995: 168). Anti-ERA activists flooded legislators with letters and lobbied relentlessly, often using memorable tactics such as delivering loaves of homemade bread to legislators, "from the breadmakers to the breadwinners" (Martin 1996: 162). Countermovement forces successfully opposed the ERA in key states, despite the fact that a majority of the public supported the amendment. When the 1982 deadline for passage of the proposed amendment expired, the New Right could claim a major victory over the women's movement.

To explain this outcome, scholars have examined how the issues were framed and what symbolic meaning the ERA held for activists on both sides. Many supporters framed the ERA in terms of the abstract values of equality, justice, and individual rights, and this frame helped to secure public support for the amendment (Mansbridge 1986; Mathews and De Hart 1990: 125). In addition to serving as a powerful symbolic statement of the country's commitment to equal rights for women, supporters expected the amendment to make substantive changes in women's lives, such as reducing economic inequalities in employment. In fact, as Mansbridge (1986) argues, the ERA may not have had much direct substantive impact, particularly since court decisions had accomplished much of what the amendment was expected to do by the time of its defeat in 1982, but it would likely have had indirect effects. However, the countermovement successfully shifted the terms of the debate away from abstract rights to issues of gender and family.

ERA opponents expressed fears that the ERA would eliminate women's "special privileges" and deny them the choice to be housewives. They argued that the ERA threatened women's traditional role as wife and mother by releasing men from their responsibilities as breadwinners, exploiting fears related to societal trends such as increased divorce rates. Phyllis Schlafly asked women to "consider a wife in her 50's whose husband decides he wants to divorce her and trade her in on a younger model . . . If ERA is ratified, and thereby wipes out the state laws that require a husband to support his wife, the cast-off wife will have to hunt for a job to support herself." Schlafly blamed the "new, militant breed of liberationist" for this predicament, while Mrs. Billy Graham argued that feminism is "turning into men's lib because we are freeing them from their responsibilities" (quoted in Klatch 1987: 136–137).

Conservative women clearly did not trust men to fulfill their responsibilities; they had to be forced to support women, and feminists were helping to release men from their duties as breadwinners. Although the ERA would likely have had little practical impact on homemakers, the issue came to symbolize for opponents the decline in status of women's traditional roles (Mansbridge 1986). As Barbara Ehrenreich (1983: 146) notes, "what was at stake in the battle over the ERA was the *legitimacy* of women's claims on men's incomes." Anti-ERA activists complained that "the women's liberation movement looks down on the housewife" and that women who used to be proud of being homemakers now say "I'm just a housewife" (Klatch 1987: 131–132). Anti-ERA activists thus blamed feminism for making women who preferred traditional gender roles less secure by arguing for "equal rights" that were not really in women's interests.

Most housewives did not in fact oppose the ERA; those housewives who were active in the anti-ERA movement were not representative of housewives in general, but were much more likely to be members of the Christian Right (Daniels et al. 1982). Nor did anti-ERA activists seem to be people who were slipping in socio-economic status. Although they tended to have lower incomes and educations than pro-ERA activists, anti-ERA activists were typically middle-class, married women who were more educated and better off than members of the general population (Arrington and Kyle 1978). Mansbridge (1986: 107–108) notes, however, that homemakers did lose an enormous amount of prestige in the late 1960s and 1970s as college-educated women began pursuing careers other than homemaking in response to new job opportunities.

Given this drop in the status of homemakers, and the fears expressed by conservative women about the decline in status suffered by the "cast-off wife," the battle over the ERA might be interpreted as an instance of status politics or cultural defense of values. That is, women who feared changes in gender roles may have been struggling to defend either their statuses or their lifestyle choices and cultural values. Scott (1985) argues that the ERA battle was a struggle over cultural dominance associated with status insofar as nonemployed women in his study were more likely than either men or employed women to feel a threat to their personal values and oppose the ERA. Although many housewives supported feminism and the ERA, employed women were more likely to support the amendment. Anti-ERA activists represented themselves as defenders of housewives and made the ERA into a symbol of threats to traditional gender roles and family life.

Feminists and conservative women both wanted to protect women's interests, but they had different ideas about what those interests were and about what it meant to be female (Klatch 1987: 139). Whereas feminists wanted freedom from oppressive gender roles, conservative women saw traditional gender roles as natural and even sacred. During the ERA battle, a number of issues were raised which pointed to the symbolic nature of the conflict. For example, opponents of the ERA argued that the amendment would lead to unisex public restrooms. Although ERA proponents mocked what they called "the potty issue," the image of unisex toilets captured for opponents the fear that women would be sexually vulnerable and that boundaries between men and women would break down. The possibility of drafting women into the military was another potent issue for ERA opponents, who feared that the ERA would lead to a denial of all distinctions on the basis of sex. Antifeminist women continually declared themselves "pleased to be women" and expressed their distaste for what they saw as the feminist goal of eliminating all differences between the sexes (Mathews and De Hart 1990: 163–166). Thus, the ERA held a great deal of symbolic meaning, which helped to make it controversial and aroused conservative women to work for its defeat.

The Abortion Conflict

Abortion is another symbolically charged issue that mobilized large numbers of activists for the New American Right beginning in the 1970s. Certainly, not all antiabortion movement supporters are conservatives; some are liberal Catholics. Much of the early organizing against legal abortion in the 1960s was initiated by Catholic activists with support from the National Conference of Catholic Bishops (Merton 1981). The National Right to Life Committee (NRLC) was founded by Catholic activists as the first national organization to oppose legal abortion. After the Supreme Court legalized abortion with its *Roe v. Wade* decision in 1973, however, "New Right leaders quickly grasped abortion's enormous symbolic value as a movement-defining issue" (Diamond 1995: 136). Right-wing antiabortionists immediately supported efforts to pass a Human Life Amendment to the U.S. Constitution, which was introduced in Congress following the 1973 Supreme Court decision. New Right PACs, such as the Life Amendment Political Action Committee and the National Pro-Life Political Action Committee, were formed to support antiabortion candidates and target liberal Democrats such as Senator Dick Clark of Iowa, who was defeated in 1978. There were some tensions between the NRLC and the New Right PACs, however, as the NRLC refused to broaden its agenda beyond the issue of abortion, whereas the New Right organizations wanted to strengthen ties with the multi-issue conservative movement. New Right activists included the abortion issue as part of a larger "pro-family" agenda, which included "larger questions of the state's role in family matters across the board" (Diamond 1995: 171).

The issue of abortion helped to mobilize many activists because it was highly emotional and symbolic of larger issues related to gender and family. In *Abortion and the Politics of Motherhood*, Kristin Luker (1984) argues that the conflict is a struggle between two groups of women over the meaning of motherhood. In a study of "pro-choice" and "pro-life" activists in California, she found that pro-choice supporters tended to be highly educated, well-paid career women who were not very religious and had one or two carefully planned children, whereas pro-life women tended to be housewives with less education and family income who were very religious and had larger families. Pro-life women were strongly committed to the traditional role of wife and mother, whereas pro-choice women saw motherhood as only one part of their lives. Pro-life women had a stake in maintaining the housewife role because their lifestyle choices made them more dependent on their husbands for support and less equipped to compete in the labor market. For pro-life women, the availability of abortion meant a devaluation of motherhood, and the availability of sex outside marriage eliminated one of the resources that women could offer men in marriage (Luker 1984: 209). Thus, the conflict over abortion, like the battle over the ERA, might be interpreted as an instance of status politics, insofar as pro-life women feel threats to their status or prestige as wives and mothers. Or it may be seen as a cultural defense of values and lifestyles that are symbolized by abortion.

Of course, many antiabortion activists also object to abortion on religious grounds, and the abortion issue became extremely important to many participants in the Christian Right, both because they believed strongly in the right to life of the fetus and because abortion symbolized larger concerns about the breakdown of morality and family life. By the late 1970s and early 1980s, fundamentalist and evangelical Christians became highly active in the New American Right as a result of the abortion issue. The Moral Majority was founded in 1979 by fundamentalist minister Jerry Falwell and his colleagues under the banner "pro-life, pro-family, pro-moral, and pro-American" (Risen and Thomas 1998: 129). Using networks of ministers, Falwell and other Moral Majority leaders urged conservative Christians to evaluate political candidates on the basis of their positions on issues such as abortion and helped to forge connections between the Christian Right and the Republican Party. With the election of Ronald Reagan in 1980, antiabortion activists hoped that *Roe v. Wade* would be overturned, but they were ultimately disappointed, and many evangelical Christians consequently became involved in militant direct-action activities. Although most of the activities were nonviolent, there was also a pattern of rising numbers of clinic bombings and arsons in the 1980s. According to Blanchard (1994: 55–56), this occurred because Reagan's election raised expectations, followed by frustration at the lack of change during his administration.

One of the most important antiabortion campaigns to mobilize evangelical Christians was Operation Rescue. Organized by Randall Terry, a fundamentalist Christian, Operation Rescue was launched in 1988 as a massive campaign to blockade abortion clinics with the bodies of antiabortion "rescuers." Operation Rescue recruited activists from evangelical churches, winning participants "by translating anti-abortion protest into their own Bible-based language of judgment and wrath" (Risen and Thomas 1998: 221). Operation Rescue staged large-scale demonstrations at abortion clinics in a number of North American cities in the late 1980s and early 1990s. In 1991, Operation Rescue mounted its largest-ever campaign in Wichita, Kansas, over 46 days, known as the "Summer of Mercy" and involving thousands of activists, centered on the abortion practice of Dr. George Tiller, one of the few doctors in the country willing to perform late-term abortions. The campaign resulted in almost 2,700 arrests and attracted activists from across the country with its "long emotional rallies" as "Wichita became a fundamentalist Woodstock" (Risen and Thomas 1998: 318).

Following this campaign, however, Operation Rescue began to decline as the movement became discredited by acts of violence and as the political opportunity structure changed under the Clinton administration. In 1993, an abortion provider, Dr. David Gunn, was murdered in Pensacola, Florida, followed by the nonfatal shooting of Dr. Tiller that same year. After this first murder occurred, the Freedom of Access to Clinic Entrances (FACE) Act was passed by Congress and signed into law by President Clinton in 1994. FACE created federal penalties for obstruction of abortion clinics and threats or violence against abortion providers. The law increased the costs of direct action against clinics and resulted in reduced numbers of clinic blockades and violence. However, threats to clinics continued, and a number of abortion providers were killed or injured in the 1990s, including Dr. Barnett Slepian, who was shot and killed in his home in a suburb of Buffalo in 1998. His was the last murder of a U.S. abortion doctor to occur until 2009, when Dr. Tiller was murdered by an antiabortionist gunman at his church in Wichita. Afterwards, Randall Terry justified the killing by calling Tiller "a mass murderer," and some observers wondered whether the latest killing would usher in a new wave of antiabortion terrorism as the murder of Dr. Gunn had done in the 1990s. Just as antiabortionists had little hope of creating change under President Clinton in the 1990s, they could expect to make little progress at the federal level under President Obama (Press 2009).

However, the federal system of government in the United States provides many venues for movement and countermovement action; as some arenas become closed to influence, activists can shift their activities to other levels and venues (Meyer and Staggenborg 1996). Abortion opponents can continue to press for regulations to make abortion more difficult at the state level, as they have done in Mississippi, where rules known as Trap laws, for Targeted Regulation of Abortion Providers, have been passed by the state legislature. For instance, doctors must offer women a brochure containing photos of fetuses, and women must wait at least 24 hours after an initial visit to a clinic to return for an abortion. While abortion rights activists continue to fight such regulations, antiabortion activists continue to press for new restrictions and to develop educational materials such as school curricula. As the head of Mississippi's Pro-Life America Network explains, "We have helped build a legal fence that helps protect women. The greater goal, even in legislation, is to influence the culture. This is a major culture war that isn't going away" (Slevin 2009).

Rhetoric about helping to "protect women" is part of the "culture war" for the hearts and minds of American women, many of whom support legal abortion and recognize the many accomplishments of the women's movement. As Schreiber (2008: 6) argues in her study *Righting Feminism*, conservative women's organizations such as Concerned Women of America "must take women's attitudes and feminism's influence into account." Antifeminist groups have in fact changed their rhetoric and goals in response to both the accomplishments of feminism and widespread changes in gender roles (Marshall 1995). For instance, organizations such as the Eagle Forum no longer reject women's employment outright but try to limit the effects of women's employment on the family with suggestions such as home-based employment (Marshall 1995: 332). Even as they oppose feminist initiatives, groups such as CWA must address feminist accomplishments and explain why they are better representatives of women's interests.

In working to restrict abortion, CWA is aware that it must appeal to "a population used to access to reproductive services but who also may feel ambivalent about abortion and its effects on women" (Schreiber 2008: 97). While CWA continues to adhere to its religious mission, and to focus on fetal rights, the group also consciously frames its arguments to appeal to women as "abortion's second victims" by pointing out how abortion harms women. Thus, CWA borrows from the women's health movement in talking about the physical and psychological consequences of abortion for women in its discussions of "post abortion syndrome." The group asserts that abortion can increase women's chances of breast cancer and that the contraceptive Norplant, considered an abortifacient by CWA, causes serious side effects in women. In opposing late-term abortions and supporting the 2003 Partial-Birth Abortion Ban Act, CWA discussed the possibilities of infection and infertility resulting from the procedure. In opposing the abortifacient RU-486, CWA emphasized the pain, nausea, and trauma experienced by women who take the drug. Similarly, CWA opposes the "morning-after pill" as unsafe for women. These "reproductive health narratives" are not unlike feminist critiques of unsafe drugs such as the birth control drug Depo-Provera, which was seen as risky by some women's health groups. The use of arguments similar to those of feminists "helps the conservative movement appear to be in sync with a range of political activists and thus has the potential to widen CWA's appeal" (Schreiber 2008: 105).

Defining Women's Interests

Concerned Women of America is one of a number of organizations of conservative women that attempt to compete with feminist groups as legitimate representatives of women's interests. Phyllis Schlafly's Eagle Forum is another socially conservative mass-based membership organization that also organizes women around issues of traditional morality.

In contrast, the Women's Freedom Network (WFN) and the Independent Women's Forum (IWF) are small organizations consisting largely of professional women who are economic rather than social conservatives. These economic conservatives strongly object to the feminist view that women are victims of sex discrimination or oppressed in any way. As successful women who feel they "made it the hard way," they believe firmly in individual accomplishment, are adamantly opposed to affirmative action of any kind, "and do not want to be tainted by what they see as the whining and man-hating women's movement" (Hardisty 1999: 87). WFN was founded in 1993 as an antifeminist research center and voice that differed from that of Christian Right groups such as CWA. IWF was founded in 1992 to support the nomination of Clarence Thomas to the Supreme Court and continued on as "a national and institutional voice for economically conservative women" (Schreiber 2008: 4). A number of conservative women associated with IWF and other antifeminist organizations have become well known through the mass media; they include Ann Coulter, who has published several books castigating liberals, and Christina Hoff Summers, who argues in her book *Who Stole Feminism?* that feminists, with their preoccupations with oppression, do not represent most women.

A number of the activists in this wing of the conservative women's movement are academics who strongly oppose women's studies and feminist influences in universities. College campuses are thus important battlegrounds where organizations such as IWF hope to attract young women to their anti-feminist positions. The Clare Boothe Luce Policy Institute (CBLPI), founded in 1993, attempts to influence college students by bringing conservative women speakers to campuses. CBLPI also publishes a student guide of alternative activities to counter the production of the popular feminist *Vagina Monologues* production because it "glorifies social deviancy and sexual perversion." The Network of Enlightened Women (NeW) was founded by students promoting "intellectual diversity on college campuses" and hoping to "bring a young female-friendly face to conservative causes" (Schreiber 2008: 22–23). In 2001, the IWF took out full-page ads in several campus newspapers to criticize feminist professors and ask students to "Take Back the Campus" and "Combat the Radical Feminist Assault on Truth" (Schreiber 2008: 2–3).

Other activities of conservative women's groups include support for conservative female political candidates to counter the funding of feminist candidates by organizations such as EMILY's List and efforts to shape public policy. Not all conservative women's groups oppose abortion; for example, WISH list raises money for pro-choice Republican women and IWF does not take a position on abortion. Both CWA and IWF work closely with the Republican Party, although neither contributes money to political candidates. IWF employs about 10 professional staff members in Washington DC who make media appearances, sponsor forums for conservatives, present awards to activists and political leaders, conduct research, and publish reports as part of their public education efforts. Conservative women's organizations also oppose public policies supported by feminists, such as the Violence Against Women Act (VAWA), which was passed by Congress and signed into law by President Clinton in 1994. IWF objects to federal intervention in the family and argues that feminists have greatly exaggerated the problems of violence against women and sexual harassment. In opposing feminist efforts to help women faced with such problems, IWF claims to be acting in women's interests by encouraging personal responsibility and allowing women to make their own decisions about relationships rather than treating them as victims (Schreiber 2008: 70–71).

As Schreiber (2008) shows, there is clearly a recognition among conservative women's groups that the feminist movement has had an impact in many areas of culture and public policy. The feminist framing of domestic violence as a widespread problem associated with institutionalized gender arrangements is widely accepted, as are other feminist views of problems such as income inequality and the need for child care. Consequently, conservative women's groups are attempting to redefine women's interests and reframe issues that have been dominated by feminists. Although the conservative women who participate in IWF dislike the gender-based identity politics of the women's movement, they themselves have chosen to organize as *women* for strategic reasons. As women's organizations, groups such as CWA and IWF enjoy credibility when they speak of women's interests, and they are helping to change public discourse about women's interests.

Antigay Campaigns

Campaigns against gay and lesbian rights rival antifeminist campaigns in their importance to the New American Right. In fact, there are important connections between antifeminist and antigay campaigns. One of the arguments made by ERA opponents was that the ERA would be used to legalize gay marriages, and Schlafly's Eagle Forum also questioned whether homosexuals could be prohibited from working in various jobs if the ERA were passed (Mansbridge 1986: 145). Like abortion, homosexuality is a symbolically charged issue that represents to some a challenge to traditional values and family life. Historically, the use of contraceptives and abortion increased opportunities for sex outside of marriage, a trend disturbing to social conservatives, and same-sex relations were part of a shift towards widespread nonreproductive sexuality outside of the control of family and community (D'Emilio and Freedman 1988). For many in the Christian Right, homosexuality is sinful behavior that also symbolizes threats to family life such as sexual liberation, changing gender roles, and the expanding youth culture on display in the leftist movements of the 1960s.

As we saw in Chapter 6, an antigay countermovement arose in the 1970s in response to the gay and lesbian rights movement. Anita Bryant's Save Our Children campaign and the effort to pass the Briggs Amendment in California were early battles in what would become a long struggle over the legitimacy of gay rights and same-sex partnerships. The early local campaigns in Florida, California, and elsewhere helped to create a network of activists opposed to gay rights and to build the organizational infrastructure of the Christian Right. Tim LaHaye became increasingly prominent as a "pro-family" activist as a result of the emerging gay rights conflicts, and the Traditional Values Coalition, which made opposition to gay rights a priority, was organized by a backer of the unsuccessful Briggs campaign (Durham 2000: 44). The Christian Values Coalition, claiming some 31,000 churches as members, went on to become a key national organization devoted to opposing gay rights (McGirr 2001: 259). Christian Voice, which became an important Christian Right organization involved in electoral politics in the 1980s, was organized by a group of ministers in Southern California who participated in antigay campaigns in the 1970s (Diamond 1995: 171).

Organizations such as Christian Voice and the Moral Majority injected opposition to gay rights into national politics in the 1980s. Christian Voice employed scorecards of the voting records of legislators on issues of concern, including gay rights, and actively campaigned for Ronald Reagan in the 1980 presidential campaign (McGirr 2001: 259). In a fundraising letter sent in the late 1970s, Christian Voice referred to the threat of "militant gays" and the possibility that "your child" might be "taught by a practicing homosexual" (Crawford 1980: 146). Christians for Reagan, a political arm of Christian Voice, ran a television advertisement accusing President Carter of "acceptance of homosexuality" and, in the 1984 elections, Christian Voice accused the Democratic Party in one of its fundraising letters of capitulating to "the lustful, sinister, and perverted demands of militant homosexuals" (Durham 2000: 44). The Moral Majority used similar rhetoric and, as the AIDS crisis came to public attention in the 1980s, sent letters highlighting the threats of homosexuality and AIDS. Christian Right organizations continued to engage in antigay campaigns at the national level in the 1980s and 1990s. They opposed Reagan's surgeon general, C. Everett Koop, for his support of education in the use of condoms to fight the AIDS epidemic. They opposed the National Endowment for the Arts during the George H. W. Bush administration for its support of gay artist Robert Mapplethorpe and other gay films and art. And they vehemently opposed the election of Bill Clinton in 1992; the Christian Action Network ran an advertisement accusing Clinton of standing for "Job Quotas for Homosexuals, Special Rights for Homosexuals, Homosexuals in the Armed Forces" (Durham 2000: 47).

It was at the state and local levels, however, that the Christian Right waged most of its antigay campaigns in the late 1980s and 1990s, by which time enough organizational decentralization of the Christian Right had occurred to allow it to mobilize grassroots activists (Diamond 1995: 171). Beginning in the late 1970s, gay and lesbian rights groups lobbied for local and state civil rights ordinances against discrimination in areas such as employment, housing, and public accommodations, finding the most success in more liberal states and more urban communities (Mucciaroni 2008: 225–227). Gay rights groups were also successful in promoting some reforms of school curricula and counseling programs in states such as California, reflecting greater acceptance of gays and lesbians (Hardisty 1999: 103). In response, antigay groups attempted to repeal or prevent antidiscrimination laws, an important activity from the early 1990s to the early 2000s, after which both sides shifted much of their attention to the battle over same-sex marriage (Mucciaroni 2008: 228). In waging campaigns against gay civil rights measures, local groups were aided by major national organizations such as Focus on the Family, Concerned Women of America, and the Christian Coalition (Hardisty 1999: 101–112).

In 1992, two high-profile battles over antigay measures that would outlaw nondiscrimination measures were waged in Colorado and Oregon. In Colorado, Amendment 2 was a statewide ballot initiative that would amend the state constitution to forbid the passage of new gay rights ordinances and repeal existing ones in various cities in the state. Amendment 2 passed with 53.4 percent of the vote but was later struck down by the U.S. Supreme Court. Ballot Measure 9 in Oregon gained only 44 percent of the vote, defeated in part because it not only prohibited recognition of gay rights but also required government agencies and public schools to "assist in setting a standard for Oregon's youth that recognizes homosexuality, pedophilia, sadism and masochism as abnormal, wrong, unnatural and perverse and that these behaviors are to be discouraged and avoided" (quoted in Herman 1997: 145). In both campaigns, frames that captured the status resentments and cultural fears of conservatives were critical to the mobilization of Christian Right activists, as were organizations and resources.

National organizations provided important support to antigay activists in both states. In Colorado, representatives of a number of national organizations involved in antigay campaigns served on the executive and advisory boards of the local sponsor of the amendment, Colorado for Family Values (CFV). Focus on the Family, which moved its operations to Colorado Springs in 1991, provided advice and in-kind contributions to CFV, including a "homosexual packet" from the Family Research Council that included a detailed strategy guide for activists (Hardisty 1999: 105–107). Other national right-wing organizations also provided support such as literature and advice. In Oregon, the campaign was organized by an affiliate of the Christian Coalition, the Oregon Citizens Alliance (OCA), and also received strategic support and materials from national organizations, including a 1992 video called *The Gay Agenda* provided by the Family Research Council (Herman 1997: 67). The video, which includes footage of extreme images from gay pride parades, was used extensively in the Oregon campaign, helping to mobilize conservative Christians by "representing gay men as hypermasculine savages" who were gaining influence in the culture (Stein 2001: 106–107).

In these and other antigay campaigns, the "special rights" frame was used effectively to convince many people that gays and lesbians were not simply seeking protection from discrimination but that they were in fact seeking "special" rights or protections. According to this logic, *civil rights* are "deserved" by groups such as blacks who have suffered discrimination based on characteristics that they cannot change, but *special rights* are "undeserved" by groups such as gays and lesbians who "choose a behavior of which society disapproves and must, therefore, live with the consequences—discrimination against them" (Hardisty 1999: 112). In an ethnographic study conducted during the 1992 Ballot Measure 9 campaign in a small logging town in Oregon, where the timber industry was in decline, Arlene Stein (2001: 125) found that the "special rights" rhetoric was very compelling to many people, even those who were sympathetic to individual gay people. Both religious and secular conservatives shared these concerns, but religious people were particularly concerned that moral values were under attack, while secular conservatives were concerned about "economics and the decline of the male breadwinner role" (Stein 2001: 111). The OCA used the rhetoric of special rights strategically to appeal to working-class people who Stein says were "justifiably anxious" about their status in a changing world. In a declining economy, they worried that they lacked the skills to get new jobs when old ones disappeared. They also worried about a "loss of standards" in the schools, blamed on permissiveness, which would make their children and grandchildren also unprepared to compete in an increasingly high-tech workforce. They resented homosexuals and others who were "getting special rights, circumventing the channels that reward those who work hard" (Stein 2001: 117). This analysis suggests a status politics explanation insofar as people who feel their own social status slipping blame gays and lesbians for their situation. Stein found that class was an important dynamic in small-town Oregon even though not all working-class people supported the OCA and many middle-class people did.

As we saw in Chapter 6, recent conflicts between gay rights activists and their opponents have centered on battles over same-sex marriage. As gay and lesbian rights groups began to achieve success through the courts in the early 1990s, a backlash against same-sex partnership recognition occurred in reaction to court decisions in Hawaii, Vermont, and Massachusetts (Mucciaroni 2008: 234; Pinello 2006). The Christian Right reacted strongly to efforts to legalize same-sex marriage owing to the symbolic importance of "traditional marriage," and gay marriage rights activists also became convinced that marriage rights were essential to full citizenship (Herdt 2009). Although Proposition 8—the ban on same-sex marriage in California that was passed as a ballot initiative in 2008 and upheld by the state Supreme Court in 2009—was a victory for the Right, legalization of same-sex marriages in several states in 2009 provided momentum for the same-sex marriage rights movement, suggesting that the battle will continue to mobilize activists in the opposing movements for years to come.

Antienvironmental Campaigns

While struggles against abortion and gay rights have been most central to the mobilization of the New American Right, countermovement campaigns have also extended to other issues, including environmentalism. Because environmentalism provides a critique of modern industrialism and calls for government intervention, it has typically been seen as a left-wing movement that "threatened core components of right-wing ideology such as the primacy of individual liberty, the absolute rights of private property, free enterprise and laissez-faire government" (Armitage 2005: 419). Thus, antienvironmentalism is an important current of the New American Right, which is supported by the extensive infrastructure of right-wing think tanks and other organizations.

Chapter 7 notes the creation of the "Wise Use" movement in the late 1980s, which helped to mobilize right-wing activists against the environmental movement, particularly in areas such as the Pacific Northwest, where disputes over logging operations pitted timber workers against environmentalists. Like issues of abortion and gay rights, environmentalism has sometimes been seen as a cultural threat that has taken on symbolic meaning. In her study of the battle over gay rights in small-town Oregon, Stein found that the heated conflict over protection of the spotted owl in the late 1980s and early 1990s was connected to resentment of gay people. Environmental efforts to protect the spotted owl from extinction led to the prohibition of logging in large areas of federal forest land, and loggers bitterly objected to the threats to their jobs and way of life. This resentment led to a common perception that various "outsiders" were the source of the problem. "Hippies, environmentalists, and homosexuals became one: immoral, dirty, lacking in self-control, and a threat to the well-being of the entire community" (Stein 2001: 122).

The Wise Use movement, which was organized nationally in the late 1980s by Ron Arnold and Alan Gottlieb, deliberately exploited such sentiments of resentment towards environmentalism. When social movements show signs of success, threatening existing interests, opponents sometimes adopt the organizational forms and strategies of the social movement. Useem and Zald (1982) found this to be the case, for example, in the battle over nuclear power in the 1970s, as proponents of nuclear energy attempted to create a pronuclear movement to compete with the increasingly successful antinuclear movement. Ironically, Ron Arnold said that he read Gerlach and Hine's (1970) book on social movements, *People, Power, Change*, and concluded "that in an activist society like ours the only way to defeat a social movement is with another social movement" (Helvarg 1994: 137). Alan Gottlieb, a former YAF member who worked with New Right activist Richard Viguerie on direct-mail fundraising, founded a think tank called the Center for the Defense of Free Enterprise (CDFE). Arnold teamed up with Gottlieb and used CDFE as a base for working with other antienvironmentalists and turning out books such as his 1988 *The Wise Use Agenda*, which outlines movement goals that include opening up federal lands for mining, logging, and the use of off-road vehicles. As Arnold recalled, "now we had a non-profit mechanism to work with and told industry, let us help you to organize our constituencies" (Helvarg 1994).

These movement entrepreneurs created a nationwide umbrella for numerous antienvironmental groups across the country. Many Wise Use groups receive industry funding and some serve as "fronts" for interests such as the mining and timber industries (Beder 2002; Burke 1995). However, there is evidence that the antienvironmental movement is wide ranging and diverse, including some genuinely grassroots mobilizations (Switzer 1997). Timber workers in California, for instance, began protesting proposed logging bans in the 1970s. In 1976, the Associated California Loggers (ACL) tied up morning rush-hour traffic on the Golden Gate Bridge with a convoy of 100 logging trucks to oppose a proposed buffer zone against logging around Redwood National Park. Following the success of that action in generating media attention, the ACL organized a second convoy of a few dozen trucks to Washington DC, where they were joined by some 300 timber workers opposed to the logging ban. Following these actions, the executive director of the ACL helped to organize a group of wives of timber workers, Women in Timber, which would eventually expand into a national organization, becoming "one of the most well-organized and powerful voices in the environmental opposition, combining grassroots activism and a strong ideological partnership with industry organizations" (Switzer 1997: 194). In the late 1980s, when the controversy over protecting the spotted owl received a great deal of publicity, there was a sharp increase in grassroots timber activism, and movement entrepreneurs had an opportunity to capitalize on the grievances of workers.

Entrepreneurs such as Arnold and Gottlieb were certainly critical in raising funds and framing issues for the antienvironmental movement. Critics argue that the Wise Use movement's primary public relations tactic is to frame complex environmental and economic issues in simplistic terms. In the conflict over the spotted owl, for example, Wise Use public relations experts coached loggers in the use of "sound bite" messages such as "jobs versus owls" (Burke 1995: 138). The countermovement effectively employed an "image of hard-working rural Americans locked in a life-or-death struggle with urban environmentalists who care more about spotted owls than about rural workers" (Micklethwait and

Wooldridge 2004: 181). Antienvironmental groups have portrayed themselves as moderate "wise users" of natural resources and they have borrowed from environmental rhetoric in framing their arguments and naming their organizations. For example, the Oregon Lands Coalition argued that people who cut down trees love the wilderness, and the Environmental Conservation Organization was actually funded by developers who wanted to drain wetlands (Burke 1995: 138–139). People for the West! borrowed its exclamation point from Earth First! and appealed to the fears of workers involved in grazing, logging, and mining that environmental restrictions on these activities would destroy their communities (Beder 2002: 58–59).

Clear organizational and ideological connections exist between the Wise Use movement and other right-wing movements. Right-wing think tanks, such as the Heritage Foundation, the American Enterprise Institute, and the Cato Institute, with financial assistance from wealthy individuals and corporations, have generated a great deal of antienvironmental literature, including work that questions predictions about global warming (Armitage 2005; Austin 2002; McCright and Dunlap 2000). McCright and Dunlap (2003) argue that major conservative think tanks served as mobilizing structures for the antienvironmental movement and played a key role in challenging the mainstream scientific consensus about global warming during the 1990s, resulting in the failure of the United States to sign on to the Kyoto Protocol. An important political opportunity, the Republican takeover of Congress in 1994, was a major factor in the ability of conservative think tanks to have this impact through means such as expert testimony at congressional hearings and increased visibility in the mass media. The ability of the countermovement to take advantage of the "balance" norm of the mass media—the media desire to appear "objective" by giving equal time to both sides—was also important to its success in challenging the scientific consensus on global warming (McCright and Dunlap 2003: 366). Antienvironmental groups, like other movements in the New American Right, maintained close ties to the Republican Party during the George W. Bush administration. President Bush renounced U.S. participation in the Kyoto Protocol in 2001 and appointed a number of officials with backgrounds in the Wise Use movement, including Secretary of the Interior Gale Norton and Secretary of Agriculture Ann Veneman (Helvarg 2004).

In addition to its connections to the larger New American Right at the national level, the Wise Use movement also has connections to state and local groups such as the Oregon Citizens Alliance, which became involved in sponsoring an initiative to undermine Oregon's land-use planning laws after its effort to pass the antigay rights Measure 9 (Burke 1995: 145). The issue of property rights, which became one of the OCA's top priorities, is central to the Wise Use movement and helps to connect the antienvironmental movement with other right-wing movements (Ramos 1995: 154). Wise Use groups are extremely concerned with protecting private property owners against any types of governmental restrictions aimed at achieving environmental goals. They have used a libertarian "regulatory takings doctrine" to fight government regulation of private property based on the contention that the Fifth Amendment of the Constitution requires the government to compensate landowners for any losses incurred as a result of government regulations. Whereas the courts have historically interpreted the relevant clause of the Fifth Amendment ("nor shall private property be taken for public use, without just compensation") to mean that the government cannot confiscate land or other property without paying a fair price for it (Ramos 1995: 147), the Wise Use movement has tried to expand the definition of government "takings." This strategy aims to make regulation prohibitively expensive by, for example, allowing developers to claim lost revenue owing to government restrictions on the ways in which they can develop property such as wetlands (Beder 2002: 60–61). Although large corporations are the main beneficiaries of such strategies, campaigns for property rights and against environmental regulations typically employ "anecdotes of individuals treated unfairly by the government, such as small landowners unable to develop their land because of regulations designed to protect wetlands or endangered species" to provoke outrage among individual supporters (Beder 2002: 48–49). The Wise Use ideology is very much in line with the individualism and antigovernment sentiments of the New American Right, and it even taps into old anticommunist themes as environmentalists are commonly called "watermelons"—green on the outside and red on the inside.

THE FUTURE OF THE NEW AMERICAN RIGHT?

With the election of liberal Democratic President Barack Obama, the Republican Party and the New American Right appeared to be in disarray. Even before the election, commentators were asking if the Republican Party and the conservative movement were running out of ideas (Packer 2008). With the fall of communism, the movement lacked a unifying focus, and many questioned the value of the ongoing "culture wars." A number of the old leaders of the movement are gone, and some remaining leaders have questioned the power of the movement to influence American culture and values. Long-time activist Paul Weyrich, one of the founders of the Moral Majority, concedes that the Right is in fact a "moral minority," telling his supporters in a letter to members of the Free Congress Foundation after President Clinton's acquittal from impeachment in the Senate that "I do not believe that a majority of Americans actually shares our values" and that "we have to look at what we can do to separate ourselves from this hostile culture" (Berke 1999).

During the George W. Bush years, the Right enjoyed a period of political opportunity with an ally on social issues in the White House. Christian conservatives helped to reelect Bush in 2004, and many activists immersed themselves in the Republican Party, "taking their talent for grassroots organization to precinct meetings and the like inside the party" (Micklethwait and Wooldridge 2004: 188). Whether or not a majority of Americans share their values, the New American Right is highly organized, with an extensive subculture that has provided mobilizing structures for the movement. In addition to the many fundamentalist and evangelical churches throughout the country, this infrastructure includes Christian schools and colleges, publications, religious television broadcasts, talk radio shows, think tanks, and numerous other organizations and networks. One question is whether evangelical Christians and other conservatives will continue to use this impressive infrastructure for political activism or whether they will retreat into their own culture and institutions. Another question is whether or not the movement will remain unified around core issues.

The issues of abortion and homosexuality were key to the mobilization of the New American Right in the 1970s and remain critical concerns for many movement constituents. While antiabortionists have made progress in banning some late-term abortions at the national level and in restricting abortions at the state level, they have not succeeded in overturning *Roe v. Wade* and it is unlikely that they will be able to do so in the foreseeable future. The battle over same-sex marriage continues to mobilize both proponents and opponents, but American culture has changed a great deal with regard to its acceptance of gay rights. As more people have personal connections to gay friends and family members, and as popular culture provides positive images of gay people, some observers suggest that political change is lagging behind cultural change. Polls show increased acceptance of gay and lesbian people and of same-sex marriage, particularly by those under the age of 40, suggesting that a generational shift is occurring (Nagourney 2009; Schafer and Shaw 2009). Some young evangelical Christians say they want to move beyond the issues of gay rights and abortion to issues such as poverty, health care, AIDS, and the environment (Banerjee 2008). A number of younger evangelical ministers, who are taking leadership of churches and organizations, are pushing for an expansion of the movement to deal with these issues.

On the issue of the environment, there is much disagreement among evangelicals and conservatives. "Green evangelicals" argue that there is "a biblical mandate for government action to stop global warming" (Kirkpatrick 2007: 60) and push the idea of "creation care," arguing that people are responsible for looking after the Earth (Sullivan 2006: 14). In 2004, the National Association of Evangelicals (NAE) voted to accept a position paper, "For the Health of the Nation," that "called upon evangelicals not only to safeguard the sanctity of life and to nurture families but also to seek justice for the poor, protect human rights, work for peace, and preserve God's creation" (Fitzgerald 2008: 29). Some leaders collected signatures for an Evangelical Climate Initiative calling for action against global warming, although others opposed it, saying there was no consensus on global warming. There are clearly divisions within the Christian Right, and more liberal evangelical activists are attempting to change the face of the movement.

At the same time, right-wing actions in response to the Obama administration demonstrate that more conservative elements of the movement are alive and well. In April, 2009, demonstrators held over 750 Tax Day "tea parties" to protest government spending in cities across the country (Robbins 2009). In the summer of 2009, rowdy demonstrators showed up at town meetings to protest health care reform, and on September 12, 2009, a large demonstration was held in Washington, DC, to protest against President Obama and his policies as well as issues such as gun rights and illegal immigration (Zeleny 2009). Right-wing protesters at these events expressed anger about the size of government and many hurled accusations of "socialism" at the President. They included racists and other extremists, some of whom questioned whether or not the first African-American president was really born in the United States, as well as more moderate conservatives opposed to big government. While noting the genuine rage of protesters, some observers have suggested that the protests were nevertheless "astroturf" demonstrations that resemble grassroots protest but rely on hidden elite backing. Tomasky (2009: 4) notes that the conservative protests are supported by corporate money, conservative radio and cable television shows and commentators, and elected officials in the Republican Party. With these resources, along with grievances stoked by leaders inside and outside of government, the New American Right is clearly capable of ongoing mobilization and broad impacts on U.S. politics and culture.

Although this chapter has focused on the right-wing movement in the United States, another important trend to note in considering the future of the movement is the globalization of the Christian Right. In reaction to the progressive international advocacy networks that have formed around issues such as women's rights and the environment, often mobilizing through UN forums (Keck and Sikkink 1998), the Christian Right is also building international issue networks with which to spread its "pro-family" message (Buss and Herman 2003; Butler 2006). Despite the right-wing distaste for international governing bodies, major Christian Right organizations such as Focus on the Family and Concerned Women of America have become active along with progressive NGOs in UN world conferences. Alarmed that progressive groups were spreading their views around the world through UN forums such as the 1995 World Conference on Women held in Beijing, Christian Right groups began to attend NGO events and push their own perspectives at meetings such as the 2000 five-year review of the Beijing Platform for Action that came out of the feminist-dominated 1995 meetings (Butler 2006: 52–54). This intervention disrupted the progress of the global women's movement in advancing its previously agreed upon agenda of women's rights. During the 2000s, the Bush administration assisted the Christian Right in becoming insiders by appointing Christian Right leaders to U.S. delegations, and the movement began pushing its own conservative "pro-family" agenda (Butler 2006: 69). Thus, the Christian Right has mounted an important challenge to global civil society, affecting the ability of the women's movement and other global movements to advance their concerns through the UN.

CONCLUSION

The above account of the rise of the New American Right points to the importance of several different types of factors emphasized by social movement theorists. Political opportunities are clearly important as right-wing activists have forged alliances with the Republican Party and enjoyed exceptional access to government in periods of Republican control of Congress and the White House. They have also taken advantage of American federalism, working in state and local as well as national venues. The New American Right has employed numerous mobilizing structures, including evangelical Christian clergy networks, churches, and schools, and the movement has created a strong organizational infrastructure, including right-wing think tanks and many other organizations. Resources have come from both grassroots and elite supporters. Movement entrepreneurs have mobilized resources through direct mail, Christian television, churches, and other channels, and they have framed issues to exploit concerns about cultural and political changes associated with the left-wing movements of the 1960s. Campaigns around moral issues, which often had symbolic dimensions related to status politics or cultural defense, were critical in mobilizing the movement. Although movement entrepreneurs, resources, organization, and political opportunity were essential, the New American Right could not have thrived without the passion of its constituents. Issues such as abortion and gay rights generated a great deal of outrage, and this emotion fuelled grassroots participation. And, in turn, right-wing movements stimulated passionate responses from their progressive opponents. The New American Right has operated as a countermovement to feminist, gay and lesbian, environmental, and other progressive movements, blocking their efforts at times, but also stimulating their ongoing campaigns. In Chapter 9, we consider a more recent progressive movement, the global justice movement, which arose in reaction to neoliberal economics and other elements of the right-wing agenda.

NOTE

1. Following McGirr (2001), who uses "New American Right" in her subtitle, I chose this label to encompass both the New Right and the Christian Right, which are each more specific labels. I also employ the more specific labels as well as the commonly used term "conservative" where appropriate in the text.

DISCUSSION QUESTIONS

1. How important is the concept of either "status politics" or "cultural defense" in explaining the mobilization of the New American Right? Are activists opposed to abortion rights and gay rights concerned about broader threats to their status or culture or are they simply acting out of religious or political belief?

2. What role have political opportunities played in the mobilization of the New American Right, and to what extent can the movement generate its own opportunities during periods such as the Obama administration?

3. Can the New American Right continue to maintain itself if countermovement campaigns around abortion and gay rights decline? What other issues might keep the movement mobilized?

SUGGESTED READINGS

Diamond, S. 1995. *Roads to Dominion: Right-Wing Movements and Political Power in the United States.* New York: Guilford Press. This book is an excellent history of right-wing American movements from the 1940s to the 1990s.

Himmelstein, Jerome L. 1990. *To the Right: The Transformation of American Conservatism.* Berkeley: University of California Press. This book provides a sociological analysis of the rise of the Right in America in the late 1970s and early 1980s.

Schreiber, Ronnee. 2008. *Righting Feminism: Conservative Women & American Politics.* New York: Oxford University Press. This is a very interesting analysis of how conservative feminists are responding to feminist frames and affecting public discourse.

CHAPTER 9

The Global Justice Movement

A seemingly new movement burst on the scene with massive demonstrations at the meetings of the World Trade Organization in Seattle in 1999. As many as 50,000 demonstrators, including environmentalists, labor unionists, human rights advocates, students, and feminists, descended on the city, resulting in major disruptions to the week-long WTO meetings, intense clashes with police, and a great deal of media attention. The "battle of Seattle" and subsequent protests in Washington DC, Quebec City, Genoa, and elsewhere were manifestations of a "movement of movements" to protest the neoliberal economic policies promoted by the WTO and other global financial institutions. International financial institutions and their policies—and global capitalism more generally—became targets for multiple movements because they were seen as worsening poverty in developing countries, burdening women and families, promoting environmental destruction, and lowering labor standards. Initially, the emerging movement was commonly known as the "antiglobalization movement" for its opposition to global capitalism, but activists gradually defined their cause as a "global justice movement" promoting global democracy rather than simply opposing globalization. From the start, the movement faced enormous difficulties in bringing together diverse participants and formulating strategies that would have an impact on global political and economic institutions. After the terrorist attacks on the United States on September 11, 2001, the movement faced even stiffer challenges in mobilizing and strategizing. Nevertheless, the global justice movement remains alive, representing an important attempt to bring together many different movement constituents to develop solutions to world problems.

This chapter begins with a description of the origins of the global justice movement and the various protests that led up to the Seattle demonstrations, including the anti–free trade movement. We then look at some key factors that help to explain how the movement was able to mobilize diverse activists, including framing activities, mobilizing structures, and international opportunities. Finally, the chapter examines some of the strategies and outcomes of the movement.

ORIGINS OF THE GLOBAL JUSTICE MOVEMENT

The Seattle demonstrations captured world attention, in part because they occurred in the United States and consequently received a great deal of media coverage, but they were not the first collective actions targeted at international institutions and their neoliberal trade and monetary policies. Jackie Smith (2008) uses the concept of a "rival transnational network" (Maney 2001) to show how a *democratic globalization network* emerged to contest the *neoliberal globalization network* that had formed among business, government, and other interests. The global justice movement grew out of earlier local, national, and international mobilizations involving many of the organizations and activists present in Seattle (Smith 2001, 2008). Neoliberal economic policies, which were promoted vigorously by the Reagan administration in the United States and the Thatcher government in Britain, provided a common target for protests around the world in the 1980s and 1990s. Moreover, cultural changes associated with globalization created threats to national and ethnic identities and local cultures, while new technologies such as the Internet promoted greater awareness of these issues and increased potential for global mobilization (della Porta et al. 2006: 14–15). Thus, global economic policies and cultural threats provided numerous targets for protests: intrusions on national identities and cultures; government cutbacks to social programs; and trade policies, economic projects, and corporations considered exploitive of workers and the environment. At the same time, activists began to see themselves as part of a global movement for social justice and a new type of "globalization from below" (della Porta et al. 2006: 14–15).

The emerging movement was highly heterogeneous, incorporating multiple movements and identities but converging around opposition to the institutions of global capitalism and supporting the right of peoples to determine their own futures quite apart from the influence of international financial institutions and transnational corporations. Among the many collective actions targeted at neoliberalism (described in Starr 2005: 20–25), "IMF riots" or "bread riots" involving general strikes and massive protests took place in some 23 countries in the 1980s. These protests were responses to the structural adjustment programs (SAPs) promoted by the International Monetary Fund (IMF) and World Bank, which required developing countries to cut social programs and privatize services and investments in order to pay down their debts while increasing private production and trade. In 1990, the African Council of Churches called for debt relief in response to neoliberal policies, and a debt relief movement known as the Jubilee 2000 campaign mobilized in a number of countries, building largely on faith-based networks of activists (Smith 2008: 101). In Europe, a variety of movements used direct action to take control of buildings, for example, and to protest policies such as welfare cuts and racism in immigration. Greenpeace London initiated an International Day of Action against McDonald's on October 16, 1985, which became an annual protest of McDonald's business practices, environmental damage, and treatment of animals. A movement of European farmers in support of family farming and sustainable farming practices mobilized in the 1980s, and in 1988 some 80,000 demonstrators from across Europe protested against the IMF meetings in Berlin.

Economic adjustment policies have particularly strong impacts on poor, indigenous peoples and, in Latin America, the adjustment process following the 1982 debt crisis provoked a variety of ethnic conflicts in states such as Bolivia, Mexico, and Peru (Brysk and Wise 1997). In Colombia, beginning in 1992, indigenous people protested against a drilling project by Occidental Petroleum until the project was finally withdrawn in 2002. In Brazil, a Landless Workers' Movement became very active in large-scale land occupations. In 1992, European and Latin American farmers created an international farmers' organization of small and medium-sized producers. In India, a long-term protest movement opposed a World Bank project, the Sardar Sarovar dam, which the Bank pulled out of in 1993; by 1997, when the Supreme Court of India ordered a halt to the Sardar Sarovar project, the antidam movement had spread to other projects. Such struggles "gained intense international attention in the context of an emerging comprehensive case against corporations" and attracted environmental organizations to the cause (Brysk and Wise 1997: 24).

In North America, the movement in the 1980s against the Canada–U.S. Free Trade Agreement (FTA) was important in creating transnational networks among activists in Canada, the United States, and Mexico. As Jeffrey Ayres (1998) describes, a coalition of "popular-sector groups" in Canada, including churches, labor unions, farmers, Aboriginals, and women's groups, organized to oppose the free trade agreement with the United States. All of these groups were affected by the economic recession of the 1980s and alarmed by the political shift to the right when the Conservatives were elected in 1984. Aroused by these grievances and threats, popular-sector groups took advantage of mobilizing opportunities created by public hearings on free trade and political opportunities in the form of divisions among levels of government and disputes between Canada and the United States, which delayed the FTA and allowed opponents time to organize. Although the movement lost the battle over the FTA, Ayres argues that the form of coalition building used by the Canadian movement diffused to the United States and Mexico and, in the battle over the extension of the free trade agreement to Mexico in the North American Free Trade Agreement (NAFTA), cooperative ties created among activists in the three countries helped form the basis for the broader global justice movement.

On January 1, 1994, the day that NAFTA took effect, an army of indigenous people and peasants in the Chiapas region of Mexico calling itself the Zapatista Army of National Liberation took over a number of towns and set up autonomous zones. The Zapatistas were protesting NAFTA and neoliberal policies of the Mexican government such as elimination of protections on coffee prices and the dismantling of a program that provided communal plots of land to indigenous farmers. Although the Mexican government met the insurrection with military force, the Zapatistas quickly mobilized national and international support, which forced the government to declare a ceasefire. The Zapatistas were able to generate support through their extensive network connections to peasant organizations and other nongovernmental organizations (NGOs) within Mexico and through connections to other activists in North America created by the anti-NAFTA coalition (Schulz 1998: 593–594). The Zapatistas also generated international solidarity through use of the Internet to win sympathy for a broad set of demands focusing on justice, democracy, and dignity. In 1996, some 3,000 activists from around the world gathered in Chiapas at a meeting hosted by the Zapatistas, which resulted in an intercontinental network of activists opposed to neoliberal policies and committed to common values such as social justice, environmentalism, and women's rights.

In the decades since World War II, the number of international nongovernmental organizations increased greatly, and NGOs have played a key role in what Keck and Sikkink (1998: 1) call *transnational advocacy networks*, which are "distinguishable largely by the centrality of principled ideas or values in motivating their formation." International NGOs have formed advocacy networks around human rights, peace, environmental, women's rights, and economic justice issues (Keck and Sikkink 1998; Smith 2008). Many of the participants in these advocacy networks are professionals who lend expertise and legitimacy to international campaigns, which have helped to institutionalize new international norms on issues such as human rights. Advocacy networks have worked through institutional structures such as the UN, but they have also supported, and expanded with, grassroots movements. In recent decades, transnational social movement organizations have expanded greatly and become more decentralized, in part because new communications technologies have decreased the need for centralized and hierarchical organizational structures and allowed local and national groups to connect with international networks (Smith 2008: 124).

Around the world, local and national movements diffused internationally and supported emerging global justice networks, with a large number of protests occurring in the wake of the founding of the World Trade Organization in 1995 (Starr 2005: 25–26). In Nigeria, the Ogoni people had been waging a long struggle against exploitation in their homeland, but gained little notice until Ken Saro-Wiwa and other activists formed the Movement for the Survival of the Ogoni People (MOSOP) to fight for political autonomy and against ethnic, economic, and environmental exploitation by the Nigerian government and Royal Dutch/ Shell, the major oil company operating in the region (Bob 2005: 54). In 1995, large demonstrations were organized to protest the execution of Ken Saro-Wiwa and eight other MOSOP activists by the government of Nigeria following a trial on trumped up charges and despite world condemnation. In France, the largest demonstrations since May 1968 took place in December 1995 in the form of massive strikes by workers, students, women's groups, and others in protest of government plans to reform social security and in support of the welfare state; in 1998, some of the same organizations joined together to create the Association for the Taxation of Financial Transaction for the Aid of Citizens, known as ATTAC (Ancelovici 2002: 432). ATTAC became an "international movement for democratic control of financial markets and their institutions" with branches in over 30 countries (www.attac.org).

In many cities, local movement activity picked up in the 1990s, involving participants in causes that would feed into the global justice movement. In what Janet Conway (2004) calls the "activist city" of Toronto, for example, a group created in 1992, called the Metro Network for Social Justice, brought together unions, community-based social service agencies, housing and antipoverty activists, feminists, and others who connected local problems such as cutbacks in municipal services with larger issues of free trade and neoliberal economic policies. In London, the anti-roads movement that originally protested motorway construction and the takeover of cities by cars developed a broader anticorporate critique. Joining with other countercultural groups, anti-roads activists promoted Reclaim the Streets parties in the 1990s as a way of reclaiming public spaces (Klein 1999: 312–313). Reclaim the Streets also spread internationally, and in May 1998 a global street party was held simultaneously in cities around the world (rts.gn.apc. org). Police reaction to the parties varied greatly, in some cities resulting in riots but arousing everywhere a great deal of emotion regarding the power of the movement (Klein 1999: 320–321). The mobilization of such local movements made a scale shift to the international protests in Seattle and elsewhere possible, and the stability of local organizations provided a place for local activists to return after participating in episodic transnational activism (Tarrow 2005).

Among the transnational networks of activists forming, Peoples' Global Action (PGA), inspired by the Zapatista vision, was created in 1998. The coalition sponsored the first "global day of action" in May 1998 to coincide with the meetings of the G-8[1] in Birmingham, England, and the WTO in Geneva (Wood 2005a, 2005b). The second global day of action was called by PGA to protest the June 1999 meeting of the G-8 in Germany, and the third global day of action was called to protest the WTO meetings in Seattle in November of that year. Thus, numerous protests organized by various networks of activists occurred around the world before the events in Seattle in 1999. The dramatic protests in Seattle did create new momentum for the movement, and a record number of organizations participated in the protests, both in Seattle and in cities around the world. After the Seattle protests, PGA and other activist networks continued to organize protests to coincide with the meetings of international financial organizations such as the WTO and to target corporate symbols of global capitalism such as McDonald's and Nike. Although the events of September 11, 2001, slowed the momentum of the movement, particularly in the United States, a massive protest took place in over 150 cities worldwide against the WTO meetings in Qatar as soon as November 2001 (Wood 2005a: 80). Despite a brief pause in protests in response to the terrorist attacks of 2001, the global justice movement continued to be active worldwide after 9/11, and in fact the ranks of the movement were expanded by antiwar activists around the world after the U.S. invasions of Afghanistan and Iraq (Podobnik 2005).

A number of important changes have occurred in transnational activism since the late 1990s in the "post-Seattle era," including increased activism in the global South, decentralization of organizations, a shift to locally oriented sites of protest, and an emphasis on issue campaigns, often organized through the Internet, rather than a focus on global institutions (Smith 2008: 127). However, the movement also continues to target international institutions, and the world economic crisis that intensified in 2008 generated a great deal of anger against institutional symbols of greed and power. Large demonstrations were organized in 2009 at the site of the G-20 meetings in London, where the "financial district was an obvious target," and at the site of NATO meetings in Strasbourg, France, where protesters objected to spending on military campaigns rather than social welfare (Castle and Erlanger 2009). Under the banner of "jobs, justice and climate," the London demonstrations were organized by a coalition called Put People First, which included the Jubilee Debt Campaign, environmental groups, trade justice groups, unions, and religious groups (Kingsnorth 2009; www.putpeoplefirst.org.uk). Following the protests, the coalition planned to pursue these issues in a framework linking the urgency for economic justice to climate change. At a second meeting of the G-20 in Pittsburgh later in 2009, activists again linked concerns about economic justice and the urgency of climate change in a week of demonstrations and educational events.

MOBILIZING FRAMES, STRUCTURES, AND OPPORTUNITIES

Theories of social movements suggest some key factors that help to explain how and why the global justice movement emerged when it did. Global economic changes and the advocacy of neoliberal policies created widespread *grievances* and *threats* in both developed and developing countries. Conflicts over the consequences of these policies became widespread in the 1980s and 1990s, and—significantly for the creation of a transnational movement—activists in different locations began linking various socioeconomic and political problems to neoliberal policies. In other words, they were creating a *master frame* that diagnosed specific problems as consequences of neoliberalism and its practice by international financial institutions (Ayres 2004, 2005). This "broadly interpretive, increasingly transnationally-shared diagnostic frame" helped to mobilize a global movement by linking different types of social problems worldwide to the rise of neoliberalism (Ayres 2004: 12). Thus, problems such as rising debt loads in developing countries, cuts to social programs and rising unemployment in both developed and developing countries, and instability in the international economy could all be attributed to neoliberalism. As a result, activists working on a variety of projects were able to adopt a common *collective identity* as global actors opposed to neoliberalism and seeking social and environmental justice and democracy from below (della Porta et al. 2006).

Not only was it possible to trace many different problems to neoliberal policies, but political opportunities for transnational protest were expanded by **internationalism**, which Tarrow (2005: 25) defines as the "structure of relations among states, non-state actors, and international institutions, and the opportunities this produces for actors to engage in collective action at different levels of this system." Tarrow expands earlier political process theories to analyze how the

international opportunity structure has changed with the enlarged role of institutions such as the World Bank and the European Union (EU). Although international institutions often represent the interests of global capitalism, they "also offer an opportunity space within which opponents of global capitalism and other claimants can mobilize" (Tarrow 2005: 26). Thus, the transnational global justice movement network continually interacts with international institutions (Smith 2008). In the past few decades, as international governmental institutions and activities such as high-profile international summits have proliferated, so have parallel summits and global movements (Pianta 2003). International institutions are key targets and arenas for transnational activism and, as in the case of national governments, actors within these institutions may be divided in their sympathies, creating both opportunities and obstacles for protestors.

Tarrow (2005: 32) identifies some of the important political processes involved in transnational contention. In some instances, collective action occurs in a domestic arena, but with global connections the process of **global framing** involves the use of "international symbols to frame domestic conflicts" and **internalization** is "a response to foreign or international pressures within domestic politics." Both of these processes were involved when French farmers blockaded Euro-Disney in 1992 to protest EU agricultural reforms and the "Americanization" of Europe (Bush and Simi 2001; Tarrow 2005: 31). In **diffusion**, forms of contention spread from one site to others, as with Reclaim the Streets parties. In **scale shift**, coordination of collective action shifts to a different level, as in the case of a local group like ATTAC becoming international. Two other processes identified by Tarrow occur at the international level. **Externalization** involves "the vertical projection of domestic claims onto international institutions or foreign actors," as in the case of a Renault plant closure in Belgium that activists brought to the attention of the EU (Tarrow 2005: 32). **Transnational coalition formation** involves creating a network or coalition among actors from different countries, such as Peoples' Global Action or the World Social Forum (WSF).

The WSF originated in 2001 through "upward scale shift" as activists engaged in local struggles created the annual global justice summit as an alternative to the World Economic Forum; since then, there has been a "downward scale shift" with the proliferation of regional, local, and national forums modeled on the WSF (Tarrow 2005: 128–134). Smith (2008: 199) argues that the WSF process provides a space in which global justice activists from diverse movements can come together to experiment with new forms of participation, share ideas, develop skills, and cultivate a collective identity. She notes numerous difficulties in this process, including the problems of making connections between the local and the global, creating understandings between activists from the global North and South and dealing with resource disparities, and managing the large numbers of activists who began coming to the annual forums. However, the WSF has provided a space for activists to come together and develop a shared analysis along with particular issue campaigns. And, most critically, it has helped activists to develop a global collective identity.

Activists at different levels built on a variety of *mobilizing structures*, including both formal and informal, movement and nonmovement, organizational structures as they began to create an international global justice movement (Smith 2008: 112). For instance, contacts in intergovernmental agencies and the meetings of international institutions served as informal and formal mobilizing structures outside the movement, while activist networks and transnational movement organizations provided structures within the movement. A large number of NGOs have been very important to the global justice movement, providing professional expertise and organizational stability to movement campaigns. Nevertheless, with the crucial help of new communications technologies, informal networks of groups and individual activists may be the most critical type of mobilizing structure for the transnational movement (Smith 2008: 113).

To create a movement of movements, activists used *collective action frames* that linked the concerns of different social movements. Gerhards and Rucht analyze these processes of mobilization in two protest campaigns in West Germany, against U.S. president Ronald Reagan's visit to Berlin in 1987 and against the meetings of the IMF and the World Bank in Berlin in 1988, which included an alternative conference critiquing the policies of the international financial institutions. To explain how the campaigns mobilized, Gerhards and Rucht look at what they term the "micromobilization" and "mesomobilization" actors that formed the mobilizing structure for the protest activities. **Micromobilization actors** are the various groups that mobilize individuals to participate in protest, including trade unions and environmental, religious, neighborhood, student, peace, and women's groups. In the case of the anti-Reagan demonstration, participants were all part of a large network of local Berlin groups, whereas in the anti-IMF campaign local groups were joined by national groups, including the Green Party. **Mesomobilization actors**, who work to integrate participating groups, formed coordinating groups to organize the micromobilization actors (Gerhards and Rucht 1992: 558). One of the critical tasks they performed was the creation of collective action frames that allowed individual groups to engage in **frame bridging** to connect their particular concerns to the larger concerns of the campaigns (Gerhards and Rucht 1992: 584–586). Thus, in an early example of what would become a unifying antineoliberalism frame, the IMF and World Bank were portrayed as agents of a world economic order that exploits developing countries. This frame helped mobilize numerous groups such as ecological groups, which focused on how projects of the IMF and World Bank led to the destruction of rain forests, and women's groups, which emphasized that women bear the brunt of the burden created by economic policies that increase poverty in developing countries.

To be successful in linking together actors from different movements and at different levels, movements need effective mesomobilization actors and frames that bridge movement concerns and link local, national, and international issues. In the global justice movement, local activists have engaged in global framing to enhance the appeal of local issues, in some instances strengthening their causes by connecting to international organizations and resources. For example, Clifford

Bob (2005) shows how the Ogani, a little-known ethnic group in Nigeria facing a hostile domestic environment, sought international help in their struggle for ethnic autonomy and against degradation of their environment. The Movement for the Survival of the Ogoni People initially failed to convince major international NGOs such as Greenpeace and Amnesty International to take up the Ogoni cause, but MOSOP eventually learned to frame its concerns in ways that were more appealing to international environmental and human rights groups. By focusing on Shell Oil's environmental abuses of the Niger Delta, and aided by widespread concerns generated by deepening state repression, MOSOP convinced international NGOs to lend resources and generate publicity.

International networks of NGOs and coalition organizations such as ATTAC and the PGA have served as mesomobilization actors for the global justice movement, helping to build organizations within countries and to mobilize transnational protests such as global days of action. Networks of cooperating organizations have encouraged not only participation in protests but also active participation within the network organizations, which have stressed participatory forms of internal decision making (della Porta et al. 2006). These heterogeneous networks of organizations have been able to work together within the global justice movement because participants share a collective identity that is inclusive of diverse groups. In an extensive study of global justice networks in Europe, Donatella della Porta and colleagues show that this identity was constructed by the movement through counter-summits and documents, which stress a number of values and commitments, including global citizenship, diversity, democracy from below, ecopacifism, and opposition to neoliberalism and global capitalism. This master frame resonates with activists, who share a collective identity based on these ideas (della Porta et al. 2006: 82–84).

Although master framing helps to unite a diverse movement, resource inequalities and other North–South differences make it extremely difficult to create and maintain coalitions that include participants from both developed and developing countries. The PGA has attempted to deal with these problems by creating "a structure and process explicitly aimed at avoiding Northern domination of the coalition" (Wood 2005b: 99). Thus, participation by those from the developed global North at conferences is sometimes limited; the Conveners Committee, which is the PGA's only central decision-making body, is regionally balanced in its composition; and the overall structure of the coalition is decentralized to allow grassroots participation (Wood 2005b: 100–101). While there are ongoing struggles over organizational processes in the PGA, the coalition has worked to create collective identity among participants through practices such as the drafting of "living documents" that are revised at each gathering. This process allows participants "to challenge any perceived consolidation of power" and to "build trust by reworking the basis of their collaboration in new ways." Despite differences, "movements participating in the PGA increasingly see themselves as part of a connected global struggle against neoliberalism" (Wood 2005b: 111–113).

In addition to creating workable mobilizing structures and unifying collective action frames, the global justice movement has organized with the aid of the mass media and particularly the Internet. The Internet has become a critical strategic tool for global justice activists that allows individuals and groups within the decentralized network structure of the movement to coordinate global protests and to send information around the world quickly and cheaply (Smith 2008: 126). Use of the Internet helped to bring together "a variety of national and regional anti-neoliberal collective action frames" and to develop a critique of neoliberalism through the use of email and Web sites as well as face-to-face meetings (Ayres 2004: 19). The Zapatistas built national and international support and inspired global justice activists around the world through mass media coverage and dissemination of their messages on e-mail lists and Web sites. For example, their proposal for an international communication and resistance network was posted on a German "Initiatives Against Neoliberalism" Web site, which linked the Zapatista proposal with a wide variety of other struggles such as the European March against Unemployment (Schulz 1998: 603).

The Internet became increasingly important in North American campaigns against free trade and neoliberalism. In 1998, the Council of Canadians (COC), a public interest group with 100,000 members, was instrumental in defeating the Multilateral Agreement on Investment (MAI) through a campaign that relied heavily on the Internet to disseminate information on the MAI and to communicate with other anti-MAI activists around the world (Ayres 1999). Whereas earlier campaigns by the COC and its allies against the FTA and NAFTA had relied on costly and time-consuming mailings and cross-country meetings, the anti-MAI campaign could quickly reach a national and global audience with up-to-date information at little cost (Ayres 1999: 140). In advance of the Seattle protests in 1999, Web sites and e-mail lists were used extensively to mobilize participants.

Internet use became even more sophisticated in ongoing mobilization against the Free Trade Area of the Americas (FTAA), a proposal to extend free trade throughout the Americas. The campaign, which brought tens of thousands of demonstrators to Quebec City in April 2001, used the Internet to disseminate information about the FTAA, to communicate strategies, and to pressure authorities (Ayres 2005). Prior to the Quebec City demonstrations, electronic mailing lists available in English, French, Spanish, and Portuguese, together with a protest Web site, posted updates on demonstration plans, rider boards for those looking to share rides to Quebec City, information on what to bring and expect, and "action alerts" from groups such as Public Citizen in the United States and the COC in Canada encouraging participation in call-ins, letter-writing campaigns, and e-mail protests directed at the U.S. and Canadian governments (Ayres 2005: 47). Internet communications helped to bring together activists from different cultures and geographic regions by creating solidarity and a sense of common purpose, spreading tactical innovations and coordinating strategies (Ayres 2005: 48). Internet communications also aided in the creation of a coalition organization called the Hemispheric Social Alliance (HSA) and in the drafting of an *Alternatives for the Americas* document, which provided movement alternatives to the FTAA (Ayres 2005: 48–51).

Della Porta and her colleagues investigated a number of issues related to use of the Internet in the cases of global justice demonstrations at the G8 meetings in Genoa in 2001 and at the European Social Forum in Florence in 2002. They found that the Internet played a major role in the organization of logistics and in the development of documents and ideas via Web sites and e-mail. Web sites available in English, French, German, Italian, Portuguese, and Spanish disseminated a steady stream of information about the events and recruited international volunteers (della Porta et al. 2006: 96–97). Although della Porta and colleagues found some evidence of a "digital divide" or inequality with regard to those who have access to the Internet and skills in using it and those who are less privileged (Rucht 2005), they also found that movement organizations helped to socialize members in the use of the Internet (della Porta et al. 2006: 98). Beyond using the Internet to coordinate protests and as a source of information about the movement, activists used the Internet as a means of protest through activities such as online petitions and "net strikes" in which large numbers of people jam Web sites at prearranged times (della Porta et al. 2006: 105–106). Activists also developed their collective identities via the Internet insofar as they actively participated in online forums and mailing lists to discuss issues and ideas as well as form new social ties (della Porta et al. 2006: 108–111).

Thus, the Internet provides social movements with an alternative to other mass media in reaching large numbers of potential constituents, and it seems to hold great potential for movement organization and development. Nevertheless, in addition to the digital divide, limitations to its use include a lack of quality control regarding the information posted on the Internet (Rucht 2005). While the Internet facilitates the mobilization of long-term campaigns, it may also produce relatively weak ideological ties and collective identity (Bennett 2003). The Internet clearly does not replace face-to-face organizing, and global justice campaigns and projects typically combine use of the Internet and other new technologies with other forms of organizing. Independent media centers (IMCs), for example, have been established in a number of cities around the world since the first IMC was set up in Seattle during the WTO demonstrations in 1999. Because the mainstream mass media often focus on violence by a minority of demonstrators and fail to present movement claims fully or fairly, IMCs decided to enlist activists to report, film, and photograph events to provide a movement perspective and information about protests (Smith 2008: 134). Many IMCs are active centers of local activity that are also part of the international Indymedia network of independent journalists and activists, which maintains a Web site (www.indymedia.org) and attempts to support the global justice movement by providing alternative, noncorporate coverage of local, national, and international issues and movements (Halleck 2003; Rucht 2005).

Although the Internet has been critical to the global justice movement, the conventional mass media also remain important. Securing favorable coverage in the established press is always a challenge for social movements, as the mass media often focus on drama and violence rather than on the content of movement demands. Nevertheless, mass media coverage of the global justice movement has aided its spread, and some coverage has helped to publicize movement concerns. In the case of the Zapatistas, the dramatic January 1, 1994, guerrilla attacks immediately captured media attention and brought the group to world attention. The movement's articulate and charismatic spokesperson, a masked leader calling himself Subcomandante Marcos, gave many press conferences and interviews and disseminated numerous manifestos and communiqués, resulting in a great deal of international media attention (Bob 2005: 127–134). The Jubilee 2000 debt campaign, with extensive involvement of churches and other organizations, also received a great deal of media coverage (Pianta 2003: 252). And, despite generally negative reporting of disruptive public protests, media coverage of movement issues in the 1999 Seattle protests was fairly extensive, owing to factors such as the novelty of the protests, President Clinton's statements of support for some movement demands, and the presence of unions and church organizations that were "credible media sources" (Bennett 2003: 162). Moreover, mass media reports continue to attract movement participants. For example, a survey of protestors in Germany against the Iraq War in 2003 found that, among the one or more sources of information they reported, about 55 percent heard of the demonstrations through newspapers, about 51 percent heard through radio or television, and only about 11 percent learned of the protest through the Internet (Rucht 2005: 82). In a study of Australian anticapitalist activists, twice as many saw the mainstream mass media as central to recruitment as saw the Internet as a way to expand the movement (Bramble and Minns 2005).

MOVEMENT STRATEGIES AND OUTCOMES

The global justice movement has experienced significant success but also faces strategic difficulties in achieving its goals. Among the successes, large demonstrations at the meetings of international financial institutions and governmental groups put new concerns on the public agenda. Activists articulated a critique of neoliberal policies, created linkages among struggles around the world, and increased public awareness of the role of international trade and monetary policies in problems such as the exploitation of workers and the environment. The various movements and organizations that make up the global justice movement have used a combination of political strategies and new cultural forms in their attempts to challenge global capitalism. Nevertheless, the movement faces major challenges in maintaining coalitions, agreeing on solutions to the problems identified, and devising strategies that have a real impact.

The creation of a master frame opposing the neoliberal policies of state and institutional actors is, as we have seen, an important accomplishment of the movement. In combination with the Internet, counter-summits known as parallel summits or People's Summits, held in response to international meetings such as the WTO and G8, are an innovative tactic for developing the critique of neoliberalism and crafting documents such as *Alternatives for the Americas* in response to the FTAA proposal. Through this process, the movement created a master frame with the "breadth and capacity to absorb and accommodate the variety of movement and region specific frames that had spurred collective action against neoliberal agreements and institutions" (Ayres 2005: 18). Protests against neoliberal targets, such as the WTO in Seattle in 1999 and the FTAA negotiations in Quebec City in 2001, involved parallel summits as well as numerous other tactics, such as blockades, teach-ins, street theatre, rallies, and marches. The protests and counter-summits generated numerous discussions, position papers, and proposals for further action. The World Social Forums, held in most years since 2001, most frequently in Brazil, have attracted large numbers of participants and helped to expand the movement geographically, involving increasing numbers of participants from the global South and helping to build a transnational collective identity (Smith 2008).

While movement frames and tactics clearly mobilized the movement, it is less clear how much impact they have had on targets. Part of the difficulty is that it is easier for the movement to articulate a critique of international institutions and policies than it is to propose workable solutions. As Ayres (2005: 20) argues, movement activists have generally agreed on a "diagnostic frame" that focuses on the shortcomings of neoliberalism, but they have had a more difficult time agreeing on a "prognostic frame" that would direct challenges to neoliberalism and present alternatives. Instead, a variety of different solutions have been proposed, ranging from reform of institutions such as the WTO to a complete dismantling of global capitalism. Through the WSF process, however, the movement continues to generate new campaigns and alternatives to neoliberalism and global capitalism, including local economic initiatives such as community-supported agriculture and cooperatives (Smith 2008: 220–221).

The Seattle protests and others that followed have had some impact in terms of a reform agenda aimed at making international institutions and intergovernmental meetings more inclusive and open to public scrutiny. As a result of large-scale protests, some world leaders called for greater openness in the process of trade negotiations and other global decision making. In Seattle, then U.S. president Bill Clinton met with WTO protestors to hear the concerns of farmers and others about world trade liberalization and made a speech saying people were protesting in part because they have never been allowed inside WTO deliberations. The agendas of various intergovernmental bodies targeted by protestors were also affected. For example, the G8 meeting in Genoa, Italy, in July 2001 included the issues of AIDS and African development on its agenda, and invited addresses by the South African president and the head of the World Health Organization in an attempt to show concern for a broad range of global issues (*Gazette* July 20, 2001). Public opinion in Europe and North America also showed strong support for movement positions, and leaders of the G8 made some concessions on the issues of AIDS and debt relief in response to public acceptance of movement demands

(*Gazette* July 19, 2001). Moreover, a decade after the Seattle protests, movement claims about global inequality and the problems with free markets had diffused widely, and activists protesting at the G-20 summit in London in 2009 found "their arguments echoed, however insincerely, by prime ministers, presidents and CEOs" (Kingsnorth 2009).

Despite progress in spreading movement concerns and raising issues of accountability and democratic process in international institutions and intergovernmental bodies, however, many activists began to question the value of ongoing demonstrations at international meetings—which some activists derided as "summit hopping." Policing of the protests became increasingly effective in curbing demonstrations with escalated use of force, despite the largely nonviolent orientation of movement activists (della Porta et al. 2006). After 9/11, a number of meetings were held at remote locations that were inaccessible to protestors, such as the 2002 meeting of the G-8 in Kananaskis, Alberta. Although protests and parallel summits continue to be held at the sites of international meetings, simultaneous events such as the WSF are also organized around the world, and activists continue to work on local and national as well as global campaigns. While searching for a long-term global strategy, activists have mounted campaigns against corporate abuses of workers, against environmentally destructive projects, and in support of fair trade policies.

One of the most promising strategies of the global justice movement involves the targeting of corporations that symbolize the abuses of global capitalism. Antisweatshop, living wage, and fair trade movements picked up steam in the 1990s as labor unions, students, religious groups, and community organizations attempted to counter the impacts of global capitalism on workers. In the United States since the mid-1990s, living wage campaigns led by unions and community organizations convinced a number of cities and counties to pass "living wage" legislation requiring private-sector firms with government business to provide wages above the federal minimum wage (Levi et al. 2004). Activists have also pushed for a "global living wage" that pays workers enough to allow them to live at an adequate local standard of living (Shaw 1999). The fair trade movement has flourished in countries around the world, coordinated by networks such as the World Fair Trade Organization (www.wfto.com). The movement works to secure fair prices for the goods of economically disadvantaged producers and to promote gender equity, environmental sustainability, and safe working conditions.

The antisweatshop movement, backed by unions, churches, students, and other supporters, is active in a number of industrialized countries. The movement encourages consumer boycotts of products produced in sweatshops, pressures corporations to adopt codes of conduct for their suppliers, and attempts to monitor their compliance. University students, coordinated by groups such as United Students Against Sweatshops (USAS) in the United States and the Ethical Trading Action Group (ETAG) in Canada, became quite active in the 1990s in pressuring their universities to adopt plans that ensure that clothing with university logos is produced in "no-sweat" conditions (Cravey 2004; Ross 2005).

Canadian author and activist Naomi Klein provided one source of inspiration for anticorporate activity among students and others with her book *No Logo* (1999), which analyzes the spread of brands such as Coca-Cola, McDonald's, Nike, and Starbucks and how the production of these products is related to the exploitation of workers and the environment. Because their images are so important to them, corporations are vulnerable to attacks on their brands, leading activists to target well-known corporate brands to call attention to issues of working conditions and trade practices.

Beginning in the early 1990s, activists launched one of the most significant anticorporate campaigns, against Nike, for sweatshop abuses by its subcontractors in countries such as Indonesia (see Shaw 1999 for a detailed account). As a major manufacturer of sports shoes and clothing and a company with a very positive image in North America, Nike represented an extremely important and difficult target for antisweatshop activists. Activists struggled for a number of years before managing to get some mainstream media coverage of Nike's abuses in publications such as the *New York Times*, aided by the extensive publicity created by revelations that the clothing line of talk-show host Kathie Lee Gifford was produced in Honduran sweatshops. After the anti-Nike campaign received media publicity, and with the media know-how of organizations such as the San Francisco–based human rights organization Global Exchange, the campaign was able to build momentum. The campaign gained international support from unions, religious groups, students, and women's organizations, which played an important role in publicizing abuses of the largely female labor force in sweatshops. The anti-Nike campaign was eventually able to secure some genuinely important concessions from Nike, which suffered a major blow to its image from the campaign, although organizations such as Global Exchange continue to monitor Nike practices (Shaw 1999: 93).

Beginning in 2003, unions and other groups called for a boycott of Coca-Cola, accusing the company of international human rights, labor, and environmental abuses (Blanding 2006). As part of this campaign, a number of unions and universities banned Coke, and activists protested at stockholder meetings and sports events where Coke is sold. Although companies such as Nike and Coke responded to protestors with announcements of new workplace standards— and advertising campaigns to refurbish their images—long-term, persistent campaigns are required to produce real and lasting change in corporate practices. Extensive resources are also required to maintain organizations such as the Workers Rights Consortium (WRC), which was created in 2000 to monitor factories. And, despite some efforts to provide "sweat-free" alternative products, the lack of easily accessible alternatives remains an impediment to widespread consumer boycotts of companies with questionable human rights and environmental records (La Botz 2002). More recently, antisweatshop activists have switched from a focus on economic boycotts to efforts to build coalitions with labor that can pressure companies to improve working conditions in their factories (Smith 2008: 223).

Antisweatshop and fair trade organizing helped to forge alliances between groups such as unions, environmentalists, students, and community activists. Such alliances are both an important accomplishment of the global justice movement and an ongoing challenge. Although the antineoliberalism frame creates some common ground among the different movements that make up the global justice movement, many ideological and strategic differences exist within the movement. These include differences over whether to reform or abolish international institutions and conflicts over tactics. Violence and the unruly tactics of some activists at protest events have created internal conflict, particularly after the 2001 terrorist attacks, when more moderate groups in the movement were anxious to distance themselves from any form of violence. Different elements of the global justice movement also have different types of constituents and varying concerns. Although much was made of the "blue–green" alliance that seemed to emerge with the Seattle protests, symbolized by the image of "Teamsters and Turtles" coming together, coalition work between unions and environmentalists was not terribly extensive (Gould et al. 2005). After Seattle, environmental concerns became less central to the movement than social justice and global inequality themes, but to attract a broad constituency the movement needs to develop an inclusive discourse and ideology that includes environmental concerns (Buttel and Gould 2005). With the 2009 protests at the G-20 summits in London and Pittsburgh, concerns about climate change were again being linked to economic justice, as activists pushed for a "Green New Deal" in response to the world economic crisis (Kingsnorth 2009: 30).

The global justice movement has clearly enjoyed some successes, but it also continues to be divided over its political and organizational direction. Pleyers (2009) notes that the movement remains "more united in what it has been against than what it should now be for" and identifies three different ideas about how the movement should go forward. One approach is the "local approach" in which activists focus on participatory self-government, following the example of the Zapatistas, or engage in local sustainability and "critical consumption" initiatives. A second approach is the "advocacy approach" in which activists participate in single-issue networks around issues such as the protection of water supplies from privatization, which can be used to explore larger issues about public goods, the role of corporations, and efficiency of the public sector. In the third "state approach," the movement supports the efforts of progressive government leaders to implement policies such as social programs favoring the poor. Pleyers argues that these approaches might be combined in a shared approach and suggests that the WSF can play an important role in allowing activists to formulate such a strategy.

CONCLUSION

The global justice movement has generated some of the most exciting social movement activity since the decline of the protest cycle of the 1960s. Feminists, environmentalists, labor activists, students, community activists, and others have joined together in at least temporary coalitions out of concern about the impacts of neoliberal economic policies and the practices of global capitalism. As a result of movement activities, public consciousness has increased regarding the exploitation of women, workers, and the environment connected to these policies and practices, and international institutions and governmental bodies are subject to greater public scrutiny. Although large-scale demonstrations are necessarily sporadic, the movement has diffused widely to many different venues, using a variety of strategies. New generations of activists, together with veterans of the movements of the 1960s, are continuing to use a repertoire of collective action to promote social change. New mobilizing structures such as the WSF, aided by the Internet, have helped to maintain the movement, initiating new campaigns and providing educational space for people to learn about global issues and develop identities as transnational activists (Smith 2008: 224). The extent to which the movement succeeds depends on its ability to develop long-term campaigns with solutions to the problems that global justice activists have identified. As this chapter has shown, an international opportunity structure, together with movement frames, mobilizing structures, and collective action tactics, are central to that process.

NOTE

1. The Group of Eight, known as the G-8, is an annual gathering of the heads of eight major industrialized democracies—Canada, Britain, France, Germany, Italy, Japan, Russia, and the United States. The group began as the G-6 in 1975, becoming the G-7 with the addition of Canada in 1976 and the G-8 with the addition of Russia in 1997. The G-20 was created in 1999 as an annual meeting of finance ministers and central bank governors from both industrialized and developing countries.

DISCUSSION QUESTIONS

1. How can collective action framing help to unite a "movement of movements" such as the global justice movement?
2. What are the central challenges facing transnational coalitions and how might these be resolved?
3. What strategies are likely to be most effective in keeping the global justice movement mobilized and advancing its goals?

SUGGESTED READINGS

della Porta, Donatella, Massimiliano Andretta, Lorenzo Mosca, and Herbert Reiter. 2006. *Globalization from Below: Transnational Activists and Protest Networks*. Minneapolis, MN: University of Minnesota Press. Based on studies of European protests, this study analyzes how the global justice movement emerged, how it mobilizes participants, and how it interacts with elite targets.

Smith, Jackie. 2008. *Social Movements for Global Democracy*. Baltimore: Johns Hopkins University Press. This study captures the interactions of rival international networks and places ongoing global justice campaigns in historical context.

Tarrow, Sidney. 2005. *The New Transnational Activism*. New York: Cambridge University Press. This is an important assessment of transnational contention, offering many theoretical concepts and propositions.

CHAPTER 10

Conclusion: Social Movements and Social Change

The histories of women's, gay and lesbian, environmental, right-wing, and global justice movements provide but a few examples of the importance of social movements and collective action to social change. Social movements have had major impacts on social policies, cultural norms, and public opinion. They often profoundly affect the lives of movement participants and others who are touched by the movement and its outcomes. Social movement theories help to explain the extent to which movements are able to bring about social changes and the obstacles that they face in doing so. In this concluding chapter, I briefly revisit the successes and challenges of the movements discussed in the book in light of some of the theoretical ideas about social movements outlined in earlier chapters. I conclude by noting the ongoing challenges facing social movements as they try to bring about social changes.

LARGE-SCALE CHANGES, GRIEVANCES, AND OPPORTUNITIES

All of the major theories of social movements point to the effects of large-scale socioeconomic and political changes on the emergence and outcomes of social movements. Macro-level societal changes often create widespread grievances and political or cultural opportunities. Although grievances and opportunities alone do not mobilize collective action, they can be exploited by movement activists who build on the organizational changes that accompany large-scale social change. In the case of the American civil rights movement, economic changes and the resulting urbanization of southern blacks made it possible to organize a movement through the black churches. International and domestic political conditions, including the Cold War and the breakup of previous electoral alliances, created new political opportunities. Grievances had long existed, but there were now more opportunities for people to share them and new opportunities to be heard. Demographic changes were also important to the New Left student movement of the 1960s, as large numbers of students entered universities. In many ways, these students were privileged members of society who might not be expected to have major grievances, but they were also part of a generation that was alarmed by issues of nuclear arms proliferation, racism, and the Vietnam War. At the same time, conservative students were also mobilized around issues such as communism and big government. Once the cycle of protest of the 1960s was under way, new movements were inspired to mobilize and new countermovements also organized in their wake.

One of the movements spurred by the protest cycle of the 1960s, the women's movement, was clearly aided by large-scale transformations such as changes in labor markets and declining birth rates. Women's increased participation in the workforce and in higher education created new interests and grievances, and as women participated in more areas of social and political life, they experienced sexism that fuelled their participation in the women's movement. They also had political opportunities in democratic polities as political parties came to see the value of the women's vote. Women's movements in Western countries made great advances and, in fact, their successes may partly explain the relative decline of the movement in recent years insofar as women in these countries have fewer grievances. The maintenance of some second-wave groups and the rise of third-wave feminism show, however, that ongoing issues such as violence against women and reproductive rights continue to involve new generations of women in the feminist movement. Although a countermovement has opposed feminist gains on issues such as abortion, the opposition has also helped to keep the movement mobilized. Moreover, feminists in the North have increasingly joined feminists in the South in an expanded global women's movement.

Before the rise of gay liberation movements, gay men and lesbians met with a great deal of repression and few obvious political opportunities, but cultural changes accompanying the protest cycle of the 1960s created greater public space for sexual minorities. As in the case of the women's movement, strong opposition to the movement helped to further mobilize it, providing countermovement targets and opportunities for media exposure. Federal systems such as the United States and Canada provided political openings at different levels of government in various states and provinces, whereas in more centralized systems, such as Great Britain, opportunities arose when sympathetic governments were in power. The creation of the European Union also brought political opportunities in Europe, where the movement has enjoyed a great deal of success in winning gay rights. In relatively tolerant countries such as Canada, the gay and lesbian movement might, like the women's movement, be faced with perceptions that the battle has been won.

The environmental movement also built on the activism of the protest cycle rather than on clear political openings. Environmental threats have created grievances that helped to stimulate a sense of urgency among the public in the 1960s and 1970s and that continue to arouse activists concerned with issues such as toxic waste, the destruction of forests, and global warming. Public support has helped to create political openings, particularly in countries such as Germany with successful Green parties. Large environmental organizations, which can boast extensive constituent support, have enjoyed some access to government officials, but they are criticized for being overly institutionalized and subject to co-optation by government and business interests. Large-scale economic structures that rely on carbon-fuelled economic growth are major impediments to the ability of the movement to deal with major environmental problems.

In the case of the New American Right, the threat of communism during the Cold War was a large-scale political development that created unity among diverse groups. The gains of the civil rights movement also created grievances among many conservatives concerned about affirmative action, busing, and private property. Although adherents of the New American Right did not reject modern American society, with its intensive consumerism, they were concerned about threats to the "American way of life." The movement reacted strongly to the progressive movements of the 1960s and the social changes that accompanied them. Support from insiders in the Republican Party, conservative corporations, and evangelical churches and clergy networks provided opportunities for the New Right to achieve extensive political and cultural changes in the United States.

Expanding internationalism brought political opportunities for a new global justice movement, and neoliberal policies created new grievances around the world. By generating public support and some sympathy among elites, the movement was able to force some changes in the operation of international institutions and win some concessions from corporations. Widespread grievances and threats related to neoliberal policies helped to mobilize a transnational movement, but the movement faces major obstacles in tackling global capitalism and building more democratic and equitable political and economic structures.

MOVEMENT ORGANIZATION AND STRATEGY

Movements face different types of cultural and political contexts and varying opportunities. However, all opportunities must be perceived, and movements have to interpret threats and grievances to mobilize people for collective action. Movements also have to use and develop mobilizing structures to bring potential constituents together and to remain mobilized over time. The agency of movement leaders and other activists is essential for effective organizing, framing, and strategizing. The protest cycle of the 1960s popularized a repertoire of strategies that appear over and over in subsequent social movements as activists engage in many contentious performances (Tilly 2008). For example, movements continue to use mass demonstrations and street theatre, various types of teach-ins and sit-ins (with creative variations such as "kiss-ins" by gay activists, "tree-sits" by environmentalists, and "die-ins" first by opponents of nuclear war and later by AIDS activists). Activists from the sixties generation have continued to join with those from new generations, most recently in the global justice movement. Some long-standing organizational structures have been maintained and new movement organizations have formed. Collective action frames, such as the civil rights master frame, have been adapted by various movements, and new frames, such as the master frame opposing neoliberalism, have been developed. The successes of movements depend on their ability to employ innovative strategies and frame grievances effectively as well as to take advantage of political and cultural opportunities.

The women's movement successfully transformed problems such as rape and domestic violence, which were once seen as private concerns, into political issues, framing "the personal as political." The movement targeted numerous types of authorities and issues and developed within many institutions, such as universities and churches. Although many women's movement organizations have declined, some have remained active and new organizations have formed. Third-wave feminists have developed new cultural projects and used new media for spreading movement ideas, including zines and Web sites. Globally, the women's movement has organized through UN mobilizing structures and developed international women's rights networks. Despite the difficulties involved in creating international coalitions, the movement has developed frames that unite feminists around problems such as poverty and violence against women.

The gay and lesbian rights movement adapted to the decline of the sixties protest cycle by building community structures and a collective identity that helped to maintain the movement. Although the movement has had difficulty pursuing some of the liberationist goals of its early years, gay rights activists made great gains in using a civil rights frame and quasi-ethnic group identity to pursue legal rights. New forms of activism, such as Queer Nation, helped to expand the movement to include more bisexual and transgendered people. With victories such as the right to marriage in a number of countries and U.S. states, the movement has had an important cultural influence. Finding strategies to tackle repression in many countries around the world remains a major challenge for the movement.

The environmental movement has used a range of organizational forms and strategies to pursue its goals, including large, formalized organizations capable of lobbying governments and decentralized, radical groups able to engage in risky direct-action tactics. The formalized organizations have helped to maintain the movement over many years, and the radical groups have prodded the movement to innovate strategically. Grassroots environmentalists have invigorated the movement with antilogging blockades, protest camps, and bike-ins to reclaim city streets from cars. Public support for environmentalism is strong, and consumer boycotts have at times been used effectively, but the movement also faces obstacles in changing consumer lifestyles and addressing complicated issues through the mass media. The environmental movement also faces countermovement opposition to lifestyle changes and corporate opposition to the major structural changes needed to address global warming and other major issues. Environmentalists have formed alliances with unions and indigenous peoples, and they have worked to promote new understandings of sustainable development in searching for solutions to environmental problems.

The New American Right has organized at both the national and local levels, through the Republican Party and through grassroots community and church networks. By allying with the Christian Right and waging campaigns around the Equal Rights Amendment, abortion, gay rights, the environment, and numerous other social issues, the New Right was able to expand greatly and win a number of victories. Movement leaders skillfully framed issues to appeal to constituents who felt threatened by cultural changes in gender and family relations and to mobilize people on the basis of their religious beliefs. Antifeminist groups compete with feminist groups to represent women's interests by forming women's organizations and employing similar rhetoric. Antigay campaigns effectively employ the "special rights" frame to compete with the movement's quest for equal rights. The anti-environmental movement capitalizes on the grievances of workers concerned about loss of jobs and economic interests in "property rights." The New American Right faces new challenges with external changes in the political climate and with internal divisions in the movement, but the movement also has the opportunity to expand its constituency by tackling new issues and to extend its extensive organizational infrastructure internationally.

The global justice movement created a unifying collective action frame that connects various types of problems and inequities to global capitalism and neo-liberal economic policies. The movement has made excellent use of the Internet to organize activists around the world. Although it is difficult to sustain global alliances, the movement has created some durable coalitions and other mobilizing structures, such as independent media centers. The movement has developed some innovative strategies, such as parallel summits, antisweatshop boycotts, and fair trade initiatives. Public awareness of issues associated with global economic policies has increased as a result of movement initiatives, but the movement must struggle to maintain its momentum and to come up with workable solutions to the large-scale problems identified. The movement also faces the challenge of keeping many local activists connected during lulls in global campaigns.

CONCLUSION

Social movements have helped to bring about many political and cultural transformations, but they also face numerous challenges in effecting change. Movements typically confront powerful adversaries and long-standing structural arrangements, and they rely on cultural and political openings to afford the possibility of success. In democratic polities, the mobilization of public support helps movements to influence government officials and other elites. The mass media are critical in reaching masses of supporters, but movements have to use dramatic tactics and attractive packages to convey their messages through the mass media. Coalitions of different types of constituents strengthen movements, but they are difficult to form and maintain. Movements need leadership and vision to create the collective action frames, organizational vehicles, and strategies and tactics needed for ongoing and effective campaigns. Despite the many obstacles to effective social movements, however, the movements discussed in this book provide examples of how significant change can be achieved through collective action.

Abbreviations

ACL	Associated California Loggers
ACT UP	AIDS Coalition to Unleash Power
ATTAC	Association for the Taxation of Financial Transaction for the Aid of Citizens
CBLPI	Clare Boothe Luce Policy Institute
CDFE	Center for the Defense of Free Enterprise
CFV	Colorado for Family Values
COC	Council of Canadians
CRA	California Republican Assembly
CSFC	Committee for the Survival of a Free Congress
CWA	Concerned Women of America
DAWN	Development Alternatives with Women for a New Era
EEOC	Equal Employment Opportunity Commission
ERA	Equal Rights Amendment
ETAG	Ethical Trading Action Group
EU	European Union
FACE	Freedom of Access to Clinic Entrances Act
FTA	Canada-US Free Trade Agreement
FTAA	Free Trade Area of the Americas
GLF	Gay Liberation Front
HSA	Hemispheric Social Alliance
IMC	Independent Media Center
IMF	International Monetary Fund
ISA	Ideologically Structured Action
IWF	Independent Women's Forum
MAI	Multilateral Agreement on Investment
MOSOP	Movement for the Survival of the Ogoni People
NAACP	National Association for the Advancement of Colored People
NAE	National Association of Evangelicals
NAFTA	North American Free Trade Agreement
NATO	North Atlantic Treaty Organization
NAWSA	National American Women's Suffrage Association
NCPAC	National Conservative Political Action Committee

NeW	Network of Enlightened Women
NGLTF	National Gay and Lesbian Task Force
NGO	nongovernmental organization
NIMBY	Not in My Back Yard
NOW	National Organization for Women
NRLC	National Right to Life Committee
NWP	National Women's Party
OCA	Oregon Citizens Alliance
PAC	Political Action Committee
PGA	Peoples' Global Action
SAP	Structural Adjustment Program
SDS	Students for a Democratic Society
SMO	Social Movement Organization
SNCC	Student Nonviolent Coordinating Committee
SUPA	Student Union for Peace Action
UFW	United Farm Workers
UN	United Nations
USAS	United Students Against Sweatshops
VAWA	Violence Against Women Act
WCTU	Women's Christian Temperance Union
WFN	Women's Freedom Network
WRC	Workers Rights Consortium
WSF	World Social Forum
WTO	World Trade Organization
WVS	World Values Survey
YAF	Young Americans for Freedom

Glossary

abeyance A period in which a movement is not highly visible or very active, but is maintained by an organization or other processes (Taylor 1989).

adherents Those who believe in a cause and want to see movement goals achieved.

beneficiary constituents Aggrieved persons or groups that stand to benefit from the successes of a movement.

bureaucratization (formalization) Characteristic of movement organizations with established procedures for decision making, a developed division of labor, explicit criteria for membership, and rules governing subunits such as standing committees or chapters.

bystander public A public that defines issues from a bystander's perspective, but may become involved in a conflict.

campaigns Public interactions among movement actors, their targets, the public, and other relevant actors.

centralization Characteristic of movement organizations in which there is a single center of decision-making power.

charivari A traditional form of collective action directed towards individuals who transgressed community norms.

claim-making performances Public gatherings of collective actors using familiar tactics, making claims on the interests of targets (Tilly 2008).

collective action frames Interpretations of issues and events that inspire and legitimate collective action.

collective behavior theory A theoretical approach to social movements that focuses on the grievances or strains that are seen as leading to collective behaviors outside of established institutions and politics.

collective campaign An "aggregate of collective events or activities that appear to be oriented toward some relatively specific goal or good, and that occur within some proximity in space and time" (Marwell and Oliver 1984: 12).

collective good A public good, which cannot be withheld from any members of a group or population, regardless of whether or not they work to achieve it.

collective identity A sense of shared experiences and values connecting individuals to movements and making them feel capable of effecting change through collective action.

conscience constituents Persons or groups who contribute to movements but do not personally benefit from their achievements.

constituents Supporters who contribute resources to a movement.

contentious politics Episodic, public interactions of claim makers and their targets, typically government authorities, based on claims related to the interests of social movement actors or other claim makers; includes both *contained contention* by established political actors and *transgressive contention,* which involves at least some "newly self-identified political actors" and/or "innovative collective action" by at least some parties (McAdam et al. 2001: 7–8).

countermovement A "set of opinions and beliefs in a population opposed to a social movement" (McCarthy and Zald 1977: 1217–1218).

critical events Events that focus the attention of movement supporters, members of the public, and authorities on particular issues, creating threats and opportunities that influence movement mobilization and outcomes.

cultural defense Conflict based on the desire of a group or collectivity to defend its cultural values, beliefs, and lifestyle, typically involving symbolic politics.

cultural opportunity structure Elements of cultural environments, such as ideologies, that facilitate and constrain collective action.

cycle of contention (protest cycle) A period of heightened conflict when a number of social movements are mobilized and engaged in collective action.

diffusion The spread of forms of contention from one site to others.

discourse analysis Textual analysis of language and meanings in rhetoric and documents.

discursive opportunity structure Factors, such as cultural context and mass media norms, that shape movement discourse.

externalization "[T]he vertical projection of domestic claims onto international institutions or foreign actors" (Tarrow 2005: 32).

frame bridging Extension of collective action frames to connect together the concerns of different groups or movements.

framing perspective Emphasizes the role of movements in constructing cultural meanings, as movement leaders and organizations frame issues in particular ways to identify injustices, attribute blame, propose solutions, and motivate collective action.

free-rider problem The problem of getting individuals to participate in social movements or other collective action when they will reap the benefits of the collective action regardless of their personal participation or contributions.

global framing The use of international symbols in the framing of domestic issues.

ideologically structured action Activities inspired by or promoting movement ideology that take place in everyday life and within organizations and institutions.

initiator movement A movement that comes early in a cycle of protest and demonstrates to others that protest tactics can be used effectively.

institutionalization The tendency of movement organizations that survive over many years to develop bureaucratic structures, rely on professional staff, and cultivate relations with government officials and other elites.

internalization A "response to foreign or international pressures within domestic politics" (Tarrow 2005: 32).

internationalism The "structure of relations among states, non-state actors, and international institutions, and the opportunities this produces for actors to engage in collective action at different levels of this system" (Tarrow 2005: 25).

international opportunity structure The international space created by international institutions.

mass society theory A theory of collective behavior as a response to social isolation occurring in societies lacking in the secondary groups needed to bind people together and keep them attached to the mainstream society.

master frames Generic types of frames available for use by a number of different social movements.

material incentives Selective incentives that involve tangible rewards such as money.

mesomobilization actors Coordinating groups that integrate participating groups into a movement or campaign.

micromobilization actors The various groups that mobilize individuals to participate in protest.

mobilization The process whereby a group that shares grievances or interests gains collective control over tangible and intangible resources.

mobilizing structures The formal and informal networks, groups, and organizational vehicles that movements use to recruit participants and organize action campaigns.

movement entrepreneurs Social movement leaders who take the initiative to mobilize people with similar preferences into a movement or movement organization.

multiorganizational field The total set of organizations with which movement organizations might interact, including those that might either oppose or support the movement.

new social movement theory A theoretical approach focusing on the new types of social movements emerging in "postindustrial" or "advanced capitalist" society, thought to differ in structure, type of constituents, and ideology from older movements.

political opportunity structure (political opportunities) Features of the political environment that influence movement emergence and success, including the extent of openness in the polity, shifts in political alignments, divisions among elites, the availability of influential allies, and repression or facilitation by the state.

political process theory A theoretical approach focusing on the interactions of social movement actors with the state and the role of political opportunities in the mobilization and outcomes of social movements.

professionalized movements Movements that have paid leaders who work full-time for movement organizations and that often attract conscience constituents rather than beneficiaries and rely on financial contributions rather than activism from large numbers of participants.

purposive incentives Selective incentives that come from the sense of satisfaction at having contributed to the attainment of a worthwhile cause.

rational choice theory A theoretical approach that focuses on the costs and benefits of collective action for individuals.

recruitment The process of getting individuals to commit resources, such as time, money, and skills, to a movement.

relative deprivation theory A theory that collective behavior is most likely when conditions start to improve and expectations rise, but the rate of improvement does not match expectations and people feel deprived relative to others.

repertoire of collective action The limited set of protest forms familiar during a given time.

resource mobilization theory A theoretical approach focusing on the resources, organization, and opportunities needed for social movement mobilization and collective action.

resources The tangible and intangible assets available to social movement organizations and other actors.

scale shift The shifting of coordination of collective action to a different level.

selective incentives Benefits available exclusively to those who participate in collective action.

social movement Alternatively defined as "collective challenges, based on common purposes and social solidarities, in sustained interaction with elites, opponents, and authorities" (Tarrow 1998: 4) or "a set of opinions and beliefs in a population which represents preferences for changing some elements of the social structure and/or reward distribution of a society" (McCarthy and Zald 1977: 1217–1218).

social movement community Networks of political movement organizations, individuals, cultural groups, alternative institutions, and institutional supporters in a social movement.

social movement industry The collection of social movement organizations within a movement.

social movement organization (SMO) A "complex, or formal, organization which identifies its goals with the preferences of a social movement or a countermovement and attempts to implement those goals" (McCarthy and Zald 1977: 1218).

social movement sector All of the social movement industries in a society.

solidary incentives Selective incentives that come from associating with a group.

spinoff movement A movement that comes late in a protest cycle, modeled on earlier movements.

status politics Conflict based on a battle over the status or social prestige of a group or collectivity, which is connected to its culture or lifestyle, involving symbolic politics.

symbolic interactionism A social-psychological theory that focuses on the ways in which actors construct meanings through social interaction.

symbolic politics Status politics or cultural defense where an issue such as abortion symbolizes broader concerns such as changing gender roles.

transnational coalition formation The creation of a network or coalition among actors from different countries.

References

Adam, Barry D. 1995. *The Rise of a Gay and Lesbian Movement*, Revised Edition. New York: Twayne.

Adamson, Nancy, Linda McPhail, and Margaret Briskin. 1988. *Feminist Organizing for Change: The Contemporary Women's Movement in Canada*. Toronto: Oxford University Press.

Adkin, Laurie E. 1992. "Counter-Hegemony and Environmental Politics in Canada." pp. 135–156 in *Organizing Dissent*, edited by William K. Carroll. Toronto: Garamond Press.

Aho, James A. 1990. *The Politics of Righteousness: Idaho Christian Patriotism*. Seattle: University of Washington Press.

Allitt, Patrick. 2009. *The Conservatives: Ideas and Personalities Throughout American History*. New Haven, CT: Yale University Press.

Almeida, Paul. 2003. "Opportunity Organizations and Threat-Induced Contention: Protest Waves in Authoritarian Settings." *American Journal of Sociology* 109(2):345–400.

_____. 2008. *Waves of Protest: Popular Struggle in El Salvador, 1925–2005*. Minneapolis, MN: University of Minnesota Press.

Ancelovici, Marcos. 2002. "Organizing against Globalization: The Case of ATTAC in France." *Politics & Society* 30(3):427–463.

Andrews, Kenneth T. 2004. *Freedom Is a Constant Struggle*. Chicago: University of Chicago Press.

Antrobus, Peggy. 2004. *The Global Women's Movement: Origins, Issues and Strategies*. London: Zed Books.

Armitage, Kevin C. 2005. "State of Denial: The United States and the Politics of Global Warming." *Globalizations* 2(3):417–427.

Armstrong, Elizabeth A. 2002. *Forging Gay Identities: Organizing Sexuality in San Francisco, 1950–1994*. Chicago: University of Chicago Press.

Armstrong, Elizabeth A., and Suzanna M. Crage. 2006. "Movements and Memory: The Making of the Stonewall Myth." *American Sociological Review* 71:724–751.

Arrington, T. S., and P. A. Kyle. 1978. "Equal Rights Amendment Activists in North Carolina." *Signs* 3(Spring):660–680.

Austin, Andrew. 2002. "Advancing Accumulation and Managing its Discontents: The U.S. Antienvironmental Countermovement." *Sociological Spectrum* 22:71–105.

Ayres, Jeffrey M. 1998. *Defying Conventional Wisdom: Political Movements and Popular Contention against North American Free Trade*. Toronto: University of Toronto Press.

_____. 1999. "From the Streets to the Internet: The Cyber-Diffusion of Contention." *Annals, Academy of Political and Social Sciences* 566:132–143.

_____. 2004. "Framing Collective Action against Neoliberalism: The Case of the 'Anti-Globalization' Movement." *Journal of World-Systems Research* 10(1):11–34.

_____. 2005. "From 'Anti-Globalization' to the Global Justice Movement: Framing Collective Action Against Neoliberalism." pp. 9–27 in *Transforming Globalization*, edited by B. Podobnik and T. Reifer. Leiden: Brill.

Banerjee, Neela. 2008. "Taking Their Faith, but Not Their Politics, to the People." *The New York Times*, June 1.

Barakso, Maryann. 2004. *Governing NOW*. Ithaca, NY: Cornell University Press.

Bashevkin, Sylvia. 1998. *Women on the Defensive: Living Through Conservative Times*. Toronto: University of Toronto Press.

Baumgardner, Jennifer, and Amy Richards. 2000. *Manifesta: Young Women, Feminism and the Future*. New York: Farrar, Straus and Giroux.

Beder, Sharon. 2002. *Global Spin: The Corporate Assault on Environmentalism*, Revised Edition. Totnes, UK: Green Books.

Bell, Daniel, ed. 1963. *The Radical Right*. Garden City, NY: Doubleday.

Benford, Robert D. 1993. "Frame Disputes within the Nuclear Disarmament Movement." *Social Forces* 71(3):677–701.

Benford, Robert D., and David A. Snow. 2000. "Framing Processes and Social Movements: An Overview and Assessment." *Annual Review of Sociology* 26:611–639.

Bennett, W. Lance. 2003. "Communicating Global Activism: Strengths and Vulnerabilities of Networked Politics." *Information, Communication & Society* 6(2):143–168.

Berke, Richard L. 1999. "The Far Right Sees the Dawn of the Moral Majority." *The New York Times*, February 21.

Bernstein, Mary. 1997. "Celebration and Suppression: The Strategic Uses of Identity by the Lesbian and Gay Movement." *American Journal of Sociology* 103(3):531–565.

Blanchard, Dallas A. 1994. *The Anti-Abortion Movement and the Rise of the Religious Right: From Polite to Fiery Protest*. New York: Twayne.

Blanding, Michael. 2006. "The Case against Coca-Cola." *The Nation* 282(17):13–17.

Blee, Kathleen M. 1991. *Women of the Klan: Racism and Gender in the 1920s*. Berkeley, CA: University of California Press.

_____. 2002. *Inside Organized Racism: Women in the Hate Movement*. Berkeley, CA: University of California Press.

Blee, Kathleen M., and Verta Taylor. 2002. "Semi-Structured Interviewing in Social Movement Research." pp. 92–117 in *Methods of Social Movement Research*, edited by B. Klandermans and S. Staggenborg. Minneapolis, MN: University of Minnesota Press.

Blumer, Herbert. 1951. "Collective Behavior." pp. 166–222 in *Principles of Sociology*, edited by A. M. Lee. New York: Barnes and Noble.

Bob, Clifford. 2005. *The Marketing of Rebellion: Insurgents, Media, and International Activism*. New York: Cambridge University Press.

Bosso, Christopher J. 2005. *Environment, Inc.: From Grassroots to Beltway*. Lawrence, KS: University Press of Kansas.

Brady, David W., and Kent L. Tedin. 1976. "Ladies in Pink: Religion and Political Ideology in the Anti-ERA Movement." *Social Science Quarterly* 56(4):564–575.

Bramble, Tom, and John Minns. 2005. "Whose Streets? Our Streets! Activist Perspectives on the Australian Anti-Capitalist Movement." *Social Movement Studies* 4(2): 105–121.

Branch, Taylor. 1988. *Parting the Waters: America in the King Years 1954-63*. New York: Simon & Schuster.

Brick, Philip, and R. McGreggor Cawley. 2008. "Producing Political Climate Change: The Hidden Life of US Environmentalism." *Environmental Politics* 17(2):200–218.

Brooke, James. 1999. "Loggers Find Canada Rain Forest Flush with Foes." *The New York Times*, October 22.

Brown, Michael P. 1997. *Replacing Citizenship: AIDS Activism and Radical Democracy*. New York: Guilford Press.

Brown, Michael, and John May. 1991. *The Greenpeace Story*. New York: Dorling Kindersley.

Brownmiller, Susan. 1975. *Against Our Will: Men, Women, and Rape*. New York: Bantam Books.

Bruce, Steven. 1988. *The Rise and Fall of the New Christian Right: Conservative Protestant Politics in America, 1978-1988*. New York: Oxford University Press.

Brulle, Robert J. 2000. *Agency, Democracy, and Nature: The U.S. Environmental Movement from a Critical Theory Perspective*. Cambridge, MA: MIT Press.

Brulle, Robert J., and David N. Pellow. 2006. "Environmental Justice: Human Health and Environmental Inequalities." *Annual Review of Public Health* 27:3–24.

Brulle, Robert J., and J. Craig Jenkins. 2006. "Spinning Our Way to Sustainability." *Organization & Environment* 19(1):82–87.

Bryner, Gary. 2008. "Failure and Opportunity: Environmental Groups in the US Climate Change Policy." *Environmental Politics* 17(2):319–336.

Brysk, Alison, and Carol Wise. 1997. "Liberalization and Ethnic Conflict in Latin America." *Studies in Comparative International Development* 32(2):76–104.

Buechler, Steven M. 1990. *Women's Movements in the United States*. New Brunswick, NJ: Rutgers University Press.

_____. 1995. "New Social Movement Theories." *Sociological Quarterly* 36(3):441–464.

_____. 2000. *Social Movements in Advanced Capitalism*. New York: Oxford University Press.

_____. 2002. "Toward a Structural Approach to Social Movements." *Sociological Views on Political Participation in the 21st Century* 1:1–45.

Burke, William Kevin. 1995. "The Wise Use Movement: Right-Wing Anti-Environmentalism." pp. 135–145 in *Eyes Right! Challenging the Right Wing Backlash*, edited by C. Berlet. Boston: South End Press.

Burstein, Paul, Rachel L. Einwohner, and Jocelyn A. Hollander. 1995. "The Success of Political Movements: A Bargaining Perspective." pp. 275–295 in *The Politics of Social Protest*, edited by J. C. Jenkins and B. Klandermans. Minneapolis, MN: University of Minnesota Press.

Bush, Evelyn, and Pete Simi. 2001. "European Farmers and Their Protests." pp. 97–121 in *Contentious Europeans*, edited by D. Imig and S. Tarrow. Lanham, MD: Rowman & Littlefield.

Bush, Rod. 1999. *We Are Not What We Seem: Black Nationalism and Class Struggle in the American Century*. New York: New York University Press.

Buss, Doris, and Didi Herman. 2003. *Globalizing Family Values: The Christian Right in International Politics*. Minneapolis, MN: University of Minnesota Press.

Butler, Jennifer S. 2006. *Born Again: The Christian Right Globalized*. London: Pluto Press.

Buttel, Frederik, and Kenneth Gould. 2005. "Global Social Movements at the Crossroads: An Investigation of Relations Between the Anti-Corporate Globalization and Environmental Movements." pp. 139–155 in *Transforming Globalization*, edited by B. Podobnik and T. Reifer. Leiden: Brill.

Calhoun, Craig. 1993. " 'New Social Movements' of the Early Nineteenth Century." *Social Science History* 17(3):385–427.

Carden, Maren Lockwood. 1974. *The New Feminist Movement*. New York: Russell Sage Foundation.

Carmin, Joann, and Deborah B. Balser. 2002. "Selecting Repertoires of Action in Environmental Movement Organizations." *Organization & Environment* 15(4): 365–388.

Carroll, William K., and R. S. Ratner. 1995. "Old Unions and New Social Movements." *Labour/Le Travail* 35(Spring):195–221.

_____. 1996. "Master Framing and Cross-Movement Networking in Contemporary Social Movements." *Sociological Quarterly* 37(4):601–625.

_____. 1999. "Media Strategies and Political Projects: A Comparative Study of Social Movements." *Canadian Journal of Sociology* 24(1):1–34.

Carson, Clayborne. 1981. *In Struggle: SNCC and the Black Awakening of the 1960s*. Cambridge, MA: Harvard University Press.

Carson, Rachel. 1962. *Silent Spring*. Boston: Houghton Mifflin.

Cassidy, Sean. 1992. "The Environment and the Media: Two Strategies for Challenging Hegemony." pp. 159–174 in *Democratic Communications in the Information Age*, edited by J. Wasko and V. Mosco. Toronto: Garamond.

Castle, Stephen, and Steven Erlanger. 2009. "Riots Erupt Near Bridge That Links 2 Countries." *The New York Times*, April 5.

Caute, David. 1988. *The Year of the Barricades: A Journey through 1968*. New York: Harper and Row.

Chafetz, Janet S., and Anthony G. Dworkin. 1986. *Female Revolt: The Rise of Women's Movements in World and Historical Perspective*. Totowa, NJ: Rowman & Littlefield.

Chauncey, George. 2004. *Why Marriage?* New York: Basic Books.

Connell, Robert W. 1990. "A Whole New World: Remaking Masculinity in the Context of the Environmental Movement." *Gender & Society* 4(4):452–478.

Conway, Janet M. 2004. *Identity, Place, Knowledge: Social Movements Contesting Globalization*. Halifax: Fernwood.

Costain, Anne N. 1992. *Inviting Women's Rebellion: A Political Process Interpretation of the Women's Movement*. Baltimore, MD: Johns Hopkins University Press.

Cravey, Altha J. 2004. "Students and the Anti-Sweatshop Movement." *Antipode* 36(2):203–208.

Crawford, Alan. 1980. *Thunder on the Right: The "New Right" and the Politics of Resentment*. New York: Pantheon Books.

Cuneo, Michael W. 1989. *Catholics against the State: Anti-Abortion Protest in Toronto*. Toronto: University of Toronto Press.

Curtis, Russell L., Jr, and Louis Zurcher Jr. 1973. "Stable Resources of Protest Movements: The Multi-organizational Field." *Social Forces* 52:53–61.

Dale, Stephen. 1996. *McLuhan's Children: The Greenpeace Message and the Media*. Toronto: Between the Lines.

Dalton, Russell J. 2005. "The Greening of the Globe? Cross-national Levels of Environmental Group Membership." *Environmental Politics* 14(4):441–459.

Daniels, Mark R., Robert Darcy, and Joseph W. Westphal. 1982. "The ERA Won—At Least in the Opinion Polls." *PS: Political Science and Politics* 15(4):578–584.

Davies, James C. 1962. "Toward a Theory of Revolution." *American Sociological Review* 27:5–19.

———. 1971. *When Men Revolt and Why*. New York: Free Press.

della Porta, Donatella. 1995. *Social Movements, Political Violence, and the State*. Cambridge: Cambridge University Press.

della Porta, Donatella, Massimiliano Andretta, Lorenzo Mosca, and Herbert Reiter. 2006. *Globalization from Below: Transnational Activists and Protest Networks*. Minneapolis, MN: University of Minnesota Press.

della Porta, Donatella, and Olivier Fillieule. 2004. "Policing Social Protest." pp. 217–241 in *The Blackwell Companion to Social Movements*, edited by D. A. Snow, S. A. Soule, and H. Kriesi. Oxford: Blackwell Publishing.

D'Emilio, John. 1983. *Sexual Politics, Sexual Communities: The Making of a Homosexual Minority in the United States, 1940–1970*. Chicago: University of Chicago Press.

D'Emilio, John, and Estelle B. Freedman. 1988. *Intimate Matters: A History of Sexuality in America*. New York: Harper & Row.

Devall, Bill. 1992. "Deep Ecology and Radical Environmentalism." pp. 51–62 in *American Environmentalism: The U.S. Environmental Movement, 1970–1990*, edited by Riley E. Dunlap and Angela G. Mertig. Philadelphia, PA: Taylor and Francis.

Diamond, Sara. 1995. *Roads to Dominion: Right-Wing Movements and Political Power in the United States*. New York: Guilford Press.

Diani, Mario. 1992. "The Concept of Social Movement." *Sociological Review* 40(1):1–25.

Doherty, Brian. 1999. "Paving the Way: The Rise of Direct Action against Road-building and the Changing Character of British Environmentalism." *Political Studies* 47(2):275–291.

Dowie, Mark. 1995. *Losing Ground: American Environmentalism at the Close of the Twentieth Century*. Cambridge, MA: MIT Press.

Downs, Anthony. 1972. "Up and Down with Ecology—The 'Issue-Attention Cycle'." *Public Interest* 28:38–50.

Downton, James V., Jr, and Paul E. Wehr. 1991. "Peace Movements: The Role of Commitment and Community in Sustaining Member Participation." *Research in Social Movements, Conflicts and Change* 13:113–134.

Duberman, Martin B. 1993. *Stonewall*. New York: Dutton.

Duchen, Claire. 1994. *Women's Rights and Women's Lives in France, 1944–1968*. New York: Routledge.

Dufour, Pascale, and Isabelle Giraud. 2007. "The Continuity of Transnational Solidarities in the World March of Women, 2000 and 2005: A Collective Identity-Building Approach." *Mobilization* 12(3):307–322.

Dunlap, Riley E. 2006. "Show Us the Data." *Organization & Environment* 19(1):88–102.

Dunlap, Riley E., and Richard York. 2008. "The Globalization of Environmental Concern and the Limits of the Postmaterialist Values Explanation: Evidence from Four Multinational Surveys." *The Sociological Quarterly* 49:529–563.

Durham, Martin. 2000. *The Christian Right, the Far Right and the Boundaries of American Conservatism.* Manchester, UK: Manchester University Press.

Earl, Jennifer. 2004. "The Cultural Consequences of Social Movements." pp. 508–530 in *The Blackwell Companion to Social Movements*, edited by D. A. Snow, S. A. Soule, and H.Kriesi. Oxford: Blackwell Publishing.

Earl, Jennifer, and Alan Schussman. 2003. "The New Site of Activism: On-Line Organizations, Movement Entrepreneurs, and the Changing Location of Social Movement Decision Making." *Consensus Decision Making, Northern Ireland and Indigenous Movements* 24:155–187.

Echols, Alice. 1989. *Daring to Be Bad: Radical Feminism in America, 1967–1975.* Minneapolis, MN: University of Minnesota Press.

Edwards, Bob, and John D. McCarthy. 2004. "Resources and Social Movement Mobilization." pp. 116–152 in *The Blackwell Companion to Social Movements*, edited by D. A. Snow, S. A. Soule, and H. Kriesi. Oxford: Blackwell Publishing.

Ehrenreich, Barbara. 1983. *Hearts of Men: American Dreams and the Flight from Commitment.* New York: Anchor Press.

Engel, Stephen M. 2001. *The Unfinished Revolution: Social Movement Theory and the Gay and Lesbian Movement.* Cambridge: Cambridge University Press.

Enke, Anne. 2007. *Finding the Movement: Sexuality, Contested Space, and Feminist Activism.* Durham, NC: Duke University Press.

Epstein, Barbara. 1991. *Political Protest and Cultural Revolution: Nonviolent Direct Action in the 1970s and 1980s.* Berkeley, CA: University of California Press.

———. 2001. "What Happened to the Women's Movement?" *Monthly Review* 53(1):1–13.

Epstein, Steven. 1999. "Gay and Lesbian Movements in the United States: Dilemmas of Identity, Diversity, and Political Strategy." pp. 30–90 in *The Global Emergence of Gay and Lesbian Politics*, edited by B. D. Adam, J. W. Duyvendak, and A. Krouwel. Philadelphia, PA: Temple University Press.

Evans, Sara. 1979. *Personal Politics: The Roots of Women's Liberation in the Civil Rights Movement and the New Left.* New York: Vintage Books.

———. 2003. *Tidal Wave: How Women Changed America at Century's End.* New York: Free Press.

Eyerman, Ron, and Andrew Jamison. 1989. "Environmental Knowledge as an Organizational Weapon: The Case of Greenpeace." *Social Science Information* 28(1):99–119.

Fairclough, Adam. 1987. *To Redeem the Soul of America: The Southern Christian Leadership Conference and Martin Luther King, Jr.* Athens, GA: University of Georgia Press.

Faux, Marian. 1988. *Roe v. Wade: The Untold Story of the Landmark Supreme Court Decision That Made Abortion Legal.* New York: Macmillan.

Ferree, Myra Marx, and Carol McClurg Mueller. 2004. "Feminism and the Women's Movement: A Global Perspective." pp. 576–607 in *The Blackwell Companion to Social Movements*, edited by D. A. Snow, S. A. Soule, and H. Kriesi. Oxford: Blackwell Publishing.

Ferree, Myra Marx, William Anthony Gamson, Jürgen Gerhards, and Dieter Rucht. 2002. *Shaping Abortion Discourse: Democracy and the Public Sphere in Germany and the United States.* Cambridge: Cambridge University Press.

Fetner, Tina. 2008. *How the Religious Right Shaped Lesbian and Gay Activism*. Minneapolis, MN: University of Minnesota Press.

Findlen, Barbara, ed. 2001. *Listen Up: Voices from the Next Feminist Generation*, 2nd ed. Emeryville, CA: Seal Press.

Fireman, Bruce, and William A. Gamson. 1979. "Utilitarian Logic in the Resource Mobilization Perspective." pp. 8–44 in *The Dynamics of Social Movements: Resource Mobilization, Social Control, and Tactics*, edited by M. N. Zald and J. D. McCarthy. Cambridge, MA: Winthrop.

Fitzgerald, Frances. 2008. "The New Evangelicals." *The New Yorker*, June 30, 28–34.

Flacks, Richard. 2005. "The Question of Relevance in Social Movement Studies." pp. 3–19 in *Rhyming Hope and History: Activists, Academics, and Social Movement Scholarship*, edited by D. Croteau, W. Hoynes, and C. Ryan. Minneapolis, MN: University of Minnesota Press.

Francome, Colin. 1984. *Abortion Freedom—A Worldwide Movement*. Winchester, MA: Allen and Unwin.

Fraser, Ronald. 1988. *1968: A Student Generation in Revolt*. London: Chatto & Windus.

Freeman, Jo. 1972. "The Tyranny of Structurelessness." pp. 285–299 in *Radical Feminism*, edited by A. Koedt, E. Levine, and A. Rapone. New York: Quadrangle Press.

———. 1975. *The Politics of Women's Liberation*. New York: Longman.

———. 1979. "Resource Mobilization and Strategy: A Model for Analyzing Social Movement Organization Actions." pp. 167–189 in *The Dynamics of Social Movements: Resource Mobilization, Social Control, and Tactics*, edited by M. N. Zald and J. D. McCarthy. Cambridge, MA: Winthrop.

Gamson, Josh. 1989. "Silence, Death, and the Invisible Enemy: AIDS Activism and Social Movement 'Newness'." *Social Problems* 36(4):351–367.

Gamson, William A. 1990. *The Strategy of Social Protest*, 2nd ed. Belmont, CA: Wadsworth. (1st ed. 1975.)

———. 1998. "Social Movements and Cultural Change." pp. 57–77 in *From Contention to Democracy*, edited by M. Giugni, D. McAdam, and C. Tilly. Lanham, MD: Rowman & Littlefield.

Gamson, William A., and David S. Meyer. 1996. "Framing Political Opportunity." pp. 275–290 in *Comparative Perspectives on Social Movements: Political Opportunities, Mobilizing Structures, and Cultural Framings*, edited by D. McAdam, J. D. McCarthy, and M. N. Zald. Cambridge: Cambridge University Press.

Gamson, William A., and Gadi Wolfsfeld. 1993. "Movements and Media as Interacting Systems." *Annals, Academy of Political and Social Science* 528:114–125.

Gans, Herbert J. 1979. *Deciding What's News: A Study of CBS Evening News, NBC Nightly News, Newsweek and Time*. New York: Vintage Books.

Ganz, Marshall. 2000. "Resources and Resourcefulness: Strategic Capacity in the Unionization of California Agriculture, 1959–1966." *American Journal of Sociology* 105(4):1003–1062.

Garrow, David J. 1986. *Bearing the Cross: Martin Luther King, Jr. and the Southern Christian Leadership Conference*. New York: Vintage Books.

Gazette (Montreal). 2001. "Protesters Make Dent in Agenda." July 19.

———. 2001. "Unlikely Allies Descend on Italy." July 20.

Gerhards, Jurgen, and Dieter Rucht. 1992. "Mesomobilization: Organizing and Framing in Two Protest Campaigns in West Germany." *American Journal of Sociology* 98(3):555–595.

Gerlach, Luther, and Virginia H. Hine. 1970. *People, Power, Change: Movements of Social Transformation*. Indianapolis, IN: Bobbs-Merrill.

Giele, Janet Zollinger. 1995. *Two Paths to Women's Equality: Temperance, Suffrage, and the Origins of Modern Feminism*. New York: Twayne Publishers.

Gillham, Patrick F., and John A. Noakes. 2007. "'More than a March in a Circle': Transgressive Protests and the Limits of Negotiated Management." *Mobilization* 12(4):341–357.

Gilmore, Stephanie. 2005. "Bridging the Waves: Sex and Sexuality in a Second Wave Organization." pp. 97–116 in *Different Wavelengths: Studies of the Contemporary Women's Movement*, edited by J. Reger. New York: Routledge.

Gitlin, Todd. 1980. *The Whole World Is Watching: Mass Media and the Making of the New Left*. Berkeley, CA: University of California Press.

————. 1987. *The Sixties: Years of Hope, Days of Rage*. New York: Bantam Books.

Giugni, Marco G. 1998. "Was It Worth the Effort? The Outcomes and Consequences of Social Movements." *Annual Review of Sociology* 98:371–393.

Globe and Mail (Toronto). 1994. "Myth of Eternal Forest Toppled." July 14, A1, A3.

Goddu, Jenn. 1999. "'Powerless, Public-Spirited Women', 'Angry Feminists', and 'The Muffin Lobby': Newspaper and Magazine Coverage of Three National Women's Groups from 1980 to 1995." *Canadian Journal of Communication* 24:105–126.

Goodwin, Jeff, and James M. Jasper. 1999. "Caught in a Winding, Snarling Vine: The Structural Bias of Political Process Theory." *Sociological Forum* 14(1):27–54.

Goodwin, Jeff, James M. Jasper, and Francesca Polletta, eds. 2001. *Passionate Politics: Emotions and Social Movements*. Chicago: University of Chicago Press.

Gould, Deborah B. 2002. "Life during Wartime: Emotions and the Development of Act Up." *Mobilization* 7(2):177–200.

Gould, Kenneth, Tammy Lewis, and J. Timmons Roberts. 2005. "Blue-Green Coalitions: Constraints and Possibilities in the Post 9/11 Political Environment." pp. 123–138 in *Transforming Globalization*, edited by B. Podobnik and T. Reifer. Leiden: Brill.

Gurney, Joan Neff, and Kathleen J. Tierney. 1982. "Relative Deprivation and Social Movements: A Critical Look at Twenty Years of Theory and Research." *Sociological Quarterly* 23(1):33–47.

Gurr, Ted Robert. 1970. *Why Men Rebel*. Princeton, NJ: Princeton University Press.

Gusfield, Joseph R. 1981. "Social Movements and Social Change: Perspectives of Linearity and Fluidity." *Social Movements, Conflict and Change* 4:317–339.

————. 1986. *Symbolic Crusade: Status Politics and the American Temperance Movement*, 2nd ed. Urbana, IL: University of Illinois Press.

Habermas, Jürgen. 1984. *The Theory of Communicative Action*, vol. 1, trans. Thomas McCarthy. Boston: Beacon Press.

————. 1987. *The Theory of Communicative Action*, vol. 2, trans. Thomas McCarthy. Boston: Beacon Press.

Hacket, Robert A., and Richard Gruneau. 2000. *The Missing News: Filters and the Blind Spots in Canada's Press*. Aurora, ON: Garamond Press.

Halleck, DeeDee. 2003. "Gathering Storm: Cyberactivism after Seattle." pp. 202–214 in *Media, Profit, and Politics: Competing Priorities in an Open Society*, edited by J. Harper and T. Yantek. Kent, OH: Kent State University Press.

Hallin, Daniel C. 1989. *The "Uncensored War": The Media and Vietnam*. Berkeley, CA: University of California Press.

Hardisty, Jean. 1999. *Mobilizing Resentment: Conservative Resurgence from the John Birch Society to the Promise Keepers.* Boston: Beacon Press.

Hartmann, Susan M. 1998. *The Other Feminists: Activists in the Liberal Establishment.* New Haven, CT: Yale University Press.

Hawkesworth, Mary. 2004. "The Semiotics of Premature Burial: Feminism in a Postfeminist Age." *Signs* 29(4):961–985.

Heirich, Max. 1968. *The Spiral of Conflict: Berkeley, 1964.* New York: Columbia University Press.

Helvarg, David. 1994. *The War Against the Greens: The "Wise-Use" Movement, the New Right, and Anti-Environmental Violence.* San Francisco: Sierra Club Books.

_____. 2004. "'Wise Use' in the White House: Yesterday's Fringe, Today's Cabinet Official." *Sierra*, September/October, 49–50.

Henry, Astrid. 2004. *Not My Mother's Sister: Generational Conflict and Third-Wave Feminism.* Bloomington, IN: Indiana University Press.

_____. 2005. "Solitary Sisterhood: Individualism Meets Collectivity in Feminism's Third Wave." pp. 81–96 in *Different Wavelengths: Studies of the Contemporary Women's Movement*, edited by J. Reger. New York: Routledge.

Herdt, Gilbert. 2009. "Gay Marriage: The Panic and the Right." pp. 157–204 in *Moral Panics, Sex Panics: Fear and the Fight over Sexual Rights*, edited by G. Herdt. New York: New York University Press.

Herman, Didi. 1997. *Antigay Agenda: Orthodox Vision and the Christian Right.* Chicago: University of Chicago Press.

Heywood, Leslie, and Jennifer Drake, eds. 1997. *Third Wave Agenda: Being Feminist, Doing Feminism.* Minneapolis, MN: University of Minnesota Press.

Himmelstein, Jerome L. 1990. *To the Right: The Transformation of American Conservatism.* Berkeley, CA: University of California Press.

Hoffer, Eric. 1951. *The True Believer.* New York: Harper.

Hofstadter, Richard. [1955] 1963. "The Pseudo-Conservative Revolt." pp. 75–95 in *The Radical Right*, edited by D. Bell. Garden City, NY: Doubleday.

Hole, Judith, and Ellen Levine. 1971. *Rebirth of Feminism.* New York: Quadrangle Books.

Hull, Kathleen E. 2006. *Same-Sex Marriage: The Cultural Politics of Love and Law.* Cambridge: Cambridge University Press.

Hunter, Robert. 2004. *The Greenpeace to Amchitka: An Environmental Odyssey.* Vancouver: Arsenal Pulp Press.

Inglehart, Ronald. 1990. *Culture Shift in Advanced Industrial Society.* Princeton, NJ: Princeton University Press.

_____. 1995. "Public Support for Environmental Protection: Objective Problems and Subjective Values in 43 Societies." *PS: Political Science and Politics* 28(1):57–72.

Jasper, James M. 1998. "The Emotions of Protest: Affective and Reactive Emotions in and around Social Movements." *Sociological Forum* 13(3):397–424.

Jasper, James M., and Jane Poulsen. 1993. "Fighting Back: Vulnerabilities, Blunders, and Countermobilization by the Targets in Three Animal Rights Campaigns." *Sociological Forum* 8(4):639–657.

Jenkins, J. Craig. 1981. "Sociopolitical Movements." pp. 81–154 in *Handbook of Political Behavior*, vol. 4, edited by S. L. Long. New York: Plenum Publishers.

_____. 1983. "Resource Mobilization Theory and the Study of Social Movements." *Annual Review of Sociology* 9:527–553.

Jenkins, J. Craig, and Charles Perrow. 1977. "Insurgency of the Powerless: Farm Workers Movements 1946–1972." *American Sociological Review* 42:249–268.

Jenkins, J. Craig, David Jacobs, and Jon Agnone. 2003. "Political Opportunities and African-American Protest, 1948–1997." *American Journal of Sociology* 109(2):277–303.

Kaplan, Laura. 1995. *The Story of Jane: The Legendary Underground Feminist Abortion Service*. New York: Pantheon Books.

Katzenstein, Mary Fainsod. 1998. *Faithful and Fearless: Moving Feminist Protest inside the Church and Military*. Princeton, NJ: Princeton University Press.

Keck, Margaret E., and Kathryn Sikkink. 1998. *Activists Beyond Borders: Advocacy Networks in International Politics*. Ithaca, NY: Cornell University Press.

Kennedy, Elizabeth L., and Madeline D. Davis. 1993. *Boots of Leather, Slippers of Gold: The History of a Lesbian Community*. New York: Penguin Books.

Kielbowicz, Richard B., and Clifford Scherer. 1986. "The Role of the Press in the Dynamics of Social Movements." *Research in Social Movements, Conflicts and Change* 9:71–96.

Killian, Lewis M. 1994. "Are Social Movements Irrational or Are They Collective Behavior?" pp. 273–280 in *Disasters, Collective Behavior, and Social Organization*, edited by R. R. Dynes and K. J. Tierney. Newark, DE: University of Delaware Press.

Kingsnorth, Paul. 2009. "London Calls the Street Rebels." *New Statesman*, March 30, 30–31.

Kirkpatrick, David D. 2007. "The Evangelical Crackup." *The New York Times Magazine*, October 28, 38–45, 60, 64, 66.

Klandermans, Bert. 1986. "New Social Movements and Resource Mobilization: The European and American Approach." *International Journal of Mass Emergencies and Disasters* 4:13–37.

_____. 1992. "The Social Construction of Protest and Multiorganizational Fields." pp. 77–103 in *Frontiers in Social Movement Theory*, edited by A. D. Morris and C. M. Mueller. New Haven, CT: Yale University Press.

_____. 1994. "Transient Identities: Changes in Collective Identity in the Dutch Peace Movement." pp. 168–185 in *New Social Movements: From Ideology to Identity*, edited by H. Johnston, J. Gusfield, and E. Larana. Philadelphia, PA: Temple University Press.

_____. 1997. *The Social Psychology of Protest*. Oxford: Blackwell Publishing.

Klandermans, Bert, and Jackie Smith. 2002. "Survey Research: A Case for Comparative Designs." pp. 3–31 in *Methods of Social Movement Research*, edited by B. Klandermans and S. Staggenborg. Minneapolis, MN: University of Minnesota Press.

Klandermans, Bert, and Suzanne Staggenborg, eds. 2002. *Methods of Social Movement Research*. Minneapolis, MN: University of Minnesota Press.

Klatch, Rebecca E. 1987. *Women of the New Right*. Philadelphia, PA: Temple University Press.

_____. 1999. *A Generation Divided: The New Left, the New Right, and the 1960s*. Berkeley, CA: University of California Press.

Kleidman, Robert. 1993. *Organizing for Peace: Neutrality, the Test Ban, and the Freeze*. Syracuse, NY: Syracuse University Press.

Klein, Naomi. 1999. *No Logo*. New York: Picador.

Koopmans, Ruud, and Dieter Rucht. 2002. "Protest Event Analysis." pp. 231–259 in *Methods of Social Movement Research*, edited by B. Klandermans and S. Staggenborg. Minneapolis, MN: University of Minnesota Press.

Kornhauser, William. 1959. *The Politics of a Mass Society*. New York: Free Press.

Kostash, Myrna. 1980. *Long Way from Home: The Story of the Sixties Generation in Canada*. Toronto: James Lorimer.

Kriesi, Hanspeter, Rudd Koopmans, Jan Willem Duyvendak, and Marco G. Giugni. 1995. *New Social Movements in Western Europe: A Comparative Analysis*. Minneapolis, MN: University of Minnesota Press.

Kurzman, Charles. 2004. "The Poststructuralist Consensus in Social Movement Theory." pp. 111–120 in *Rethinking Social Movements*, edited by Jeff Goodwin and James M. Jasper. Lanham, MD: Rowman & Littlefield.

Kutchins, Herb, and Stuart A. Kirk. 1997. *Making Us Crazy*. New York: Free Press.

La Botz, Dan. 2002. "After a Decade of Antisweatshop Organizing, Activists Say It's Time They Pulled Together." (June 28, 2002) www.organicconsumers.org/clothes/sweatshop_movement.cfm

Lang, Kurt, and Gladys E. Lang. 1961. *Collective Dynamics*. New York: Thomas Y. Crowell.

Le Bon, Gustav. 1895. *The Crowd*. New York: Viking.

Leiserowitz, Anthony A., Robert W. Kates, and Thomas M. Parris. 2005. "Do Global Attitudes and Behaviors Support Sustainable Development?" *Environment* 47(9):22–38.

Lent, Adam. 2003. "The Transformation of Gay and Lesbian Politics in Britain." *British Journal of Politics and International Relations* 5(1):24–49.

Levi, Margaret, David J. Olson, and Erich Steinman. 2004. "Living Wage Movement." pp. 1471–1481 In *Encyclopedia of American Social Movements*, vol. 4, edited by I. Ness. Armonk, NY: Sharpe Reference.

Levitt, Cyril. 1984. *Children of Privilege: Student Revolt in the Sixties: A Study of Student Movements in Canada, the United States, and West Germany*. Toronto: University of Toronto Press.

Lichterman, Paul. 1996. *The Search for Political Community: American Activists Reinventing Commitment*. Cambridge: Cambridge University Press.

———. 2002. "Seeing Structure Happen: Theory-Driven Participant Observation." pp. 118–145 in *Methods of Social Movement Research*, edited by B. Klandermans and S. Staggenborg. Minneapolis, MN: University of Minnesota Press.

Liebman, Robert C. 1983. "Mobilizing the Moral Majority." pp. 49–73 in *The New Christian Right*, edited by R. Liebman and R. Wuthnow. New York: Aldine Publishing Co.

Lindsay, D. Michael. 2007. *Faith in the Halls of Power: How Evangelicals Joined the American Elite*. New York: Oxford University Press.

Lipset, Seymour M., and Earl Raab. 1978. *The Politics of Unreason, Second Edition: Right-Wing Extremism in America, 1790–1977*. Chicago: University of Chicago Press.

Lofland, John. 1979. "White-Hot Mobilization: Strategies of a Millenarian Movement." pp. 157–166 in *The Dynamics of Social Movements*, edited by M. N. Zald and J. D. McCarthy. Cambridge, MA: Winthrop.

Lowe, Philip, and Jane Goyder. 1983. *Environmental Groups in Politics*. London: George Allen & Unwin.

Lowndes, Joseph E. 2008. *From the New Deal to the New Right: Race and the Southern Origins of Modern Conservatism*. New Haven, CT: Yale University Press.

Luders, Joseph. 2006. "The Economics of Movement Success: Business Responses to Civil Rights Mobilization." *American Journal of Sociology* 111(4):963–998.

Luker, Kristin. 1984. *Abortion and the Politics of Motherhood*. Berkeley, CA: University of California Press.

MacKinnon, Catharine A. 1979. *Sexual Harassment of Working Women: A Case of Sex Discrimination.* New Haven, CT: Yale University Press.

Maney, Gregory M. 2001. "Rival Transnational Networks and Indigenous Rights: The San Blas Kuna in Panama and the Yanomami in Brazil." *Social Movements, Conflicts and Change* 23:103–144.

Mansbridge, Jane J. 1986. *Why We Lost the ERA.* Chicago: University of Chicago Press.

Marshall, Susan. 1995. "Confrontation and Co-optation in Antifeminist Organizations." pp. 323–335 in *Feminist Organizations*, edited by Myra Marx Ferree and Patricia Yancey Martin. Philadelphia, PA: Temple University Press.

Martin, William. 1996. *With God on Our Side: The Rise of the Religious Right in America.* New York: Broadway Books.

Marwell, Gerald, and Pamela Oliver. 1984. "Collective Action Theory and Social Movements Research." *Research in Social Movements, Conflicts and Change* 7:1–27.

_____. 1993. *The Critical Mass in Collective Action: A Micro-Social Theory.* Cambridge: Cambridge University Press.

Marwick, Arthur. 1998. *The Sixties: Cultural Revolution in Britain, France, Italy, and the United States.* New York: Oxford University Press.

Marx, Gary T., and James L. Wood. 1975. "Strands of Theory and Research in Collective Behavior." *Annual Review of Sociology* 1:363–428.

Mathews, Donald G., and Jane Sherron De Hart. 1990. *Sex, Gender, and the Politics of ERA: A State and the Nation.* New York: Oxford University Press.

Matthews, J. Scott. 2005. "The Political Foundations of Support for Same-Sex Marriage in Canada." *Canadian Journal of Political Science* 38(4):841–866.

Mayo, Marjorie. 2005. *Global Citizens: Social Movements and the Challenge of Globalization.* New York: Zed Books.

McAdam, Doug. 1983. "Tactical Innovation and the Pace of Insurgency." *American Sociological Review* 48(6):735–754.

_____. 1986. "Recruitment to High-Risk Activism: The Case of Freedom Summer." *American Journal of Sociology* 92(1):64–90.

_____. 1988. *Freedom Summer.* New York: Oxford University Press.

_____. 1994. "Culture and Social Movements." pp. 36–57 in *New Social Movements: From Ideology to Identity*, edited by E. Larana, H. Johnston, and J. R. Gusfield. Philadelphia, PA: Temple University Press.

_____. 1995. "'Initiator' and 'Spin-off' Movements: Diffusion Processes in Protest Cycles." pp. 217–239 in *Repertoires and Cycles of Collective Action*, edited by M. Traugott. Durham, NC: Duke University Press.

_____.1996. "The Framing Function of Movement Tactics: Strategic Dramaturgy in the American Civil Rights Movement." pp. 338–355 in *Comparitive Perspectives on Social Movements: Political Opportunities, Mobilizing Structures and Cultural Framings*, edited by Doug McAdam, John D. McCarthy, and Mayer N. Zald. Cambridge: Cambridge University Press.

_____. 1999. *Political Process and the Development of Black Insurgency*, 2nd ed. Chicago: University of Chicago Press. (1st ed. 1982.)

McAdam, Doug, and Debra Friedman. 1992. "Collective Identity and Activism: Networks, Choices, and the Life of a Social Movement." pp. 156–173 in *Frontiers in Social Movement Theory*, edited by Aldon D. Morris and Carol M. Mueller. New Haven, CT: Yale University Press.

McAdam, Doug, and Dieter Rucht. 1993. "The Cross-National Diffusion of Movement Ideas." *Annals, American Academy of Political and Social Science* 528:56–74.

McAdam, Doug, John D. McCarthy, and Mayer N. Zald. 1988. "Social Movements." pp. 695–737 in *Handbook of Sociology*, edited by N. J. Smelser. Newbury Park, CA: Sage.

_____, eds. 1996. *Comparative Perspectives on Social Movements*. New York: Cambridge University Press.

McAdam, Doug, Sidney Tarrow, and Charles Tilly. 2001. *Dynamics of Contention*. Cambridge: Cambridge University Press.

McCammon, Holly J. 2001. "Stirring Up Suffrage Sentiment: The Formation of the State Women's Suffrage Organizations, 1866–1914." *Social Forces* 80(2): 449–480.

McCarthy, John D., and Mayer N. Zald. 1973. *The Trend of Social Movements in America: Professionalization and Resource Mobilization*. Morristown, NJ: General Learning Press.

_____. 1977. "Resource Mobilization and Social Movements: A Partial Theory." *American Journal of Sociology* 82(6):1212–1241.

_____. 2002. "The Enduring Vitality of the Resource Mobilization Theory of Social Movements." pp. 533–565 in *Handbook of Sociological Theory*, edited by H. T. Jonathan. New York: Kluwer Academic/Plenum Publishers.

McCloskey, Michael. 1992. "Twenty Years of Change in the Environmental Movement: An Insider's View." pp. 77–88 in *American Environmentalism: The U.S. Environmental Movement, 1970–1990*, edited by Riley E. Dunlap and Angela G. Mertig. Philadelphia, PA: Taylor and Francis.

McComas, Katherine, and James Shanahan. 1999. "Telling Stories about Global Climate Change." *Communication Research* 26(1):30–57.

McCright, Aaron M., and Riley E. Dunlap. 2000. "Challenging Global Warming as a Social Problem: An Analysis of the Conservative Movement's Counter-Claims." *Social Problems* 47(4):499–522.

_____. 2003. "Defeating Kyoto: The Conservative Movement's Impact on U.S. Climate Change Policy." *Social Problems* 50(3):348–373.

McGirr, Lisa. 2001. *Suburban Warriors: The Origins of the New American Right*. Princeton, NJ: Princeton University Press.

McKenzie, Judith I. 2002. *Environmental Politics in Canada: Managing the Commons into the Twenty-First Century*. Toronto: Oxford University Press.

McKinley, Jesse. 2008. "Across U.S., Big Rallies For Same-Sex Marriage." *The New York Times*, November 16.

Meier, August, and Elliott Rudwick. 1973. *CORE: A Study of the Civil Rights Movement, 1942–1968*. Urbana, IL: University of Illinois Press.

Melucci, Alberto. 1988. "Getting Involved: Identity and Mobilization in Social Movements." *International Social Movement Research* 1:329–348.

_____. 1989. *Nomads of the President: Social Movements and Individual Needs in Contemporary Society*. Philadelphia, PA: Temple University Press.

_____. 1996. *Challenging Codes: Collective Action in the Information Age*. Cambridge: Cambridge University Press.

Merton, Andrew H. 1981. *Enemies of Choice: The Right-to-Life Movement and Its Threat to Abortion*. Boston: Beacon Press.

Meyer, David S. 2004. "Protest and Political Opportunities." *Annual Review of Sociology* 30:125–145.

Meyer, David S., and Nancy Whittier. 1994. "Social Movement Spillover." *Social Problems* 41(2):277–298.

Meyer, David S., and Suzanne Staggenborg. 1996. "Movements, Countermovements, and the Structure of Political Opportunity." *American Journal of Sociology* 101(6): 1628–1660.

Meyer, David S., and Suzanne Staggenborg. 1998. "Countermovement Dynamics in Federal Systems: A Comparison of Abortion Politics in Canada and the United States." *Research in Political Sociology* 8:209–240.

Micklethwait, John, and Adrian Wooldridge. 2004. *The Right Nation: Conservative Power in America*. New York: Penguin Books.

Mitchell, Allyson, Lisa Bryn Rundle, and Lara Karaian, eds. 2001. *Turbo Chicks: Talking Young Feminisms*. Toronto: Sumach Press.

Mitchell, Robert Cameron. 1979. "National Environmental Lobbies and the Apparent Illogic of Collective Action." pp. 87–136 in *Collective Decision Making: Applications from Public Choice Theory*, edited by C. S. Russel. Baltimore, MD: Johns Hopkins University Press.

———. 1984. "Public Opinion and Environmental Politics in the 1970's and 1980's." pp. 51–74 in *Environmental Policy in the 1980's: Reagan's New Agenda*, edited by J. V. Norman and M. E. Kraft. Washington, DC: Congressional Quarterly Press.

Mitchell, Robert Cameron, Angela G. Mertig, and Riley E. Dunlap. 1992. "Twenty Years of Environmental Mobilization: Trends among National Environmental Organizations." pp. 11–26 in *American Environmentalism: The U.S. Environmental Movement, 1970–1990*, edited by Riley E. Dunlap and Angela G. Mertig. Philadelphia, PA: Taylor and Francis.

Moghadam, Valentine M. 2005. *Globalizing Women*. Baltimore, MD: Johns Hopkins University Press.

Morgen, Sandra. 2002. *Into Our Own Hands: The Women's Health Movement in the United States, 1969–1990*. New Brunswick, NJ: Rutgers University Press.

Morris, Aldon D. 1981. "Black Southern Student Sit-In Movement: An Analysis of Internal Organization." *American Sociological Review* 46(4):744–767.

———. 1984. *The Origins of the Civil Rights Movement: Black Communities Organizing for Change*. New York: Free Press.

———. 1999. "A Retrospective on the Civil Rights Movement: Political and Intellectual Landmarks." *Annual Review of Sociology* 25:517–539.

———. 2000. "Reflections on Social Movement Theory: Criticisms and Proposals." *Contemporary Sociology* 29:445–454.

Morris, Aldon D., and Cedric Herring. 1987. "Theory and Research in Social Movements: A Critical Review." *Annual Review in Political Science* 2:137–198.

Morris, Aldon D., and Suzanne Staggenborg. 2004. "Leadership in Social Movements." pp. 171–196 in *The Blackwell Companion to Social Movements*, edited by D. A. Snow, S. A. Soule, and H. Kriesi. Malden, MA: Blackwell Publishing.

Moser, Susanne C. 2007. "In the Long Shadows of Inaction: The Quiet Building of a Climate Protection Movement in the United States." *Global Environmental Politics* 7(2):124–144.

Mucciaroni, Gary. 2008. *Same Sex, Different Politics: Success and Failure in the Struggles over Gay Rights*. Chicago: University of Chicago Press.

Mueller, Carol McClurg. 1987. "Collective Consciousness, Identity Transformation, and the Rise of Women in Public Office in the United States." pp. 89–108 in *The Women's Movements in the United States and Western Europe: Consciousness, Political Opportunity and Public Policy*, edited by M. F. Katzenstein and C. M. Mueller. Philadelphia, PA: Temple University Press.

_____. 1994. "Conflict Networks and the Origins of Women's Liberation." pp. 234–263 in *New Social Movements*, edited by E. Larana, H. Johnston, and J. R. Gusfield. Philadelphia, PA: Temple University Press.

Myers, Daniel J. 1994. "Communication Technology and Social Movements: Contributions of Computer Networks to Activism." *Social Science Computer Review* 12(2):250–260.

Nagel, Joane. 1994. "Constructing Ethnicity: Creating and Recreating Ethnic Identity and Culture." *Social Problems* 41(1):152–176.

_____. 1996. *American Indian Ethnic Renewal: Red Power and the Resurgence of Identity and Culture*. New York: Oxford University Press.

Nagourney, Adam. 2009. "Political Shifts on Gay Rights Are Lagging Behind Culture." *The New York Times*, June 28.

Nepstad, Sharon Erickson, and Christian Smith. 2001. "The Social Structure of Moral Outrage in Recruitment to the U.S. Central America Peace Movement." pp. 158–174 in *Passionate Politics: Emotions and Social Movements*, edited by J. Goodwin, J. M. Jasper, and F. Polletta. Chicago: University of Chicago Press.

Noonan, Rita K. 1995. "Women against the State: Political Opportunities and Collective Action Frames in Chile's Transition to Democracy." *Sociological Forum* 10(1):81–111.

Nordhaus, Ted, and Michael Shellenberger. 2007. *Breakthrough: From the Death of Environmentalism to the Politics of Possibility*. New York: Houghton Mifflin.

Obach, Brian K. 2004. *Labor and the Environmental Movement: The Quest for Common Ground*. Cambridge, MA: MIT Press.

Oberschall, Anthony. 1973. *Social Conflict and Social Movements*. Englewood Cliffs, NJ: Prentice-Hall.

_____. 1978. "The Decline of the 1960s Social Movements." *Research in Social Movements, Conflicts, and Change* 1:257–289.

Oliver, Pamela E., Jorge Cadena-Roa, and Kelley D. Strawn. 2003. "Emerging Trends in the Study of Protest and Social Movements." *Research in Political Sociology* 12:213–244.

Olson, Mancur. 1965. *The Logic of Collective Action: Public Goods and the Theory of Groups*. Cambridge, MA: Harvard University Press.

Owram, Doug. 1996. *Born at the Right Time: A History of the Baby-Boom Generation*. Toronto: University of Toronto Press.

Packer, George. 2008. "The Fall of Conservatism." *The New Yorker*, May 26, 47–55.

Page, Ann L., and Donald A. Clelland. 1978. "The Kanawha County Textbook Controversy: A Study of the Politics of Life Style Concern." *Social Forces* 57 (1):265–281.

Park, Robert E., and Ernest W. Burgess. 1921. *Introduction to the Science of Sociology*. Chicago: University of Chicago Press.

Peckham, Michael. 1998. "New Dimensions of Social Movement/Countermovement Interaction: The Case of Scientology and Its Internet Critics." *Canadian Journal of Sociology* 23(4):317–347.

Perrow, Charles. 1979. "The Sixties Observed." pp. 192–211 in *The Dynamics of Social Movements*, edited by Mayer N. Zald and John D. McCarthy. Cambridge, MA: Winthrop.

Pianta, Mario. 2003. "Democracy vs Globalization. The Growth of Parallel Summits and Global Movements." pp. 232–256 in *Debating Cosmopolitics*, edited by D. Archibugi. London: Verso.

Pichardo, Nelson A. 1997. "New Social Movements: A Critical Review." *Annual Review of Sociology* 23:411–430.

Pierceson, Jason. 2005. *Courts, Liberalism, and Rights: Gay Law and Politics in the United States and Canada*. Philadelphia, PA: Temple University Press.

Pinello, Daniel R. 2006. *America's Struggle for Same-Sex Marriage*. New York: Cambridge University Press.

Piven, Frances Fox and Richard A. Cloward. 1977. *Poor People's Movements: Why They Succeed, How They Fail*. New York: Vintage Books.

Pleyers, Geoffrey. 2009. "World Social Forum 2009: A Generation's Challenge." *Open Democracy* (www.opendemocracy.net).

Podobnik, Bruce. 2005. "Resistance to Globalization: Cycles and Trends in the Globalization Protest Movement." pp. 51–68 in *Transforming Globalization*, edited by B. Podobnik and T. Reifer. Leiden: Brill.

Polletta, Francesca. 1997. "Culture and Its Discontents: Recent Theorizing on the Cultural Dimensions of Protest." *Sociological Inquiry* 67(4):431–450.

_____. 2002. *Freedom Is an Endless Meeting*. Chicago: University of Chicago Press.

_____. 2004. "Culture in and Outside of Institutions." *Research in Social Movements, Conflicts and Change* 25:161–183.

Polletta, Francesca, and James M. Jasper. 2001. "Collective Identity and Social Movements." *Annual Review of Sociology* 27:283–305.

Polletta, Francesca, and M. Kai Ho. 2006. "Frames and their Consequences." pp. 187–209 in *The Oxford Handbook of Contextual Political Analysis*, edited by R. E. Goodin and C. Tilly. Oxford: Oxford University Press.

Press, Eyal. 2009. "A Culture War Casualty." *The Nation*, June 22, 6–7.

Raeburn, Nicole C. 2004. *Changing Corporate America from Inside Out: Lesbian and Gay Workplace Organizing*. Minneapolis, MN: University of Minnesota Press.

Ramos, Tarso. 1995. "Regulatory Takings and Private Property Rights." pp. 146–154 in *Eyes Right! Challenging the Right Wing Backlash*, edited by C. Berlet. Boston: South End Press.

Rayside, David. 1998. *On the Fringe: Gays and Lesbians in Politics*. Ithaca, NY: Cornell University Press.

Rebick, Judy. 2005. *Ten Thousand Roses: The Making of a Feminist Revolution*. Toronto: Penguin Canada.

Reger, Jo, ed. 2005. *Different Wavelengths: Studies of the Contemporary Women's Movement*. New York: Routledge.

Reger, Jo, and Lacey Story. 2005. "Talking about My Vagina: Two College Campuses and *The Vagina Monologues*." pp. 139–160 in *Different Wavelengths: Studies of the Contemporary Women's Movement*, edited by J. Reger. New York: Routledge.

Reger, Jo, and Suzanne Staggenborg. 2006. "Patterns of Mobilization in Local Movement Organizations: Leadership and Strategy in Four National Organization for Women Chapters." *Sociological Perspectives* 49(3):297–323.

Revkin, Andrew C. 2009. "Environmental Issues Slide in Poll of Public's Concerns." *The New York Times*, January 22.

Ricard, François. 1994. *The Lyric Generation: The Life and Times of the Baby Boomers*, trans. Donald Winkler. Toronto: Stoddart.

Rimmerman, Craig A. 2002. *From Identity to Politics: The Lesbian and Gay Movements in the United States*. Philadelphia, PA: Temple University Press.

Risen, James, and Judy L. Thomas. 1998. *Wrath of Angels: The American Abortion War* New York: Basic Books.

Robbins, Liz. 2009. "Tax Day is Met with Tea Parties." *The New York Times*, April 16.

Rome, Adam. 2003. "'Give Earth a Chance': The Environmental Movement and the Sixties." *Journal of American History* 90(2):525–554.

Rootes, Christopher. 1999. *Environmental Movements: Local, National and Global*. London: Frank Cass.

_____. 2004. "Environmental Movements." pp. 608–640 in *The Blackwell Companion to Social Movements*, edited by D. A. Snow, S. A. Soule, and H. Kriesi. Malden, MA: Blackwell Publishing.

Rosen, Ruth. 2000. *The World Split Open: How the Modern Women's Movement Changed America*. New York: Penguin Books.

Ross, Robert J. S. 2005. "From Anti-Sweatshop, to Global Justice, to Anti-War: Student Participation in Globalization Protests." pp. 112–121 in *Transforming Globalization*, edited by B. Podobnik and T. Reifer. Leiden: Brill.

Roth, Benita. 2004. *Separate Roads to Feminism: Black, Chicana, and White Feminist Movements in America's Second Wave*. Cambridge: Cambridge University Press.

Rucht, Dieter. 1988. "Themes, Logics, and Arenas of Social Movements: A Structural Approach." *International Social Movement Research* 1:305–328.

_____. 1995. "Ecological Protest as Calculated Law-breaking: Greenpeace and Earth First! in Comparative Perspective." pp. 66–89 in *Green Politics Three*, edited by R. Wolfgang. Edinburgh: Edinburgh University Press.

_____. 2004. "Movement Allies, Adversaries, and Third Parties." pp. 197–216 in *The Blackwell Companion to Social Movements*, edited by D. A. Snow, S. A. Soule, and H. Kriesi. Oxford: Blackwell Publishing.

_____. 2005. "The Internet as a New Opportunity for Transnational Protest Groups." pp. 70–85 in *Economic and Political Contention in Comparative Perspective*, edited by M. Kousis and C. Tilly. Boulder, CO: Paradigm Publishers.

Rucht, Dieter, and Jochen Roose. 1999. "The German Environmental Movement at a Crossroads?" *Environmental Politics* 8(1):59–80.

_____. 2001. "Neither Decline Nor Sclerosis: The Organizational Structure of the German Environmental Movement." *West European Politics* 24(4):55–81.

Rupp, Leila J. 1997. *Worlds of Women: The Making of an International Women's Movement*. Princeton, NJ: Princeton University Press.

Rupp, Leila J., and Verta Taylor. 1987. *Survival in the Doldrums: The American Women's Rights Movement, 1945 to the 1960s*. New York: Oxford University Press.

_____. 1999. "Forging Feminist Identity in an International Movement: A Collective Identity Approach to Twentieth-Century Feminism." *Signs* 24(2):363–386.

Saad, Lydia. 2006. "Americans Still Not Highly Concerned about Global Warming." *The Gallup Poll* (April):20–22.

Sale, Kirkpatrick. 1973. *SDS*. New York: Random House.

_____. 1993. *The Green Revolution*. New York: Hill and Wang.

Schafer, Chelsea, E. and Greg. M. Shaw. 2009. "Trends: Tolerance in the United States." *Public Opinion Quarterly* 73(2):404–431.Schreiber, Ronnee. 2008. *Righting Feminism: Conservative Women & American Politics*. New York: Oxford University Press.

Schudson, Michael. 2003. *The Sociology of News*. New York: Norton.

Schulz, Markus S. 1998. "Collective Action across Borders: Opportunity Structures, Network Capacities, and Communicative Praxis in the Age of Advanced Globalization." *Sociological Perspectives* 41(3):587–616.

Scott, Wilbur J. 1985. "The Equal Rights Amendment as Status Politics." *Social Forces* 64(2):499–506.

Seidman, Gay W. 2000. "Adjusting the Lens: What Do Globalizations, Transnationalism, and the Anti-apartheid Movement Mean for Social Movement Theory?" pp. 339–357 in *Globalizations and Social Movements*, edited by J. A. Guidry, M. D. Kennedy, and M. N. Zald. Ann Arbor, MI: University of Michigan Press.

Shaw, Randy. 1999. *Reclaiming America: Nike, Clean Air, and the New National Activism*. Berkeley, CA: University of California Press.

Shellenberger, Michael, and Ted Nordhaus. 2004. "The Death of Environmentalism: Global Warming Politics in a Post-Environmental World." At www.thebreakthrough.org/images/Death_of_Environmentalism.pdf.

Shorter, Edward. 1975. *The Making of the Modern Family*. New York: Basic Books.

Sigal, Leon V. 1973. *Reporters and Officials: The Organization and Politics of Newsmaking*. Lexington, MA: D.C. Heath.

Skrentny, John D. 1998. "The Effect of the Cold War on African-American Civil Rights: America and the World Audience, 1945–1968." *Theory and Society* 27:237–285.

Slevin, Peter. 2009. "Antiabortion Efforts Move to the State Level." *The Washington Post*, June 8.

Smelser, Neil J. 1962. *Theory of Collective Behavior*. New York: Free Press.

_____. 1970. "Two Critics in Search of a Bias: A Response to Currie and Skolnick." *Annals, American Academy of Political and Social Science* 391:46–55.

Smith, Jackie. 2001. "Globalizing Resistance: The Battle of Seattle and the Future of Social Movements." *Mobilization* 6(1):1–19.

_____. 2008. *Social Movements for Global Democracy*. Baltimore, MD: Johns Hopkins University Press.

Smith, Miriam. 1998. "Social Movements and Equality Seeking: The Case of Gay Liberation in Canada." *Canadian Journal of Political Science* 31(2):285–309.

_____. 1999. *Lesbian and Gay Rights in Canada*. Toronto: University of Toronto Press.

_____. 2005. "The Politics of Same-Sex Marriage in Canada and the United States." *PS: Political Science and Politics* 38(2):225–228.

Snow, David A. 2001. "Collective Identity." pp. 2212–2219 in *International Encyclopedia of the Social and Behavioral Sciences*, edited by Neil J. Smelser and Paul B. Baltes. London: Elsevier.

_____. 2004. "Social Movements as Challenges to Authority: Resistance to an Emerging Conceptual Hegemony." *Research in Social Movements, Conflicts and Change* 25:3–25.

Snow, David A., and Robert D. Benford. 1992. "Ideology, Frame Resonance and Participant Mobilization." *International Social Movement Research* 1:197–217.

Snow, David A., Louis A. Zurcher Jr, and Sheldon Ekland-Olson. 1980. "Social Networks and Social Movements: A Microstructural Approach to Differential Recruitment." *American Sociological Review* 45(5):787–801.

Snow, David A., Sarah A. Soule, and Hanspeter Kriesi, eds. 2004. *The Blackwell Companion to Social Movements*. Malden, MA: Blackwell Publishing.

Snyder, David, and William R. Kelly. 1979. "Strategies for Investigating Violence and Social Change: Illustrations from Analyses of Racial Disorders and Implications for Mobilization Research." pp. 212–237 in *The Dynamics of Social Movements: Resource Mobilization, Social Control, and Tactics*, edited by M. N. Zald and J. D. McCarthy. Cambridge, MA: Winthrop.

Soule, Sarah A. 2004. "Going to the Chapel? Same-Sex Marriage Bans in the United States, 1973–2000." *Social Problems* 51(4):453–477.

Springer, Kimberly. 2005. *Living for the Revolution: Black Feminist Organizations, 1968–1980.* Durham, NC: Duke University Press.

Staggenborg, Suzanne. 1986. "Coalition Work in the Pro-Choice Movement: Organizational and Environmental Opportunities and Obstacles." *Social Problems* 33(5):374–390.

_____. 1988. "The Consequences of Professionalization and Formalization in the Pro-Choice Movement." *American Sociological Review* 53:585–605.

_____. 1989. "Stability and Innovation in the Women's Movement: A Comparison of Two Movement Organizations." *Social Problems* 36(1):75–92.

_____. 1991. *The Pro-Choice Movement: Organization and Activism in the Abortion Conflict.* New York: Oxford University Press.

_____. 1993. "Critical Events and the Mobilization of the Pro-Choice Movement." *Research in Political Sociology* 6:319–345.

_____. 1995. "Can Feminist Organizations Be Effective?" pp. 339–355 in *Feminist Organizations: Harvest of the New Women's Movement*, edited by Myra Marx Ferree and Patricia Yancey Martin. Philadelphia, PA: Temple University Press.

_____. 1998. "Social Movement Communities and Cycles of Protest: The Emergence and Maintenance of a Local Women's Movement." *Social Problems* 45(2):180–204.

_____. 2001. "Beyond Culture versus Politics: A Case Study of a Local Women's Movement." *Gender & Society* 15(4):507–530.

Staggenborg, Suzanne, and Josée Lecomte. 2009. "Social Movement Campaigns: Mobilization and Outcomes in the Montreal Women's Movement Community." *Mobilization* 14(2): 405–422.

Staggenborg, Suzanne, and Verta Taylor. 2005. "Whatever Happened to the Women's Movement?" *Mobilization* 10(1):37–52.

Starr, Amory. 2005. *Global Revolt: A Guide to the Movements against Globalization.* New York: Zed Books.

Stein, Arlene. 2001. *The Stranger Next Door: The Story of a Small Community's Battle Over Sex, Faith, and Civil Rights.* Boston: Beacon Press.

Steinberg, Marc W. 1998. "Tilting the Frame: Considerations on Collective Action Framing from a Discursive Turn." *Theory and Society* 27(6):845–872.

Steinhart, Peter. 1987. "The Longer View." *Audubon* 89(2):10–13.

Stewart, Keith. 2003. "If I Can't Dance: Reformism, Anti-Capitalism and the Canadian Environmental Movement." *Canadian Dimension* 37(5):41–43.

Sullivan, Amy. 2006. "Base Running." *The New Republic*, May 29, 12–16.

Swerdlow, Amy. 1993. *Women's Strike for Peace*. Chicago: University of Chicago Press.

Switzer, Jacqueline Vaughn. 1997. *Green Backlash: The History and Politics of Environmental Opposition in the U.S.* Boulder, CO: Lynne Rienner.

Szasz, Andrew. 1994. *Ecopopulism: Toxic Waste and the Movement for Environmental Justice*. Minneapolis, MN: University of Minnesota Press.

Tarrow, Sidney. 1989. *Democracy and Disorder: Protest and Politics in Italy, 1965–1975*. Oxford: Oxford University Press.

_____.1998. *Power in Movement: Social Movements and Contentious Politics*, 2nd ed. Cambridge: Cambridge University Press.

_____. 2005. *The New Transnational Activism*. New York: Cambridge University Press.

Taylor, Verta. 1989. "Social Movement Continuity: The Women's Movement in Abeyance." *American Sociological Review* 54:761–775.

Taylor, Verta, and Leila J. Rupp. 1993. "Women's Culture and Lesbian Feminist Activism: A Reconsideration of Cultural Feminism." *Signs* 19(1):32–61.

Taylor, Verta, and Nancy E. Whittier. 1992. "Collective Identity in Social Movement Communities: Lesbian Feminist Mobilization." pp. 104–129 in *Frontiers in Social Movement Theory*, edited by A. D. Morris and C. M. Mueller. New Haven, CT: Yale University Press.

Taylor, Verta, Katrina Kimport, Nella Van Dyke, and Ellen Ann Andersen. 2009. "Culture and Mobilization: Tactical Repertoires, Same-Sex Weddings, and the Impact on Gay Activism." *American Sociological Review* 74(6):865–890.

Tedin, K. L., D. W. Brady, M. E. Buxton, B. M. Gorman, and J. L. Thompson. 1977. "Social Background and Political Differences Between Pro- and Anti-ERA Activists." *American Political Quarterly* 5(July):395–408.

Tierney, Kathleen J. 1982. "The Battered Women Movement and the Creation of the Wife Beating Problem." *Social Problems* 29(3):207–220.

Tilly, Charles. 1978. *From Mobilization to Revolution*. Reading, MA: Addison-Wesley.

_____. 1984. "Social Movements and National Politics." pp. 297–317 in *Statemaking and Social Movements*, edited by H. Charles Bright and Susan Harding. Ann Arbor, MI: University of Michigan Press.

_____. 1986. "European Violence and Collective Action Since 1700." *Social Research* 53(1):159–184.

_____. 1988. "Social Movements, Old and New." *Research in Social Movements, Conflicts and Change* 10:1–18.

_____. 1995. *Popular Contention in Great Britain, 1758–1834*. Cambridge, MA: Harvard University Press.

_____. 2004a. *Contention and Democracy in Europe, 1650–2000*. New York: Cambridge University Press.

_____. 2004b. *Social Movements, 1768–2004*. Boulder, CO: Paradigm.

_____. 2008. *Contentious Performances*. New York: Cambridge University Press.

Tindall, David B. 2002. "Social Networks, Identification and Participation in an Environmental Movement: Low-medium Cost Activism within the British Columbia

Wilderness Preservation Movement." *Canadian Review of Sociology and Anthropology* 39(4):413–452.

Tomasky, Michael. 2009. "Something New on the Mall." *The New York Review of Books.* October 22 (Vol. LVI, Number 16), pp. 4–8.

Touraine, Alain. 1971. *The May Movement: Revolt and Reform.* New York: Random House.

Tuchman, Gaye. 1978. *Making News: A Study in the Construction of Reality.* New York: Free Press.

Turner, Ralph. 1981. "Collective Behavior and Resource Mobilization as Approaches to Social Movements: Issues and Continuities." *Social Movements, Conflicts and Change* 4:1–24.

Turner, Ralph, and Lewis M. Killian. 1957. *Collective Behavior.* Englewood Cliffs, NJ: Prentice-Hall.

———. 1972. *Collective Behavior,* 2nd ed. Englewood Cliffs, NJ: Prentice-Hall.

———. 1987. *Collective Behaviour,* 3rd ed. Englewood Cliffs, NJ: Prentice-Hall.

Useem, Bert, and Mayer N. Zald. 1982. "From Pressure Group to Social Movement: Organizational Dilemmas of the Effort to Promote Nuclear Power." *Social Problems* 30(2):144–156.

Useem, Michael. 1975. *Protest Movements in America.* Indianapolis, IN: Bobbs-Merrill.

Valocchi, Steve. 1999. "Riding the Crest of a Protest Wave? Collective Action Frames in the Gay Liberation Movement, 1969–1973." *Mobilization* 4(1):59–73.

———. 2001. "Individual Identities, Collective Identities, and Organizational Structure: The Relationship of the Political Left and Gay Liberation in the United States." *Sociological Perspectives* 44(4):445–467.

Van Deburg, William L. 1992. *New Day in Babylon: The Black Power Movement and American Culture, 1965–1975.* Chicago: University of Chicago Press.

Van Dyke, Nella. 2003. "Crossing Movement Boundaries: Factors that Facilitate Coalition Protest by American College Students, 1930–1990." *Social Problems* 50(2):226–250.

Vasi, Ion Bogdan. 2007. "Thinking Globally, Planning Nationally and Acting Locally: Nested Organizational Fields and the Adoption of Environmental Practices." *Social Forces* 86(1):113–136.

Voss, Kim, and Rachel Sherman. 2000. "Breaking the Iron Law of Oligarchy: Union Revitalization in the American Labor Movement." *American Journal of Sociology* 106(2):303–349.

Walker, Rebecca, ed. 1995. *To Be Real: Telling the Truth and Changing the Face of Feminism.* New York: Anchor Books.

Wall, Derek. 1999. *Earth First! and the Anti-Roads Movement: Radical Environmentalism and the Comparative Social Movements.* London: Routledge.

Wallis, Roy. 1979. *Salvation and Protest: Studies of Social and Religious Movements.* London: F. Pister.

Walsh, Edward J. 1988. *Democracy in the Shadows: Citizen Mobilization in the Wake of the Accident at Three Mile Island.* Westport, CT: Greenwood Press.

Wapner, Paul. 2002. "Horizontal Politics: Environmental Activism and Global Cultural Change." *Global Environmental Politics* 2(2):37–62.

Warner, Tom. 2002. *Never Going Back: A History of Queer Activism in Canada.* Toronto: University of Toronto Press.

Werum, Regina, and Bill Winders. 2001. "Who's 'In' and Who's 'Out': State Fragmentation and the Struggle over Gay Rights, 1974–1999." *Social Problems* 48(3):386–410.

Weyler, Rex. 2004. *Greenpeace: How a Group of Ecologists, Journalists and Visionaries Changed the World.* Vancouver: Raincoast Books.

Whittier, Nancy. 1995. *Feminist Generations: The Persistence of the Radical Women's Movement.* Philadelphia, PA: Temple University Press.

Wilcox, Clyde. 1992. *God's Warriors: The Christian Right in Twentieth-Century America.* Baltimore, MD: Johns Hopkins University Press.

Wilson, Jeremy. 2001. "Continuity and Change in the Canadian Environmental Movement: Assessing the Effects of Institutionalization." pp. 46–65 in *Canadian Environmental Policy: Context and Cases,* edited by D. L. VanNijnatten and R. Boardman. Oxford: Oxford University Press.

Wilson, John. 1973. *Introduction to Social Movements.* New York: Basic Books.

Wood, Lesley J. 2005a. "Taking to the Streets Against Neoliberalism: Global Days of Action and Other Strategies." pp. 69–81 in *Transforming Globalization,* edited by B. Podobnik and T. Reifer. Leiden: Brill.

———. 2005b. "Bridging the Chasms: The Peoples' Global Action." pp. 95–117 in *Coalitions Across Borders: Transnational Protest and the Neoliberal Order,* edited by J. Bandy and J. Smith. Lanham, MD: Rowman & Littlefield.

Zald, Mayer N. 2000. "Ideologically Structured Action: An Enlarged Agenda for Social Movement Research." *Mobilization* 5(1):1–16.

Zald, Mayer N., and Bert Useem. 1987. "Movement and Countermovement Interaction: Mobilization, Tactics, and State Involvement." pp. 247–272 in *Social Movements in an Organizational Society,* edited by M. N. Zald and J. D. McCarthy. New Brunswick, NJ: Transaction Books.

Zeleny, Jeff. 2009. "Thousands Attend Broad Protest of Government." *The New York Times,* September 13.

Zogby International. 2006. "Zogby Post-Election Poll: Dems Gained from Global Warming Debate," press release, November 16.

INDEX

CPSIA information can be obtained at www.ICGtesting.com
Printed in the USA
BVOW04s1543230713

326695BV00003B/3/P

9 780195 375084